Urban Nationalism

Urban Nationalism

A Study of Political Development in Trinidad

ALVIN MAGID

UNIVERSITY PRESSES OF FLORIDA

University of Florida Press / Gainesville

UNIVERSITY PRESSES OF FLORIDA is the central agency for scholarly publishing of the State of Florida's university system, producing books selected for publication by the faculty editorial committees of Florida's nine public universities: Florida A&M University (Tallahassee), Florida Atlantic University (Boca Raton), Florida International University (Miami), Florida State University (Tallahassee), University of Central Florida (Orlando), University of Florida (Gainesville), University of North Florida (Jacksonville), University of South Florida (Tampa), University of West Florida (Pensacola).

ORDERS for books published by all member presses should be addressed to University Presses of Florida, 15 NW 15th Street, Gainesville, FL 32603.

Library of Congress Cataloging in Publication Data

Magid, Alvin, 1937–
  Urban nationalism.

  Bibliography: p.
  Includes index.
  1. Trinidad and Tobago—Politics and government.
2. Nationalism—Trinidad—History. 3. Trinidad—
Ethnic relations. I. Title.
F2119.M34   1987   972.98′3   86-33978
ISBN 0–8130–0853–0

To Sally and our family,
my parents,
and Enos Sewlal

Contents

Table and Maps

Preface

FOR SOME TIME now my interests as a political scientist have centered on the urban factor in political change, on nationalism in colonial societies under European rule, and on Trinidad and Tobago, formerly a British Crown Colony. *Urban Nationalism* is an attempt to merge the three interests.

My early interest in urban life, deriving from my upbringing in New York City, was reinforced by William Hanna, especially by his own admirable research on comparative urbanism and on urban politics. I arrived at a scholarly interest in Trinidad and Tobago by accident. Fieldwork some years ago in northern Nigeria first brought me into contact with archival materials pertaining to the late Sir Hugh Clifford, who served as governor of Nigeria from 1919 to 1925. Clifford came quickly to fascinate me—his strong personality, his abundant fictional writings, mostly adventure stories drawing upon his early years in the Malay Civil Service, and his considerable administrative achievement in colonial Nigeria as successor to Sir Frederick (later Lord) Lugard. I resolved to prepare someday a full-length biography of Clifford, research for which, I reckoned, would take me to all the territories in which he had built his long, distinguished career as a servant of the British Empire. Subsequently, I journeyed to Trinidad and Tobago, where Clifford served as colonial secretary from 1903 to 1907. At the National Archives in Port-of-Spain, I was distracted by the rich colonial history of that society, particularly by what in this study I refer to as the period of urban nationalism, from 1895 to 1914. My interest in the colonial politics of Trinidad and Tobago, and in the implications of that politics for nationalism there, was deepened by subsequent archival investigations undertaken in London and at Oxford and by my immersion in a rich secondary literature. The scholarship particularly of Selwyn

D. Ryan, Eric Williams (the late prime minister of Trinidad and Tobago), and Gordon K. Lewis have aided me in my labors. The great
body of literature on nationalism that also sustained me in my
efforts needs no citation here.

I have benefited greatly from comments made on an earlier draft
of *Urban Nationalism* by Wendell Bell and Robert Dishman and from
their own scholarship on the Anglophone Caribbean. The manuscript
was guided to publication by the fine editorial hand of Judy Goffman,
managing editor of University Presses of Florida. Phillip Martin, director of University Presses, lent strong encouragement when I
needed it most.

My several archival investigations were supported generously by
grants from the American Philosophical Society, the Research Foundation of the State University of New York, and the Office of Research
at the State University of New York in Albany. I also gratefully acknowledge the assistance which I received on various occasions from
staff at the Nigerian National Archives branches in Enugu and Ka-
duna; at the Trinidad and Tobago National Archives, Port-of-Spain;
at the Public Record Office, the British Museum, and the Foreign
and Commonwealth Office Library, London; and at the Colonial
Records Project and Rhodes House Library, Oxford. Gwen Deiber
and Sally Stevenson assisted my research efforts in the library of
the State University of New York at Albany. I am grateful for their
kindness and professionalism.

I owe a special debt of gratitude to Enos Sewlal, Chief Archivist of
the Trinidad and Tobago National Archives, who, sharing my enthusiasm for *Urban Nationalism*, worked heroically to keep me supplied
in Port-of-Spain with pertinent materials. His labors and great courtesy did much to lighten my burden.

I wish to thank my typist, Addie Napolitano, for her abundant patience and skill.

And finally, there is my family—Brooke, Dawn, Glenn, Sean, and
my wife, Sally. A writer is apt to place great strain upon those closest and dearest to him. I cannot begin to estimate my debt to them.

To be aided in one's scholarship is not to share responsibility for
it. I alone am responsible for what is written in these pages.

1

Imperial Administration and the Urban Factor in Nationalism

I

AN IMPERIAL POWER exercises control over its subjects principally by the instrument of administration. Formally, control can be seen to be organized in bureaucratic functions that bind participants and interests in an unequal, hierarchical relationship. On close examination, however, we discern in the push and pull between governor and governed a political relationship that is daily reflected in their accommodation and adjustment to each other. The case of imperial Britain in the nineteenth century is instructive.

British imperial administration was organized in that century in a network that linked the Colonial Office in Downing Street with an array of colonial societies.[1] Because the flow of authority followed the pattern of hierarchical positions in the network—from the secretary of state for the colonies, who was a member of the British cabinet, or from his senior officials at the Colonial Office acting on his behalf, downward to the colonial governors and their subordinates—

it might appear that influence also flowed downward. The reality was otherwise, rendering the process of imperial control—by administration—one of great complexity. Influence, as communication, flowed in many directions: downward, upward, and horizontally (in the last instance, moving among colleagues at the same organizational levels, both in Downing Street and in the colonial governments).[2]

These streams in imperial administration were fed by others whose sources were, strictly speaking, outside the official network. The secretary of state and his Colonial Office officials had to contend, for example, with pressures exerted from time to time by the prime minister and the cabinet, who were collectively responsible for the direction of government policy; by the Treasury Department, which ordinarily kept a tight rein on imperial expenditure;[3] by Parliament backbenchers, who might rise to assail some aspect of imperial policy or to lay a claim upon it; and by special interests in Great Britain and throughout the empire (for example, church groups, which dominated educational life in the colonies; the West India Committee, which represented the interests of sugar plantocracies in the Caribbean dependencies; and dissident colonial subjects, who clamored for constitutional advance and political change).

Colonial governments were not immune from similar outside pressures. These agents of a distant metropole were at the center of colonial societies whose characters were shaped by many factors— extrinsically, for example, by the international economy and by imperial policy set in London, intrinsically by the natural environments within which the colonial societies took root and by the multifarious interests that they came to encompass. Not the least important interests in the colonies were those of the colonial governments themselves. Colonial rule in practice was a system of power in which conformity to abstract principles (for example, the Western civil-service ethic mirrored in the Weberian model of bureaucracy, the basic texts on Indirect Rule, and the philosophy of paternalistic trusteeship) was far less important than the need for give-and-take by diverse interests in colonial societies. The imperative of "good government," of "efficient administration," often required colonial officials to execute (or at least appear to execute) the role of broker, seeking to balance the conflicting claims of local groups with the divergent interests of the colony and the metropole. In the process, those officials were apt to evince their own commitment to this transcendent interest: the primacy of government in the colonial society.

Viewing colonial rule (within the larger framework of imperial administration) as a system of power, we become more sensitive to the bureaucratizing impulse of colonial governments—that is, to their efforts to expand and consolidate their power over those whose lives they regulated. As do institutions generally, colonial governments valued their own survival along with the tasks they performed.[4] Men who acquire power and try to hold on to it often have to pursue their interests under the cloak of high principle and disinterested service—a truism that appears to have eluded those commentators who stress the clash of universalistic and particularistic ethics in colonial life.[5]

Reduced to their essentials, colonial governments are more accurately seen as institutions in and around which diverse interests collected—all of them particularistic at the core and all (by their actions or their tacit consent) in varying degrees lending support to, or opposing, the bureaucratizing impulse.[6]

II

Urban Nationalism is set broadly within the framework of British imperial administration in the late nineteenth and early twentieth centuries. The focus of the study is on the interaction between, on the one hand, a particular system of colonial administration (a Crown Colony government) and public policy in one West Indies dependency, Trinidad and Tobago, and, on the other, anticolonial nationalism centered in its capital and main town, Port-of-Spain (see maps 1 and 2).[7] (Owing to the financial plight of the Crown Colony of Tobago, in 1888 the British Parliament decided to merge the island dependency with nearby Trinidad, another Crown Colony. Port-of-Spain, capital of the old Crown Colony of Trinidad, has been the capital of Trinidad and Tobago since their union. Trinidad is by far the more important of the two islands—demographically, economically, geographically, and politically. References in this book to "Trinidad," to the "Crown Colony of Trinidad," and to the "Crown Colony" apply to Trinidad alone before 1888 and to the union of Trinidad and Tobago in the century after 1888. There are also occasional specific references to the smaller island of Tobago.)

By plumbing the relationships among colonial government, public policy, and the urban factor in nationalism in one dependency, I intend also to underscore the need to correct certain imbalances as-

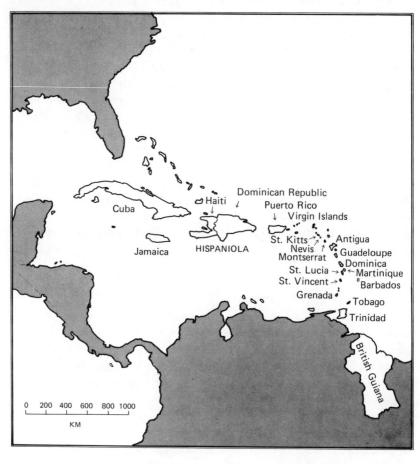

Map 1. The Islands of Trinidad and Tobago in the Caribbean Archipelago

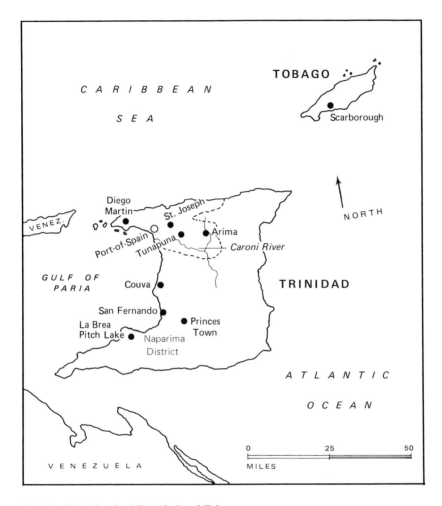

Map 2. The Islands of Trinidad and Tobago

sociated with the study of British imperial administration. Substantial literature exists on administration at the apex of the imperial network, in its nerve center at the Colonial Office;[8] on the internal organization of the Colonial Office and its procedures for recruiting and training Colonial Office and overseas staff;[9] and on relationships between the secretary of state for the colonies and his senior officials.[10] There is no dearth of literature, moreover, on the principles of colonial government;[11] on the roles and personalities of prominent colonial governors;[12] and on subordinate officials in various British dependencies.[13] Yet little is known today about administration and public policy nearer the base of the imperial network, in the colonial societies themselves. For example, we still have limited understanding of the channels through which influence and communication moved up and down between the Colonial Office and colonial governments and the distortions, either purposeful or unintentional, that may have occurred in the process; of the day-to-day relationships between colonial governments and the colonial societies of which they were a part; and of the measures taken by colonial officials to consolidate their power in the face of local resistance and demands for change.

The legacy of failure to produce heretofore a large number of studies of the "lower end" of the imperial network, in the colonies, is a constrained view of the imperial enterprise and, correlatively, of the course of political change throughout the British Empire. In that view, colonial societies were scarcely more than inventions of Europe and essentially extensions of it. I prefer to stress instead that the national histories of many societies—of the metropole and of its colonies—have their confluence in imperial administration and that, by enlarging our perspective to include both ends of the imperial network, we will be better placed not only to fill in our view of imperial administration but also to enhance our understanding of its historical corollary, anticolonial nationalism among subject peoples.

III

Urban areas, whether towns or cities, have characteristics that, taken together, make them distinct from other areas of human settlement and activity: (1) a substantial population that (2) lives permanently within a confined space and (3) is tied to a permanent structure of social and economic activity based on differentiated, albeit interdependent, roles.[14] In the long era of modern European imperialism, urban areas of varying size, population, density, and role complexity had a significant place in the life of colonial societies— as hosts for alien ideas, institutions, and technologies and as disseminators of the same to outlying populations. Networks of communication and transportation in those societies radiated from what social scientists have labeled urban "nodes" or "central places"[15] to the hinterlands, accompanied by the artifacts of modern "culture" and the mechanisms of political control. Urban areas served as key nexuses in complex systems of economic and political dependency, linking the urban and rural sectors of colonial societies to European imperial centers and, with or without the latter's consent, to the world community based on international trade and political power. The roles described for urban areas in colonial societies applied especially to their capital towns, particularly those sited on great international waterways.[16]

Occupying a strategic position in colonial societies, urban rather than rural areas were apt to be the first—or at least the main— places where political discontent was channeled into organizations of protest against one or more aspects of colonial rule and imperial policy. Even where such protest—or rebellion—was mounted in rural areas, its underlying causes were likely to be linked directly or indirectly to colonial urban areas, often to their capital towns—to tax policies and administrative regulations framed in government centers, to the dispatch of colonial officials, security forces, and missionaries to "pacify" and "civilize" outlying populations, and so forth. With a few exceptions, anticolonial nationalism was born of the discontents of town life in colonial societies; as did the perspectives and activities of their principal architects and leaders, nationalist movements typically bore the hallmark of urban origin.

Early in the history of anticolonial nationalism in societies under European rule, parochial issues of urban life—for example, house and water rates, elective municipal institutions, and expropriation of property for official use—formed the basis for what James S. Coleman has labeled "primary resistance" in the colonial situation.[17] Oppression and burdens that those issues created for town dwellers were often perceived by them as inherent in the colonial situation, so demonstrations of resentment over these issues also expressed, symbolically at least, objection to colonial rule. In some colonial societies, town dwellers in time perceived clearly the link between parochial issues and the larger issue of colonial rule itself. One such society was British Trinidad, where public life had long been dominated by the politics of its capital, Port-of-Spain. By the end of the nineteenth century, two municipal issues had impinged on the Crown Colony government, and they stood for nearly two decades as the singular expression in that small colony of anticolonial nationalism. Before turning to those issues and to explicating the concept of urban nationalism on which the analysis will proceed, it is necessary to deal briefly with the concept of nationalism.

IV

In the literature of social science and of history, one finds diverse definitions of nationalism and many kinds of cases to which that concept has been applied. Some definitions emphasize explicitly or implicitly the ideological, juridical, or cultural dimension of sociopolitical life, others some combination of the three. One also encounters diversity in typologies of nationalism. In one typology, for example, a distinction is drawn between old nationalism and new, corresponding generally to the contrast between Western and non-Western (i.e., Third World) states. Different conditions are fixed in that scheme for the phenomenon of nationalism. In the Western type, nationalism is seen to derive from the "nation," whose boundaries are customarily marked by the sharing among its members of such attributes as religion, language, music and literature, political identity, and a particular territory (or the desire therefor). In the non-Western type, conversely, nationalism is regarded not as a corollary of "nationhood" but of "anticolonialism," as the seed from which the nation may grow.[18] Among non-Western societies, the concept of "anticolonial nationalism" may refer to one or more of these conditions: to the opposition of a colonial people to imperial rule; to the affirmation by a colonial people of their sovereign independence among international states; or to the opposition of relatively poor states to their "colonial economic status"[19] vis-à-vis advanced industrial states. *Urban Nationalism* is a case study of anticolonial nationalism in the first instance; its focus is upon the opposition of a colonial people—in Trinidad—to a particular system of imperial rule—Crown Colony government.

Another typology of nationalism, constructed for non-Western societies under European rule, emphasizes the scope and explicitness of the political component in anticolonialism. Some writers evince a narrow perspective here, applying the concepts of nationalism and "nationalist activity" only to those cases where the anticolonial impulse is conveyed by political means (e.g., lobbying, party, and mass-movement activities) intended to secure avowedly political goals (e.g., internal autonomy or sovereign independence).[20] Others adopt a broad perspective, attaching the labels of nationalism and nationalist activity to all forms of anticolonial expression, including the nonpolitical and the vaguely political.[21]

Collectively, the many efforts to define and classify the phenomenon of nationalism have yielded ambivalent results. Case studies have accumulated at an impressive rate but have not dispelled confusion over basic meanings for nationalism and related concepts. Ambiguous concepts have been used in typologies of nationalism; those who use them have added to the confusion by failing to heed a cardinal principle of logical classification, that there must be a mutually exclusive and jointly exhaustive set of classes for the domain under consideration.[22] Typologies of nationalism have characteristically failed to arrange their pertinent criteria—temporal, spatial, developmental, and so on—with logical consistency. Because comparison presupposes classification in the logic of inquiry, flawed typologies have tended to inhibit the comparative study of nationalism. It behooves contemporary scholars of nationalism to bring to the tasks of concept formation and theory construction the same admirable concern for precision and detail that has usually marked the case-study approach to their subject. Arthur Stinchcombe has aptly observed, "For a social theorist ignorance is more excusable than vagueness. Other investigators can easily show that I am wrong if I am sufficiently precise. They will have much more difficulty showing what, precisely, I mean if I am vague. I hope not to be forced to weasel out with 'But I didn't really mean that.' Social theorists should prefer to be wrong rather than misunderstood. Being misunderstood shows sloppy theoretical work."[23]

V

Urban nationalism denotes a historical condition in which anticolonialism is expressed principally through parochial issues of public policy that affect the colony and its leading municipality, its capital. The anticolonial impulse is sharpened by resentment over (or "primary resistance" to) some public policy for the capital. The emotions that result in turn galvanize political opposition to the colonial status quo. Like urban "nodes" or "central places," from which modernity spreads into remote regions, the rise of urban nationalism diffuses anticolonial sentiment beyond the colonial capital. The historical condition that I have labeled *urban* nationalism points up the critical importance of the *urban factor* in anticolonialism.[24] Urban nationalism has four defining characteristics. The first is its origin in a colonial situation marked by two distinctive but connected asymmetries in relations of power and authority, that is, by relations of power and control and of dependence and subordination between the European imperial center and its overseas colony and, within the latter, between the central government and the colonial capital. The second is the presence of anticolonialism precipitated by the colonial situation. The third is a legitimizing rationale for anticolonialism—nationalism. The last is the expression of anticolonialism based on issues of municipal public policy that affect both the colony and the capital. These characteristics are elucidated with reference to Trinidad.

Asymmetries in relations of power and authority

There existed between the imperial center, Great Britain, and its colony, Trinidad, and between the government of Trinidad and the municipality of Port-of-Spain, relations of power and control and of dependence and subordination. Crown and Parliament, represented by the secretary of state and his officials at the Colonial Office and throughout the empire, were ultimately responsible for all governmental business—executive, legislative, and judicial—in the colony and for its security and general well-being.

The initiative in policy making for the Crown Colony of Trinidad—and for other dependencies in the empire—might from time to time pass between the Colonial Office and its officials in the colony, and between the secretary of state and his senior officials in Downing Street. Reliance on written communications borne by seagoing vessels in the nineteenth century often made it necessary for colonial governments to act expeditiously with only general guidance from the metropole; but as the availability of telegraph communication increased at the end of the century, the initiative came increasingly to rest with officials at the Colonial Office.[25] Throughout most of the nineteenth century, too, the policy process at the Colonial Office was dominated by senior officials who were responsible for particular geographic areas; but a strong-willed secretary of state, endowed also with political intelligence and a "grand design" for the imperial enterprise, might shift the balance to his side.[26] As we shall see, Joseph Chamberlain's long incumbency, bracketing the turn of the century, exemplified such resourceful leadership.[27]

These changing patterns of influence in the network of British imperial administration during the nineteenth century sometimes affected significantly the balance of local interests in particular Crown Colonies. But no similar effect can be seen in the relationship between those dependencies and the metropole. Paramount authority over Crown Colony affairs in Trinidad, for example, continued to be lodged formally and in fact in the imperial power and its overseas agents, not in the local population or its leading citizens and spokesmen.

Asymmetric relations were characteristic of the system of Crown Colony government, an artifact of British imperialism that, in place of responsible government in local hands in Trinidad, substituted a powerful administration of mainly foreign officials—the governor and others—under the control of the secretary of state at the Colonial Office in London. Based on a philosophy of paternalistic trusteeship, the system of colonial government in Trinidad was designed to resist pressures in the colony toward rule either by a white oligarchy or by the majority of color, all the while holding out the promise of gradual advance, constitutional and political—that advance to follow an unprescribed course toward some indeterminate goal. In fact, nearly to the twilight of colonial rule in Trinidad in the early 1960s, the philosophy of trusteeship served to slow the process of change. The hand of the Trinidad government was strengthened both by the refusal of the Colonial Office for more than a century down to the 1920s even to begin to institute the representative (elective) principle in the colony's legislature on a partial basis and by the authority the colonial government exercised over municipal affairs in the capital.

Rising anticolonialism

Contained within the pattern of hierarchical relations in the imperial network was a dialectical tendency, anticolonialism. That tendency was evidenced by a wide array of actions taken by the colonial population of Trinidad to reduce or eliminate altogether the asymmetry in relations between the imperial center and the colony and between the colony's government and Port-of-Spain. Those actions included, among other things, conventional pressure-group tactics, political agitation, riots, and violence, aimed at official institutions, persons, policies, and symbols in the Crown Colony government. Opposition to the colonial situation was also expressed symbolically, in elaborate festivals that satirized leading figures, groups, and institutions in the colonial society.

Anticolonialism in Trinidad at the beginning of the twentieth century bore the marks of contentious rivalry. Foes of the imperial status quo differed sharply among themselves over methods and goals. The proponents of peaceful change, who were often divided over public policy, personalities, and regional interests, faced a small minority who espoused a strategy of confrontation and political agitation with its attendant risk of mass violence. There was no dearth of advocates for anticolonial causes as diverse as, for example, precipitate sovereign independence; gradual social improvement; adoption of the elective principle, either wholly or partially, in the Trinidad Legislative Council; and abolition of the indenture system for immigrants from the Indian subcontinent, both to improve the lot of black workers and to weaken the influence of a foreign-dominated cane-sugar industry tied closely to the Trinidad government.

Nationalism: a legitimizing rationale for anticolonialism

Nationalism is a corollary of anticolonialism, that is, colonialism produces anticolonialism which, in turn, begets nationalism as a means of legitimizing opposition to a colonial situation marked by asymmetry in relations of power and authority. Articulated chiefly by the literati, nationalism is a people's brief for anticolonialism. But who are "the people" in a colonial situation? Are they the colonial "nation," perhaps—fully formed or in embryo? This question is not easily answered with reference to the paired concepts of anticolonialism and nationalism. For the existence of the nation, in any stage of development, need not be presumed or anticipated by anticolonialism or nationalism. *Anticolonialism* (action of any kind taken against any aspect of the prevailing systems of power and control and of dependence and subordination) and *nationalism* (the articulation of belief in the rightness or propriety of such action) may both obtain without either certifying the need for nationhood in a particular colonial society. The case of Trinidad in the period under review—of urban nationalism, from 1895 to 1914—points up the fact that a deepening sense of collective grievance over the direction of public policy may be more important than national consciousness per se in the interplay between anticolonialism and nationalism.

By the last quarter of the nineteenth century, the anticolonial camp in Trinidad had come to include some who extolled the island society as a nation distinct from the British metropole; others whose weak attraction to the idea of a nation mirrored a profound skepticism that nationhood could be achieved by a small colonial population divided by race, religion, ethnicity, and class; and still others whose attitude could be described as rudely dismissive. Years would pass before most Trinidadians were drawn even to the idea of a single national identity for their society. Only in the first decade after the Second World War—when the drive for sovereign independence was quickening and when, correlatively, the antagonistic communal nationalism of the blacks and of the Indians emerged full-blown—did there develop among the population of Trinidad the feeling that a single institution could be made to stand for a transcendent national identity: Carnival, the annual pre-Lenten bacchanal whose origins in the island colony could be traced back more than a century to the era of slavery. This passion for at least a symbolic wholeness in Trinidad was no happenstance. Nor was it an expression of prideful anticolonialism alone. Communal nationalism was the excreta of anticolonial nationalism, destined, if left unchecked, to wound and possibly destroy plural societies that colonialism had never made whole. All around the British Empire in the aftermath of the Second World War, in large decolonizing political spaces and in small ones, evidence was rapidly accumulating of its destructive potential—in India, in Palestine, in Ceylon, and in British Guiana near Trinidad. In that time, Carnival came to symbolize in Trinidad the hope that anticolonialism would sublimate the passions of communal nationalism, not be engulfed by them.[28]

In the century before the First World War, discordance over Trinidad's nationhood combined with division over methods and goals to weaken the anticolonial effort, though not the anticolonial impulse itself. Even the most intransigent foes in the anticolonial camp could generally agree at least on the need to oppose the imperial status quo and on the propriety of doing so. It is in their call to rightful action, sparked by a collective sense of grievance within the prevailing system of Crown Colony government, that we discern the urban variant of nationalism emergent in Trinidad near the end of the nineteenth century.

Intersecting issues of public policy in the colony and the capital

The fourth characteristic of urban nationalism is anticolonialism based on issues of municipal public policy that cut across the colony and its capital. The case of Trinidad illuminates anticolonialism integrating its urban and its wider territorial expressions.

The philosophy of trusteeship in Crown Colony government in nineteenth-century Trinidad drew public attention to powerful officials in the administration. Political grievances were apt to center on the attitudes and actions particularly of the governor of Trinidad and his principal official, the colonial secretary.

At the apex of the hierarchy of Crown Colony government in Trinidad, the governor served as chief executive.[29] Appointed by the Colonial Office,[30] he had wide authority in the day-to-day management of public affairs. As the Crown's representative in the colony, he alone could issue orders regarding its administration, and all public acts had to be approved either by him or in his name. A corollary of this broad authority was the assignment of legislative responsibility to the governor. In the Legislative Council, with its official and appointive unofficial members, the governor was ultimately responsible for lawmaking, through his right of assent or veto. The Legislative Council was empowered to discuss and adopt such measures as were introduced or proposed by a member or by the governor, but the Crown had to sanction ordinances passed by the legislature before they could become law. The Legislative Council could also discuss and vote the estimates for the following year, but motions for money ordinarily had to come through the governor and the estimates had always to be transmitted to the Colonial Office for its consideration and approval.

The Executive Council, composed of the leading officials of the Crown Colony under the presidency of the governor,[31] often influenced the making of public policy, but its powers did not rival those of the chief executive. In Trinidad the council was essentially a consultative body, and the governor could accept or reject its advice. In all but the most unusual circumstances he could, as a practical matter, anticipate—or command—the support of his officials in the Executive Council.[32] As we shall see, where that support was occasionally withheld, either intentionally or by miscalculation, the effect was apt to be a crisis in Crown Colony government.[33]

Appointments to all but a few public offices in the Crown Colony were made by the governor, and he alone in the colony's government could suspend or dismiss the incumbents. The unofficial members of the Legislative Council were nominated by the governor and formally approved by the secretary of state for the colonies in London. Department heads were ultimately responsible to the chief executive, who was responsible also for deploying local military forces and for disbursing funds out of the local treasury. The governor was also empowered to remit fines and to pardon offenses against the law.

Finally, the great authority and prestige of the governor were affirmed by his position in local society. A sought-after speaker at public and private functions and the patron of numerous educational, charitable, social, and religious causes, the chief executive was, with his wife, at the center of social life in the colony.

After the governor, the colonial secretary was undoubtedly the most important public official.[34] Perhaps the most incisive description of the office, and of the scope of its authority, is that of Hugh Clifford, who served as colonial secretary for part of the period of urban nationalism in Trinidad (1903–7)[35] and then in the Crown Colony of Ceylon (1907–12):

> The responsibilities thus laid upon the Governor being of so direct and personal a character, it became necessary in the Crown Colonies to devise administrative machinery that should enable him to exercise direct control and supervision over every Public Department; and to this end the Colonial Secretariat was brought into being. This Office is presided over by the Colonial Secretary, who occupies, vis-à-vis the Governor, very much the position of the Commander of a battleship in relation to her Captain. Thus it is to the Colonial Secretary, rather than to the Governor, that the Heads of Departments and prominent members of the local public go in the first instance for assistance, direction, or advice in matters of difficulty or emergency; and, where the system is working as it was designed to work, the Colonial Secretary is in such close touch with the Governor, so completely in his confidence, and so intimately acquainted with his wishes and opinions regarding public affairs that, in the majority of cases, he can deal on his own responsibility with questions brought before him which demand prompt action or decision, merely reporting to the Governor what he has done for covering sanction. Nonetheless, it was an essential feature of the Crown Colony system that the Colonial Secretary should not himself be vested with any executive authority. He is the Governor's principal adviser; his mouthpiece, through whom all his orders are issued; the official channel of communication with him, alike for the members of the public service and for the general public of the Colony;

and the principal spokesman of the Government in the Legislative Council. He has no power, however, to give any instructions to any public servant, with the exception of those serving as his immediate subordinates in the Secretariat, save in the Governor's name or by his direction; but he is the pivotal part of the administrative machine by means of which work of all the Public Departments is coordinated, supervised, and controlled. Through his agency also the Governor is kept fully informed of all that is going on in the Colony, and is enabled to exercise his authority and to discharge his responsibilities.[36]

The great weight and complexity of the role of colonial secretary in Crown Colony government are affirmed in the several offices to which it has sometimes been compared. Clifford drew an analogy to a battleship commander, Anton Bertram to a prime minister,[37] John W. Cell to a permanent undersecretary at the Colonial Office.[38]

The colonial secretary was alter ego to the governor in the public service of Trinidad: his principal adviser and closest confidant; his senior official in the Executive Council and chief spokesman for, and defender of, the government in the Legislative Council; his nominee to head special commissions occasionally established by the governor; and, whenever the chief executive was absent from the colony or was prevented by illness from performing his official duties, his surrogate as "officer administering the government." As acting governor, the colonial secretary was expected to follow closely the lines of government policy, except in emergencies or during an interregnum, when he might evince a judiciously independent spirit.

The colonial secretary was a vital nexus in two ways in Trinidad, one hierarchical, the other temporal. He was the principal link between subordinate officials, leading citizens, and the general public, on the one hand, and the governor, usually distant and detached, on the other. The colonial secretary could assert himself as a gatekeeper controlling access to the governor and exerting great influence upon the timing and content of communication among the multifarious interests that formed the colony's public life. Moreover, because the colonial secretary normally served longer in the Crown Colony than the governor, his incumbency tended to promote the continuity of policy and performance between administrations.

As the de facto head of the public service in Trinidad, the colonial secretary was responsible for ensuring the day-to-day efficiency and integrity of its operations; for establishing and maintaining records and other archives in the secretariat; and for collecting the estimates each year from government departments for incorporation (usually with modifications) into the general estimates that the governor had to submit to the Legislative Council and ultimately to the secretary of state for the colonies for his sanction.[39]

Finally, the influence and prestige of the colonial secretary were enhanced in subtle ways by the perception, widely held in the Crown Colony, that that official doubtless coveted, and might someday be rewarded with, a colonial governorship in the empire.

Pressure began to build early in Trinidad for a constitutional framework resembling that in the older British colonies. But the imperial government in London feared that the proposed concession would antagonize the majority, composed of French and Spanish settlers, and that, moreover, it would be tantamount to an endorsement of white oligarchy based on a slave economy. In order to ensure metropolitan control of the colony and to ensure the possible abolition of slavery, there was established in Trinidad in the first decade of the nineteenth century the system of Crown Colony government based on a philosophy of paternalistic trusteeship.

For most of the nineteenth century the major sources of political grievances were colonywide issues of public policy tied directly or indirectly to continuing efforts by different groups to weaken, or eliminate, Crown Colony government in Trinidad. Intense political conflict arose over such issues as tariff and immigration policies, a restrictive franchise in local elections, the launching of costly public works projects, and control by the governor and his officials of the legislative process. Throughout the century the political opposition had as its base a tiny fragment of the colony's small middle class— whites tied to mercantile and cane-sugar interests and a handful of colored professionals. Attempts to wrest control of public affairs from a government dominated by foreign-born officials would all prove futile, however, partly because of adherence to a conservative imperial policy in London and partly because of endemic differences in Trinidad among the proponents of constitutional advance and because of the ineffectuality of their principal weapon, conventional pressure-group tactics.

By the last quarter of the nineteenth century, municipal affairs in Port-of-Spain increasingly overlapped the public affairs of the Crown Colony, lending an aura of importance to the former. Two municipal issues had gained special prominence by the 1890s, the role of the Port-of-Spain Borough Council in municipal governance and the policy of the colony government regarding water supply in the capital. Together they provided a springboard for a continuing assault upon the system of Crown Colony government in Trinidad. Both issues seemed to the residents of Port-of-Spain to point up the heavy-handedness of their colonial government based on a powerful administration and, correlatively, the ineptitude of its leading officials. Municipal issues in the capital would be the rallying point for anti-colonialism down to the outbreak of the First World War. Public agitation over the Borough Council increased shortly before the end of the century and was soon after directed to the water issue, resulting on March 23, 1903, in a major riot in Port-of-Spain which destroyed the government center, Red House. That event gave impetus to a new kind of radical opposition politics based on confrontation, political agitation, and mass mobilization.

The beginning of the period of urban nationalism in 1895 coincided with the accession of Joseph Chamberlain to the office of secretary of state for the colonies. Influenced by Negrophobic sentiment in Great Britain and armed with a "grand design" for imperial renewal, Chamberlain was determined during his eight-year tenure to strengthen Crown Colony government throughout the British West Indies. By the time he resigned in 1903, the urban black population in Trinidad had begun to assert itself as a radicalized political force, one destined to spearhead the drive to independence three-score years later. (Two immigrant groups were originally brought to the Caribbean in large numbers to work in the fields. The first to arrive in slaveholding British Trinidad was of African descent; the large community of indentured laborers from the Indian subcontinent came in the first generation after black manumission in 1834. Having been the first to move into Port-of-Spain and the other main towns and to be influenced by "Western" cultural norms and behavior, it is hardly surprising that those of African descent were the first group to experience political radicalization. Despite the end of immigration of Indians as indentured labor in 1917 and the formal abolition of the indenture system five years later, most of the Indian community continued to live and work in rural districts—on the land and in small towns—where they were less susceptible to Western cultural influences and to political radicalization. But in due course they, too, would develop politically. Long restive in their low social status, the Indian community began to manifest a growing political consciousness just before the outbreak of the First World War. The black and Indian communities, which together formed the majority underclass in Trinidad, would clash politically after the Second World War.) Urban nationalism had a galvanizing effect upon urban black workers and professionals, emphasizing for them the relationship between municipal issues and the system of Crown Colony government grounded on a philosophy of paternalistic trusteeship, which had thus far failed to advance significantly their collective interest. Urban nationalism constituted the last phase in a long era of reformist nationalism which, from its inception early in the nineteenth century, had been dominated by whites. It was the formative period for new political classes—black and Indian—in Trinidad, a testing time for new political methods, and the bridge, as it were, to a new era in the history of nationalism in the colony. Organized in the half century after the First World War on the mobilization of black discontent (in trade unions and party movements), a more strident revolutionary nationalism would build under charismatic black leadership toward victory over the system of Crown Colony government.

VI

Having dealt with various matters pertaining to towns and the process of urbanization in colonial societies, with definitional problems relating to the concept of nationalism, and with the concept of urban nationalism and how it relates to the case of Trinidad, I have only to highlight what follows in the study.

Chapter 2 presents an overview of three centuries of Spanish rule in Trinidad, with attention particularly to the establishment of towns and the emergence of Port-of-Spain as the capital, to the role of the Roman Catholic Church and the secular bureaucracy in colonial administration, to changes in immigration policy and consequent economic development in the island, and to tension between municipal authority and central authority as a historical source of urban nationalism.

The rise and fall of reform politics in nineteenth-century British Trinidad is examined in chapter 3 against the backdrop of the establishment of its system of Crown Colony government. Other sources of urban nationalism are located in the deep conservatism of imperial policy, in the organizational and tactical weaknesses of the re-

formers, and in the growing importance of the Negro factor in political life.

Chapter 4 describes the evolution in the nineteenth century of
Port-of-Spain as a colonial capital. Its physical and demographic
growth are both highlighted as bases for strain in the town's social
and political life. Riots occurring in the half century before the period of urban nationalism are examined, along with tensions developing between a powerful Crown Colony government and the municipal authority in Port-of-Spain.

Subsequently, the focus of the study shifts to urban nationalism
in Trinidad, different aspects of which are examined in five chapters. Chapter 5 traces the political conflict between the municipality
of Port-of-Spain and the Trinidad government over the role of the
elective Borough Council in the capital. Culminating in the dissolution of that body and its replacement by an appointive municipal authority beholden to the central government, the conflict is seen as a
major spur to the radicalization of opposition politics in Port-of-
Spain.

The historical roots of the vexatious problem of water supply are
examined in chapter 6. Political radicalization is shown to have built
on the water issue toward the denouement of a mass riot in Port-of-
Spain on March 23, 1903.

Chapter 7 deals with the official inquiry into the water riot against
the backdrop of continuing radicalization of political life in Port-of-
Spain and elsewhere in the colony.

The establishment of a new normalcy in Trinidad—based on a
modest political advance within the constitutional status quo—is
described in chapter 8. Attention is drawn particularly to the role of
two strong figures in the public life of the Crown Colony, Governor
Sir Henry Moore Jackson and his colonial secretary, Hugh Clifford,
to the resolution of the water issue, and to efforts to resolve the festering issue of municipal governance in Port-of-Spain. All of these
developments are seen against the backdrop of the growing importance of a radicalized urban black population.

Chapter 9 deals with the resolution of the municipal question in
Port-of-Spain shortly before the outbreak of the First World War, the
further radicalization of urban blacks, and the emergence of the Indian factor in the political life of the colony.

The concluding chapter weighs the significance of the period of
urban nationalism in the history of Trinidad's nationalism—drawing the implications of major economic, social, and political develop-

ments in the two decades preceding the First World War for the nationalist struggle destined to intensify in the half century after 1919. Relationships are examined between urban nationalism and different social factors—race, class, religion, ethnicity—and the implications of those relationships drawn for various analytic perspectives on Caribbean society held by social scientists. The five perspectives on which I shall remark are social stratification, pluralism, social class analysis in the Marxist tradition, democratic revolution, and the ideology of Black Power. Finally, chapter 10 highlights the implications of *Urban Nationalism* for understanding the process of social and political change.

A brief comment is in order on the utility of the case-study approach employed. Clearly a case study of urban nationalism in the Crown Colony of Trinidad cannot be used as the basis for generalizing about anticolonial nationalism in the history of European imperialism. Nor can it provide answers to more general questions regarding conflict and change in a wide array of colonial and former colonial societies. Those objectives can be pursued only by accumulating and analyzing a rich variety of historical data about numerous societies over which the European imperial powers have held sway. But a case study of urban nationalism in Trinidad can serve four important purposes. By keeping in view both ends of the network of imperial administration—the metropole and the colony—such a study can demonstrate that there are limits to authoritarian rule and that within those limits social and political changes are apt to result as much from the actions of those who resist change as from the actions of those who instigate it. This study can also enhance our understanding of the origins and early dynamics of political radicalism in Trinidad—an important subject in the political history of the Caribbean and in British imperial history.[40] Moreover, a study of urban nationalism based on the historical record of British rule in Trinidad can help reveal the key link in that colony between the formulation and implementation of municipal public policy and anticolonial nationalism. Finally, a close reading of the historical record can aid in assessing various social science perspectives on Caribbean society. *Urban Nationalism* is intended to serve all four purposes.

2

Spanish Trinidad: Colonization, Town Life, and Constitutional Development

I

CHRISTOPHER COLUMBUS took possession of the island of Trinidad (which he so named) for the Spanish Crown on July 31, 1498, during his third voyage. Coming upon a land sparsely populated by native Amerindian groups, he remained just long enough to establish contact with some of them; less than a week later he sailed north to Hispaniola, then the principal seat of government of the Spanish Empire in the New World. During the next quarter century, Spanish traders occasionally visited this remote outpost in the southern Caribbean, usually to seize Amerindians for slave labor in the gold mines of Hispaniola and Puerto Rico. Spain did not begin to colonize Trinidad until around 1530.[1] For many years thereafter, the small body of Spanish colonists living under a weak executive authority in the island struggled to maintain their foothold in the face of repeated incursions by foreign enemies.

In 1595, Trinidad was visited by Sir Walter Raleigh, who marked the occasion by laying waste the capital founded three years earlier at San José de Oruña (hereafter St. Joseph). He soon withdrew with his force to Guiana, taking with him a prisoner, Don Antonio de Berrio y Oruña, the Spanish governor of Trinidad. (The hapless Don Antonio was later allowed to return to his colony.) Over the next century, Trinidad was attacked from time to time by English, Dutch, and French marauders, occasionally with the aid of their allies among the Amerindian population. The Dutch invaded in 1640 and captured St. Joseph but eventually withdrew from the island. In 1672, Trinidad was assaulted by a British force from Barbados under the command of Sir Tobias Bridges; the invaders withdrew after sustaining heavy losses in a futile attempt to reach the capital at St. Joseph. Five years later, a French force led by the Marquis de Maintenon was content to withdraw with its spoils after sacking the Spanish colony. In 1690, another French force, this one headed by Levassor de la Touche, tried unsuccessfully to subdue the island colony.

During the first two centuries of Spanish rule in Trinidad, a succession of colonial governors, lacking a sizable body of colonists from which to raise an effective military force, did their best to ward off foreign invaders, to exert their authority over the Spanish settlers and the Amerindians, and to appropriate the latter's wealth, especially their land. Their efforts gradually bore fruit, as evidenced by several developments.

By the end of the seventeenth century, an alien regime and its native subjects were bound closely together by ties of mutual self-interest. Many among the Amerindian population had come to regard the colonial authority in Trinidad as their protector against a common adversary, the foreign invader bent on plunder; and the colonial authority together with the Spanish colonists on the island had come to look upon the Amerindians as a docile work force to be exploited, even if harshly. Eventually labor conditions ameliorated, partly through the influence of Roman Catholicism, the religion of the conqueror, which by the end of the seventeenth century had begun to make firm its claim upon the allegiance of the remnant native population.[2] In 1687, for example, a Royal Cédula ("decree") provided, among other things, that Amerindians would become vassals of the Spanish Crown twenty years after they were baptized and that those baptized would henceforth be freed from slave labor. By 1700, slave labor by Amerindians was abolished in the colony.[3]

In another effort, the governor in 1592 established a capital at St.

Joseph, a settlement twelve miles east of present-day Port-of-Spain on the Gulf of Paria. The site was chosen largely for strategic reasons. A coastal capital, the Spanish feared, would be prey to attack by their European rivals leading to the loss of the entire island. It was thought, moreover, that inland St. Joseph, in addition to being militarily defensible and well provisioned, would have good communications with the sea and with the native population in the interior. The reason that would prove weakest of these was the defensibility of St. Joseph. In fact, the town was as vulnerable to attack as any capital on the coast would have been.

With Raleigh's withdrawal from Trinidad in 1595, the colony's government made haste to rebuild the devastated capital in accordance with the rules for new towns set down in the Royal Ordinances of 1573. On the periphery of its main plaza were plots reserved for the governor's palace, the Roman Catholic church, and the town hall and jail. In time, more plots were staked out in a gridwork pattern for new Spanish settlers in the colony. By 1637, St. Joseph consisted of about thirty houses, each one built of mud, wood, and straw. Fire broke out frequently in the town, destroying many of its rudimentary structures.

Throughout most of its history, St. Joseph has been a small, relatively unimportant community in Trinidad. Even before the end of Spanish rule in the island in 1797, the first capital of Trinidad was destined to be eclipsed, economically and politically, by its main rival, the coastal town of Port-of-Spain.

Port-of-Spain, like St. Joseph to the east, was founded originally by the Spanish on the site of a pre-Columbian Amerindian settlement. Cumucurapo, "the place of the silk-cotton tree," from which the Mucurapo quarter of modern Port-of-Spain takes its name, was chosen as the site for Puerto de España, Spain's first coastal town on the island.[4] Early Puerto de España, or Port-of-Spain, served the colony both as a port and a defensive post. A fort was built there many years before St. Joseph was designated as the capital. From its beginnings, Port-of-Spain was a key military outpost behind which Spanish control of the hinterland and its native population gradually spread. However, the town proved to be as vulnerable as St. Joseph to the ravages of foreign invasion. Earthquakes and fires also took periodic tolls. Laid waste by a great conflagration in 1678, Port-of-Spain was rebuilt south of Mucurapo along the coast, near the mouth of the Caroni River.

II

Only two towns were established in Trinidad during three centuries of Spanish rule: St. Joseph and Port-of-Spain. St. Joseph alone was officially designated a *ciudad* ("town," "city") in 1691, but despite its formal status St. Joseph continued to suffer languid development. Neither new immigrants in the colony nor settlers elsewhere on the island were drawn to the town, and even its earliest residents evinced little attachment to it. By 1757, all of the *vecinos* ("householders")[5] had abandoned the administrative capital to live on their rural estates. Dwellings in the town quickly fell into disrepair, and finally, in 1761, the *cabildo* ("town council," a body of Spanish settlers who shared with the governor responsibility for managing public affairs in the capital and the colony)[6] ordered the vecinos to rebuild their houses in St. Joseph and to reestablish residence there. The order produced a brief spurt of development, which extended also to Port-of-Spain. Within a year, thirty houses were either built or rehabilitated in each town.

But St. Joseph and Port-of-Spain both experienced slow growth for some time. For example, in 1762 Port-of-Spain was still nestled against the coast, its buildings strung along two streets, Calle de Infante and Calle del Principe (renamed Duncan Street and Nelson Street, respectively, during the era of British rule). Following a major earthquake in 1766, both towns were substantially rebuilt but only modestly expanded. Twenty years before the end of Spanish rule in Trinidad, by which time Port-of-Spain had eclipsed St. Joseph, the two towns still resembled ramshackle villages. By 1777, Port-of-Spain, the larger town, contained only eighty private dwellings, most of small or modest size and most inhabited by vecinos of poor or modest means.

The permanent populations of St. Joseph and Port-of-Spain remained small throughout the period of Spanish rule. For example, in 1688 about 100 vecinos lived in the capital, about one-tenth that number in Port-of-Spain. Each group of vecinos, holding political rights in the respective towns, was comprised of whites, *mestizos,* and *mulattoes.*[7] Counting also the wives and children of vecinos, their slaves, and the nearly 300 Amerindian adults and children who labored for the vecinos, about 750 people lived in the two towns. By 1760, the populations of St. Joseph and Port-of-Spain had grown, respectively, to 786 and 440, representing a combined increase of only 63.6 percent in nearly three-quarters of a century. By 1777, the population of St. Joseph had risen to 1,053, Port-of-Spain to 632. (Small as these figures were, they represented a substantial proportion of the total population of Trinidad at the time. In 1778, for example, the colony had only 3,432 inhabitants, up nearly 2,500 over a two-year period mainly as a result of liberal concessions granted in 1776 to French Catholic immigrants and their black slaves.)[8] Nearly half the population of Trinidad dwelt in St. Joseph and Port-of-Spain in 1778, an augury of future overcrowding in the northernmost sector of the island.[9] Slow growth and development notwithstanding, it was evident before the last quarter of the eighteenth century that long-term prospects were brighter for Port-of-Spain than for the capital. The coastal town appeared by then to have a more vital function than its inland rival.

By the beginning of the eighteenth century, the arguments for siting the colonial capital at St. Joseph had become progressively weaker because of repeated foreign attacks upon the town, a dwindling Amerindian population having to acquiesce to the Spanish imperial order, and the spread of commerce throughout the Western Hemisphere. The growth of external trade in particular made more pressing the need for a coastal capital in the colony.

Even before the decision was taken to relocate the capital in Port-of-Spain, the town had come to dominate the public life of the colony. Ignoring the strong objections of the cabildo, in 1735 Governor Don Estevan de Liñan y Vera decided to move his official residence to Port-of-Spain. By 1757, the entire retinue of royal officials in Trinidad had also taken up residence in the coastal town, leaving only the members of the cabildo in St. Joseph. With the administration of the colony now effectively divided between its commercial center, Port-of-Spain, and its nominal capital, St. Joseph, antagonism grew between the two towns and between their respective officials. This condition did not abate until August 1783, when the cabildo reluctantly convened its first meetings in Port-of-Spain. With that development, Port-of-Spain was recognized de facto as the new capital of Spanish Trinidad.[10]

III

Until the eighteenth century, Trinidad continued to stagnate in the backwater of the Spanish Empire in the New World. Imperial poli-

cies adopted long before by the Spanish Crown had worked to restrain European settlement in the colony and to perpetuate its marginal involvement in the international economy. Foreign nationals
were prohibited from settling in Trinidad and from handling any
part of its external trade; the latter prohibition produced a contra-
band trade that rivaled the legal Spanish monopoly and cut deeply
into the royal revenues. The island's economy looked bleak indeed,
brightened only occasionally by developments that seemed to augur
improvement. But those developments were usually short lived. For
example, cocoa had been successfully cultivated in Trinidad in
the late seventeenth and early eighteenth centuries. But a blight
struck the plantations around 1725, and sustained recovery was not
achieved until nearly sixty years later.

Economic prospects for the long term finally brightened in 1776.
Recognizing at last that few Spaniards from Spain or her colonies
would ever be enticed or compelled to settle in Trinidad, the Crown
decided to liberalize its policy on immigration by allowing certain
Roman Catholic foreigners to settle in the colony. The new policy
was instituted that year by granting to French Catholics the first in
a series of concessions that was intended to spur immigration, especially from the neighboring islands of Dominica, Grenada, St. Vincent, and Tobago.[11] (Those colonies had been ceded by France to
Great Britain by the Treaty of Paris in 1763. Spain was aware that
the French colonists in the four islands were discontented under
British rule and would be disposed to migrate to Trinidad under attractive conditions.) The major incentive to foreigners would be land
grants according to their economic station in the territory from
which they had emigrated. In the next two years, 2,500 immigrants
(1,000 Frenchmen and their 1,500 slaves) entered Trinidad. In 1779,
the same concessions were granted to Irish Catholics in Santa Cruz,
a Danish colony.[12] The year before, Roume de St. Laurent, a French
planter from Grenada, who would be appointed the first commissioner of population in Trinidad in 1786,[13] had occasion to visit the
Spanish colony for the first time. Struck by its fertile soil and its economic impoverishment resulting from underpopulation, he went to
Madrid to petition the Spanish Crown to liberalize its immigration
policy further. He proved to be a persuasive advocate. On November
24, 1783, the Crown promulgated a new Cédula for the Population of
Trinidad.[14] It contained a bold strategy for developing the colony
rapidly by opening it to foreign immigration.

Henceforth all Roman Catholics, whatever their nationality,

would be allowed to enter Trinidad as colonists, conditional on their taking an oath of allegiance to the Spanish Crown. After five years, the new settlers could become naturalized subjects of Spain. In fact, the ban against non-Catholic immigration was ineffectual during the long administration of the last Spanish governor of the island, Don José María Chacón; the liberal-minded, pragmatic Chacón permitted many Protestant settlers—white, black, and mulatto—to enter the colony in the period 1784–97.

The cédula regulated both the acquisition of land by these new settlers and their rights with regard to slaveholding. White settlers would be allowed twice the amount of land as free black and mulatto immigrants—a policy that, while discriminatory on the basis of race, was more tolerant than any other pursued at the time by Spain's European rivals in the West Indies.[15] Under the new dispensation, Spanish Trinidad for the first time became a slave colony.[16] Immigrants from other West Indies islands, whatever their race, were to be allowed to enter Trinidad with their slaves. The racial status of the new settlers coupled with the number of slaves they owned would determine how much land they received from the Spanish Crown: slaveholding white immigrants would be granted twice the amount of land as slaveholding immigrants of color.

With the promulgation of the Cédula of 1783, a new generation of settlers, white and free black and mulatto, descended upon Trinidad. Many colonists came from neighboring islands in the West Indies, often with black slaves. Others came from North America or Europe; by 1786 a large number of Irish tradesmen and cultivators had settled in the island. So great was the immigrant tide that barely two years after the promulgation of the cédula, Spanish Trinidad was transformed, demographically and economically, into a non-Spanish colony. By 1785, the French community in the island outnumbered the Spanish community by a 20:1 ratio.[17] Fleeing the consequences of the French Revolution in France and its West Indies colonies, French immigrants entered Trinidad at an even more accelerated rate after 1789.

The magnitude of the transformation that was wrought in Spanish Trinidad in the era of a liberalized immigration policy, 1776–97, can be seen in three sets of data.

In the initial phase of the new policy, 1776–78, the population of the colony nearly quadrupled, to 3,432. In 1784, a year after the cédula was promulgated, the population reached 6,503, nearly double that of 1778. Only six years later, in 1790, Trinidad had a population of 13,247, more than double that of 1784. In 1797, the last year of Spanish rule, the colony had 17,718 inhabitants, representing a 33.8 percent increase over the number in 1790.[18]

In the fifteen years 1782–97, the population of whites and free people of color increased, respectively, from 126 to 2,151 and from 295 to 4,476; the number of black slaves rose from 310 to 10,009. Headed for virtual extinction after three centuries of Spanish rule, the Amerindian population declined in the period 1782–97 from 2,200 to 1,082.[19]

The French community became more important after 1776 (and especially after 1783). Great Britain acquired Trinidad from Spain in 1797 and secured its claim to the island in 1802 under the Treaty of Amiens.[20] In 1802, more than half (52.5 percent) of the 1,415 white men and women in the colony's three largest European communities (English, Spanish, and French) were members of the French community. French nationality was held by nearly half (48.3 percent) of the 2,261 whites in Trinidad and by more than half (54.4 percent) of the 5,154 free men and women of color.[21]

All of these developments were keenly felt in Port-of-Spain, which experienced a population explosion in the first generation after liberal immigration was introduced. Whereas the population of that town increased 43.7 percent, from 440 to 632, in the seventeen-year period 1760–77, it increased more than sixfold (by 616.6 percent) in the next twenty years, reaching 4,525 in 1797. (Pointing up the declining importance of the former capital, St. Joseph, its population decreased in the period 1777–97 from 1,053 to 728.) Of the 4,525 inhabitants of Port-of-Spain in 1797, the last year of Spanish rule, 938 (20.7 percent) were white, 1,671 (36.9 percent) free colored, and 1,916 (42.3 percent) black slaves. (Among the 728 inhabitants of St. Joseph that year, 142 [19.5 percent] were white, 177 [24.3 percent] free colored, and 409 [56.1 percent] black slaves.)[22] Far more striking than the difference between the two towns based on status as free or slave is that based on nationality. In 1802, the year Great Britain sealed its claim to Trinidad, nearly two-thirds (63.7 percent) of the free population of Port-of-Spain was French; in contrast, the overwhelming majority (88.1 percent) of the free men in St. Joseph were Spanish.[23] Port-of-Spain had become a "French" town by the dawn of British rule in the island colony, its old rival, St. Joseph, a "Spanish" town.

Once langorous Port-of-Spain was transformed by 1788 into a robust center of administration and commerce, its business community and external trade virtually monopolized under the new dispensation to foreigners—by French and, to a lesser extent, by English, North American, and Antillean interests. In time, these interests were able to project their economic power far beyond the northernmost sector of the island, which included Port-of-Spain. As the owners of large tracts of cultivable land in the hinterland—where cane sugar and cocoa were the principal cash crops—they hastened the integration of town and countryside into the economic life of the capital. After the Spanish Crown and this small emergent foreign elite, the new colonists with more modest endowments rounded out the ranks of landowners in rural Trinidad.

Prominent among the new landowners in Spanish Trinidad were French cultivators of cocoa. The growing influence of the French in cultivation and trade, both based increasingly on cocoa, enabled them to assume an eminent role in the economic life of the colony.[24] Contemplating the rapid growth of the French community, in numbers and in influence, one historian of the period was moved to observe that "the French completely governed the destiny of Trinidad."[25]

The new wave of immigrants also became a part of the political life of Port-of-Spain and of Trinidad. Soon after the cédula took effect, three new settlers in the colony were appointed to fill seats on the cabildo. Three years later, in 1786, control of the town council passed forever from Spanish hands: among its ten members that year were eight colonists—seven French, one Irish—who had only recently arrived in the island. Following a pattern established by their Spanish predecessors on the cabildo, the new settlers holding seats on the council sought to enhance the prestige and power of that body, and of Port-of-Spain, at the expense of Governor Chacón and his royal officials.

Despite the liberal concessions made to French immigrants, their loyalty to Spain was suspect. Thus, when France and Spain were at war in 1793, many in the French community acted as if Trinidad belonged not to Spain but to the Republic of France. Employing conciliation and the threat of force in appropriate measure, the adroit Chacón managed to keep the French inhabitants of the colony in check.[26] Still, the "French factor" loomed large in Trinidad, whatever the colonial regime. Having laid a strong foundation in Trinidad's political economy in the twilight years of Spanish rule, the French community was destined to fill a major role in the public affairs of the colony and the capital even under British rule. Its once-great influence would finally slip away only in the era of mass politics and political radicalization, after 1918.[27]

The pattern of immigration after 1776 (and especially after 1783) notwithstanding, Trinidad was destined to become a colony not of France but of Great Britain. At war with Spain in 1797, Great Britain dispatched a large force from Martinique on February 12 under General Sir Ralph Abercrombie and Admiral Henry Harvey to subdue the Spanish colony. Finding his military situation hopeless, Governor Chacón capitulated six days later.[28]

IV

Spanish imperialism in the New World had two principal objectives: to Christianize and civilize the vanquished native peoples and to exploit the material resources of the colonies in the interest of Crown and country. To ensure its ultimate control over so vast an enterprise, the Spanish Crown organized imperial governance on a principle of dualism that kept separate two large and powerful bureaucracies— one secular, the other ecclesiastical. Together they comprised the overarching political organization that was established by the Crown to administer its empire in the New World.[29]

In Spain, the Council of the Indies, a judicial and advisory body founded in 1524, was responsible for making major administrative, judicial, and ecclesiastical decisions for the empire. It drafted most imperial legislation and then waited upon the Crown for its assent. In the New World, the most important administrative institution was the *audiencia,* which had several functions. As the supreme judicial body in its jurisdiction, it spoke for the interests of the Crown. It was responsible, moreover, for monitoring the activities of subordinate royal officials and for assessing the records of those officials when their terms of office had ended. Finally, it was charged with certain responsibilities for the native population.

All posts in Spanish America were filled by the Crown. But fearing that powerful audiencias far from Spain might still pose a threat to royal interests, the Crown charged viceroys to watch over those institutions. Representing the sovereign, these officials could direct the actions of audiencias in all but judicial matters. Audiencias had to report regularly to the viceroys on conditions in the colonies for which the former were responsible.

Early on, the colonies of Trinidad and Guiana together constituted one of the nine provinces under the jurisdiction of the Audiencia of Santo Domingo and the Viceroyalty of New Spain. Then, for two centuries, various schemes for administrative reorganization of Spanish America caused Trinidad to be attached to one or another audiencia and viceroyalty. Finally, in 1742, the colony's military and financial affairs were transferred to the Captaincy-General of Venezuela, which was under the Audiencia of Santo Domingo.[30]

Heading each colony within the audiencia was a governor appointed by the Spanish Crown for five years. Acting for the Crown, he was chief executive, military commander, and, for a time, chief of the highest court in the colony. Despite his accountability to the audiencia, a resourceful governor could have considerable autonomy in day-to-day affairs. He could delay the implementation of any law or command he deemed incompatible with the interests of the colony. And if his colony was far removed from the seat of the audiencia (as Trinidad was from Santo Domingo), the governor could usually be confident that higher authorities would neither restrain nor punish his actions.

Heading the ecclesiastical hierarchy was the Spanish Crown, which administered the affairs of the clergy in consultation with the Council of the Indies. The ecclesiastical hierarchy was organized in two parts, secular clergy and mission clergy. Because there were too few secular clergy in Spanish America to instruct in the Roman Catholic faith and at the same time to act as agents of the Crown, missionary orders were enlisted for those tasks. The secular clergy was supposed eventually to assume responsibility for the missions' spearhead activities, but this rarely happened.[31] Rather, a division of labor emerged in which the missions preached to the unconverted among the native population and the secular clergy preached to the Spanish colonists and to Amerindians in the *encomiendas*. (Leading Spanish colonists received an encomienda, or grant, of natives as a personal reward for service or merit; the *encomendero,* or grantholder, pledged to protect his charges and instruct them in the Catholic faith in exchange for their tribute in money, kind, or labor.)

Underlining the distinctions between the two parts of the ecclesiastical hierarchy was the method of their appointment. Secular clergy were appointed by the bishop of the appropriate diocese in Spanish America, mission clergy by the head of the missionary order in Spain—in Trinidad, by the bishop of Puerto Rico and the head of the Catalonian Capuchins, respectively.

The dual systems of secular and ecclesiastical hierarchies, the latter formed around two sets of clergy (secular and mission), was scarcely a model of administrative efficiency. But the Crown preferred securing its power to achieving imperial efficiency. By dividing jurisdictions and causing them to overlap, competing administrative interests in Spanish America had perforce to vie for the Crown's favor. Therein lay the source of royal supremacy in imperial affairs.

Near the end of the sixteenth century, the Spanish Crown made ready to enforce the territorial segregation of the various communities in Trinidad. Its principal objectives were to protect the dwindling native population, especially against physical abuse,[32] and to establish on a firm basis the secular and ecclesiastical bureaucracies that would have responsibility, respectively, for the Spanish and the Amerindian communities. Inhabitants of the colony who were of mixed race (mulattoes, mestizos, and *zambos*)[33] would be required to live among the Spanish population, in the main towns; most of the native population would live with the missionaries or with the encomenderos to whom they had been granted.

For more than a century after the inception of the new policy, Trinidad was organized so that each community had a system of private and communal land tenure based on its segregated residential location. For the Spanish community, there were royal officials, including the governor, *alcaldes* ("magistrates"), *procuradores* ("solicitors"), and *contadores* ("accountants"), along with the elected cabildo based at the capital, St. Joseph. Judicial power was lodged far away in the audiencia and in certain extraordinary military and ecclesiastical courts. Finally, the ecclesiastical hierarchy included secular clergy serving as parish priests along with cloistered religious in various convents and monasteries.

At the center of administration in the Amerindian community were the encomiendas and the *corregidores de indios*; the latter were Spanish officials who had responsibility for protecting the native population and for collecting tribute and regulating native labor under the *mita* regimen (a system of draft labor that required each native village to provide a specified number of its male members to work for fixed wages on various public works projects). Both the encomiendas and the corregidores de indios were under the control of the Spanish Crown, exercised locally by the governor. The Amerindian community also had its own conciliar body, the cabildo; judicial power was lodged in an office known as the *juzgado de indios*. Finally, the ecclesiastical hierarchy included missionaries in the missions and *curas doctrineros,* priests responsible for ensuring the conversion of the native population in the encomiendas and their instruction in the Catholic faith.

In time, two of the major institutions in the Amerindian community, the quasi-feudal encomiendas and the missions, were abolished by the Spanish Crown, the former for failing as an economic institution, the latter for zealously protecting the native population against the Crown and other interests that were bent on exploiting Amerindian labor for economic development. Nearly two centuries would pass before the administration was reorganized in Trinidad—and throughout Spanish America—to accelerate such development.[34]

V

Various administrative reforms were instituted in Trinidad in the late seventeenth and early eighteenth centuries, among them reconstituting the cabildo at St. Joseph so that it would comprise two *alcaldes ordinarios* ("magistrates"), an *alférez mayor* ("standard bearer"), four *regidores* ("councillors"), a procurador, an *alguacil* ("constable"), and an *alcalde de hermandad* ("justice of the peace for rural areas").[35] (A similar arrangement of offices and powers obtained in the cabildo after 1783, when its venue was shifted to the new capital at Port-of-Spain.) But not even all these reforms encouraged either the efficiency of government in the colony or its economic development. Despite their role as agents of the Crown, and despite their considerable autonomy vis-à-vis the audiencia, the governor and his royal officials continued to exercise little real power outside the Spanish towns in northern Trinidad. And even there executive authority was dependent upon the goodwill of the clergy and the cabildo—a political condition that the Crown had long fostered as a means of restraining the growth of independent executive power in the colony. Near the middle of the eighteenth century, the cabildo had considerable administrative power in St. Joseph: it could levy duties and taxes in and around the capital, supervise town police, markets, and streets, and license physicians and surgeons to practice. Its two alcaldes ordinarios served also as chief judges in the colony, thereby integrating the affairs of the colony and the capital in the institution of the cabildo.[36] Under this arrangement, the relationships among governor, clergy, and cabildo were characterized by persistent strain and conflict, as evidenced by several events.

In 1735, as seen, Governor Estevan de Liñan y Vera dared to defy the cabildo and take up residence in Port-of-Spain, a move that augured the eventual transfer of the capital to that town. Embittered by his initiative, the town council exploited every opportunity over the ensuing decade of his administration to assert its own powers and privileges. In 1743 it protested when the governor took temporary leave of the colony and appointed an acting governor. When Vera returned to his post, he was imprisoned by the council for eight months. During his absence from the colony and his incarceration, the government of Trinidad was in the hands of the two alcaldes ordinarios in the cabildo. Legal government was not restored in Trinidad until the viceroyalty dispatched a large force to free the hapless governor and remove the usurper alcaldes.[37]

On another occasion, in 1752, the cabildo tried to assert its power in ecclesiastical affairs, this time criticizing another governor for allowing the vicar-general to depart the understaffed community of clergy in the colony. Upon taking up his appointment, the new vicar-general was castigated by the council for failing to appear before it to present his credentials.[38]

The cabildo could act against the executive authority for other than explicitly political reasons. In 1765, it tried unsuccessfully to prevent Governor José Antonio Gil from allowing a medical practitioner to take temporary leave of Trinidad, contending that the latter's absence from the colony would further strain its inadequate medical resources.[39]

All such conflicts underscored the institutional rivalry between the governor and the cabildo. As their relationship continued to worsen throughout the eighteenth century, even the Spanish Crown came eventually to recognize that to achieve both efficient and effective administration in Trinidad would require centralization under a far stronger governor as chief executive.

VI

The imperial policy of fostering weak executive authority in the colonies was mainly responsible for the political instability that was endemic in Spanish America. And that instability, together with the restrictive policies on immigration, land tenure, and trade, caused many Spanish colonies in the New World to suffer economic distress. Clearly, these problems could not be resolved without the Crown's adoption of a new policy direction for its empire.[40]

Throughout the eighteenth century, pressures for change built within the empire and without; flushed with the Enlightenment spirit of egalitarianism and free trade, European rivals pressed hard for Spain to lower the imperial barriers it had raised against the outside world.[41] Approaching the last quarter of the century, the Spanish Crown felt constrained to adopt a more flexible approach, balancing its traditional conservatism with the need for measured change. Its initial moves were cautious and modest, for example, the decision taken in 1776 to open Trinidad to restricted French Catholic immigration. But the wall in Madrid was finally breached, setting the empire on a course of accelerated development—political, social, and economic—for two decades.

The first generation of foreign immigrants in Trinidad was joined within a decade by the flood tide unleashed by the Cédula for Population. Two events in 1783, the promulgation of the cédula and the transfer of the capital from St. Joseph to Port-of-Spain, signaled that the island colony was turning its face to the non-Spanish world. The stage was set for a major reorganization of administration in Trinidad. Spearheading that development would be the last Spanish governor of the island, Don José María Chacón. Appointed in 1784, Chacón was to serve as governor for thirteen years, longer than all but four of his thirty-eight predecessors over nearly three centuries.[42] There would be time for him to calibrate his every initiative on the administrative front with the new policy of bureaucratic centralism that was taking hold throughout Spanish America. For the first time, colonial government in Trinidad would bear the hallmark of an efficient and effective operation.

Under the Bourbons, the Spanish Crown moved to base imperial administration on the principle of intendancy. The importance of the intendants in the new system was emphasized by making them answerable only to the Crown; to enhance their effectiveness, they would have many of the administrative, judicial, and financial powers of the former governors and corregidores.[43]

Coincident with the launching of the first phase of the new immigration policy, the Intendancy of Venezuela was created in 1776; among its several provinces was the colony of Trinidad, which had the status of a *partido,* or subunit, headed by an official known as the *subdelegado.*[44] In 1781, Trinidad was elevated to an intendancy, with its governor as intendant. Hesitant still to underwrite a strong executive authority in the colony, during the period 1779–83 the governorship of Trinidad was divided into civil and military roles,[45] thereby weakening the office. But in 1783 the roles were reunited and the office of governor/intendant thus greatly strengthened.

When he became chief executive in 1784, Chacón had more authority than any of his predecessors. For a time, he had to share some of that authority (in administrative and judicial affairs) with the subdelegado who had been appointed to head the partido of Trinidad under the Intendancy of Venezuela. But with his reappointment as governor/intendant in 1789, Chacón was granted full control over agricultural, commercial, and financial affairs in Trinidad, with the power to appoint key officials of the colony in the towns and in the newly created rural *barrios* ("wards").[46]

The ecclesiastical hierarchy, having long ago lost much of its royal patronage in Spanish America, could raise no effective challenge now to Chacón's authority in Trinidad. His only potential rival among the official institutions, the cabildo in Port-of-Spain, had had its own powers sharply curtailed by 1791, rendering it essentially a municipal council in the capital. On matters of public policy affecting the whole colony, the cabildo had only an advisory role vis-à-vis the governor/intendant.[47]

In less than a decade, Chacón managed to put the stamp of his own strong leadership on the colony. As a contemporary, a free mulatto in the island, put it, "The period of the administration of Don José María Chacón was the golden age of Trinidad. Commerce flourished, justice poised in equal scale, and prejudice was driven to skulk in the dark abodes of a few illiberal earth-born breasts."[48]

But there were dimmer illuminations, too, in the "golden age" of Spanish Trinidad. For example, during his long incumbency Chacón tried to direct the energies of the growing population in the colony especially to the task of agricultural development. The results were positive but hardly spectacular. In the year of the British conquest, only 100,000 of the 800,000 acres in Trinidad were under cultivation.[49] A limited range of crops, headed by sugarcane (from which was produced rum and molasses) and cocoa, were grown in monocultural estates; the fate of these estates, which varied greatly in size, was marked by the vicissitudes of labor and capital, of nature, and of the international economy. Agriculture continued to lag far behind the development of commerce based mainly on the northern towns in the island.

VII

Chacón served as governor/intendant until his capitulation in 1797. With the passage of Trinidad into British hands, there began a new phase in the struggle between the colony and the capital which pitted their respective governments against each other. The struggle had its roots, as seen, in the institutional rivalry in Spanish Trinidad between the governor and the cabildo, the latter based initially in St. Joseph and after 1783 in the new capital at Port-of-Spain. During the nineteenth century, the municipality of Port-of-Spain often found itself in conflict with a powerful Crown Colony government, usually over issues of urban reform involving the responsibilities of the local government and the central government and over the delivery of public services locally. By the end of the first century of British rule in the island, such conflicts were being exacerbated by tensions arising from the failure of the Trinidad reform movement to achieve its larger political objectives in the colony.[50] The struggle between the colony and the capital crystallized in the two decades after 1895 as urban nationalism, where the issues of urban reform were projected by important elements in the reform movement as a corollary of the larger issue of representative government in the Crown Colony. In chapter 3, we shall examine the evolution of reform politics in nineteenth-century Trinidad as a backdrop to the crisis period of urban nationalism.

3

British Trinidad: The Rise and Fall of Reform Politics in the Nineteenth Century

I

ALMOST IMMEDIATELY upon securing Britain's claim to Trinidad under the Treaty of Amiens in 1802, the growing minority of Britons in the colony began to agitate for English civil law and a constitution modeled after those in older British colonies. Thus began, albeit inauspiciously, an era of reform politics in British Trinidad. Fearing that these reforms would pose a threat to the interests of the large, potentially rebellious French and Spanish populations in Trinidad, and fearing also that the reforms would encourage the rise in the island of a white oligarchy based upon a slave economy, the imperial government in London rejected the proposal. Ministers there were confident that the pressure for reform disguised a plot by certain economic interests in Trinidad and Great Britain to wrest control of the colony and its legislative affairs from Parliament.[1] They tended also to look upon Trinidad as a laboratory for imperial policy, especially in the matter of the institution of slavery to which they were opposed: rules and practices tried and found suitable in one colony might subsequently be adopted elsewhere in the British Empire. They believed, for example, that since Spanish law pertaining to slavery was more benevolent than English law, slave life would be more easily ameliorated in British Trinidad and in other of Great Britain's former Spanish colonies by perpetuating the regime of Spanish law.[2] They also believed that their larger cause, the abolition of slavery throughout the empire, would be advanced by nominating rather than electing the legislative institution in Trinidad and other British slave colonies.[3] For all of these reasons, near the end of the Napoleonic Wars, Parliament chose to establish a Crown Colony government in Trinidad that would be directly responsible to London.[4]

II

Soon after receiving Governor Chacón's capitulation, General Sir Ralph Abercrombie and Admiral Henry Harvey departed Trinidad for Martinique, leaving Lieutenant-Colonel (later Brigadier-General) Thomas Picton, Abercrombie's aide-de-camp, to oversee the newly acquired colony as captain-general or military governor. Picton was instructed to use Spanish law in the island as a way of mollifying the French and Spanish populations. His hand as chief executive was strengthened when he was appointed by the British Crown on June 29, 1801, as civil and military governor of Trinidad. Governor Picton then proceeded to name his Council of Advice, whose five members were drawn from the British, French, Spanish, and Irish communities in the island. The council had neither legislative responsibilities nor any control over the chief executive; it met whenever the governor needed its experience and advice. It operated concurrently with the cabildo in Port-of-Spain, causing tension between the two bodies.[5]

In 1803, Picton's successor as governor, Brigadier-General Sir Thomas Hislop, changed the name of the Council of Advice to the Council of Government, albeit without changing its advisory function. The governor was obliged merely to consult his council, which was comprised of officials only, before he promulgated any laws for the colony.

In 1803, 1811, and 1820, petitions were laid before the Crown for the adoption of English law and a British constitution in Trinidad. A Commission of Legal Enquiry was appointed in London on November 29, 1823, to travel to the colony and report on the system of land titles under the old Spanish law, the state of the civil and criminal law, the system of taxation, and the powers of the governor. Based partly on the findings of the commission, on June 20, 1831, an order-in-council was promulgated establishing a Legislative Council with twelve members, six officials and six unofficials, the latter leading proprietors in the colony. (The governor was granted a casting vote.) The Crown would make nominations to the legislature on the basis of the governor's recommendations, and all legislative ordinances would be enacted by the chief executive in the colony upon the assent of the Crown.

With the slave trade formally abolished by Great Britain in 1808,[6] and slavery itself destined soon to be abolished in the empire,[7] Spanish law in Trinidad had become an anachronism. Accordingly, the order-in-council called also for the judicial system in the Crown Colony to be streamlined and for the system of Spanish law to be eliminated almost completely. The governor was empowered to constitute inferior courts by ordinance and, with the advice and consent of the newly established Executive Council, to fix the form and proceeding in those courts. A year later, an ordinance was passed in the Legislative Council declaring the Habeas Corpus Act operative in Trinidad.[8] Consistent with the order-in-council virtually abrogating Spanish law in the colony, in 1840 the cabildo was replaced in Port-of-Spain by a town council based on the British system of municipal government.[9]

The Legislative Council established in 1831 can be seen, on balance, to have had a generally obstructive attitude toward the constitutional development of Trinidad under British rule. There was a nominally progressive aspect to the course of action adopted that year—the introduction of some legislative capacity to check executive power in the Crown Colony if the members were disposed to do so. Prior to 1831, the governor was empowered to make laws for the colony after consulting his council, but, except where there was great urgency or the need to raise the annual revenue, those laws enacted by the governor were not binding in Trinidad until they were confirmed by the King-in-Council. While this principle continued after 1831, there were so many exceptions that the governor, with the advice and consent of the ordinarily pliable legislature, was eventually empowered to make laws that were binding and took effect in the colony from the day of his assent. The governor continued to exercise control over legislative affairs.

Basing the new Legislative Council firmly on the principle of nomination strengthened executive authority in the Crown Colony. Moreover, the adoption of that principle was the harbinger of a slow evolution in the constitution of Trinidad; henceforth the Crown would proceed in the matter of constitutional development by small steps over long intervals, and usually with great reluctance. Subsequent reforms would provide, as we shall see, for a nominated unofficial majority in the Legislative Council and for a greater voice for the legislature in the financial affairs of the colony. But responsible government proved an elusive goal. Public life in Trinidad remained firmly under the control of the governor and his officials until after the First World War, and the pace of constitutional advance would not quicken until after the Second World War a generation later. The elective principle was not established for the legislature until 1925, when that body was enlarged to include twenty-six members, of whom only seven were popularly elected. A restrictive franchise based on property and income was instituted at the time. In the ensuing years, the Legislative Council and the Executive Council were both gradually democratized by the addition of elected members. All the while, pressures to accelerate constitutional progress continued to build, based principally on clamorous trade union and nationalist party movements in the colony and on kindred developments throughout the various European empires in Africa, Asia, and the West Indies. Finally, as a prelude to independence in 1962, the system of Crown Colony government in Trinidad was replaced in 1961 by a system of responsible government that incorporated the principle of bicameralism.[10]

III

Launched early in the nineteenth century on a slow course of political change, Trinidad was to experience a growing popular distemper. There developed throughout the century a pervasive sense of grievance whose main targets were the Crown Colony government and the sugar plantocracy. Each was dominated by Britons whose principal loyalty, many islanders believed, was to metropolitan interests: the governor and his officials to their superiors in London, the planters to their British shareholders. Government and plantocracy were widely suspected of allying against the interests of Trinidad. Crown Colony government and the cane-sugar interests were seen by many in Trinidad as battening on the island's limited resources. The popular mind saw easy distinctions: between government and the people, Great Britain and Trinidad, Briton and non-Briton among the colony's white population, white and nonwhite,[11] black and Indian, town and country district, rich and poor.

If this distrust, and the various polarities that were its corollary, appears in retrospect to have been exaggerated in the Trinidadian's mind, it is only necessary to recall some roots in the last century— when the colony's political life was calibrated generally with an economic struggle that pitted labor against capital and management, especially in the sugar industry. In the first generation after black manumission in 1834, planter interests based on cane sugar had persuaded the imperial government in London to adopt a harshly restrictive Crown lands policy for Trinidad. Seen in perspective, this initiative had several practical effects, short term and long. Immediately it denied access to these valuable lands to all but the most affluent classes, thereby discouraging the formation of a substantial body of small farmers among free laborers in the Crown Colony (white and black) and poorer immigrants from Europe and elsewhere, who might have been persuaded by a more liberal policy to become farmers. The long-term effect of the restrictive land policy was to block the formation of a rural yeomanry. Lacking such a class as the economic foundation of society—and as a political force to whose interest the government of the Crown Colony would some day have to attend—Trinidad at mid-nineteenth century resembled a pyramid of affluent planters, merchants, and professionals atop a broad base of marginal and impoverished laborers, free and indentured.[12] Contemplating the injustice of that arrangement and, by implication, its potential explosiveness, the Scottish Presbyterian missionary Alexander Kennedy observed in 1846 that "the present [policies for Crown lands and accelerated immigration of indentured Indian laborers] would ere long make Trinidad a human *pen* instead of a paradise as it might be."[13] Cautious liberalization of Crown lands policy in the late 1860s did not transform the basic pyramid. Rather, it strengthened the tendency toward a two-tiered social formation by encouraging the emergence of a new class of largely poor or marginal peasant cultivators—white, black, and Indian.

Rising social tension in Trinidad was also associated with Indian immigration. The rapid influx after 1845 of indentured laborers from the subcontinent, a development that was spurred by large subsidies from the Crown Colony treasury,[14] worked a radical transformation upon the ethnic and racial composition of Trinidad. (Indian immigration followed largely unsuccessful efforts to recruit Portuguese, Chinese, and West African labor for the British West Indies.)[15] Whereas the Indians constituted only 4.81 percent of the population in 1851, by 1891 their proportion had increased nearly sevenfold to 32.15 percent.[16] While day-to-day relations between the black and Indian communities were never as explosive in Trinidad as, for example, in neighboring British Guiana, cultural and religious differences were a continuing source of mutual antagonism.[17]

Another factor that deeply divided blacks and Indians in the Crown Colony evolved from the economics of free and indentured labor. The persistent high level of Indian immigration coupled with a soaring birth rate in the Indian community depressed the level of wages in the free labor market. It weighed most heavily on the black community, which formed the backbone of the free laboring class. Caught between the restrictive Crown lands policy, which denied them the status of rural yeomanry, and the desperately low level of wages for free labor on and around the sugar estates, many blacks moved off the land and into the towns. (For many former slaves and their descendants, rural labor bore the stigmata of the slave experience. Their antipathy to such labor helped fuel migration into the towns.) Economic hardship continued to stalk many of the town blacks, who suffered underemployment or outright idleness.[18] As a result, resentment grew between these new town dwellers, on one side, and the sugar planters and their indentured Indian laborers, on the other. The sugarcane planters were perceived by most landless blacks as the principal beneficiaries of an oppressive wage structure, the economic role of the Indians as a major reason for black flight to the towns. A corollary of the growing gulf between social classes and racial groups in nineteenth-century Trinidad was heightened tension between the country districts and the towns. Wage levels continued to decline with consolidation and modernization of the sugar estates in the 1870s, intensifying the strains on a heterogeneous social fabric. These tensions, originating in the first generation after manumission, continued well into the twentieth century, even after the abolition of the indenture system, as economic advances made by rural Indian landholders and shopkeepers served to widen the breach between the Indian community and town blacks.[19]

Finally, there was considerable tension in the first half of the nineteenth century among the white population of Trinidad—especially between the British and French communities. But despite basic differences between the two groups on a broad range of communal issues, including sectarian education and the official policy of Anglicization,[20] in time more and more of their members, sharing a class outlook, found it possible to effect working alliances in pursuit of common political objectives. For example, in the second half of the century French Catholic creoles[21] and a growing number of British Protestants in the colony agreed to work together to reduce the voice of the Colonial Office in Trinidad's affairs. Their deepening sense that the island society was being governed highhandedly by foreign officials, representing a remote authority, in collusion with a small local plantocracy gave impetus to the establishment in 1856 of the Legislative Reform Committee. Along with a shared political interest, in time there was even the bond of a common language. The spread of English as a lingua franca in the last quarter of the nineteenth century, promoted partly by the eventual resolution of differences over education, removed a major barrier within the polyethnic white population.

IV

The most significant of the groups that emerged in Trinidad during the nineteenth century to espouse the cause of political reform were the Legislative Reform Committee and the Trinidad Workingmen's Association.

Comprised principally of French creole cocoa interests, British merchants, and a lesser number of colored (mulatto) professionals in the main towns, the Legislative Reform Committee was united in its opposition to the official policy of encouraging Indian immigration; to the system of indentured labor (regarded by the reformers as the basis for the privileged status of the sugar interests); and to the control of governmental, economic, and financial affairs in Trinidad by officials appointed by the imperial government in London. Established in the same year that Parliament struck a major blow against the British Caribbean planters by replacing the preferential tariff on cane sugar with a system of free trade, the committee was animated by a hopeful spirit.[22] Buoyed by the free trade initiative, it began to raise a sharp protest against the great burden imposed on Trinidad's revenues by the indenture system and by the system of Crown Colony government itself.

The committee was a liberal organization in the nineteenth-century tradition of reformist political clubs and associations. As in many other middle-class, cadre-type organizations of the time in Europe, its members were leading citizens who generally preferred constitutional methods over mass action to attain their goals.[23] From its inception in 1856 to its demise nearly sixty years later, the committee was content to eschew mass appeals. It never sought or enjoyed broad popular support.

It was not until 1897, when the Trinidad Workingmen's Association was founded, that the Crown Colony had its first working-class organization nominally committed to mass-movement politics. Notwithstanding, the association failed throughout its relatively short life to achieve the large following and the organizational cohesion that such a strategy required. Among the founders of the small, loosely knit group was a colored pharmacist, Alfred Richards,[24] who pressed, among other things, for the abolition of the Indian indenture system as a means of improving the lot of black workers, for an end to expatriate control of the only electricity company in Trinidad, and for municipal reforms in Port-of-Spain. Generally ignored or scorned by government, by the Legislative Council, and by such other reform groups as the Legislative Reform Committee, the association was nevertheless able, before its dissolution at the end of the First World War, to intensify the politicization of the black working class and to instill in it the value of collective action on behalf of shared goals. Richards's eventual leadership of the organization, while largely ineffectual, did at least symbolize for many in Trinidad an emergent political alliance, finally, between black workers and colored professionals in Port-of-Spain and the other main towns.

V

Social tensions arising from a wide range of class, racial, national, religious, and geographic differences in the Crown Colony sapped the energy of the reform movement almost from its inception. The Legislative Reform Committee, which mirrored many of these deep divisions, quickly learned that it could more easily agree on broad goals than on concrete actions. The members' initial ebullience was soon displaced by a cautious, despairing mood.

Still other forces, principally economic, conspired against the reform cause in the second half of the nineteenth century. The economic incentive to press for political reform in the colony was weakened when Trinidad, better off than the other, generally impoverished Caribbean societies, managed to weather the West Indies sugar depression in the 1870s and 1880s. Along with the other sugar colonies in the West Indies, Trinidad suffered from the abolition of the preferential tariff on cane sugar in 1856. Competition from Hawaiian and Puerto Rican cane sugar and from bounty-fed European beet sugar caused Trinidad's cane sugar exports to decline sharply in the period 1856–74. The colony managed to stay afloat after 1870 with the aid of a prospering cocoa industry, mostly in French creole hands, and by oil and asphalt industries infused with foreign capital.[25] The Trinidad reform movement was further weakened in the 1870s when vast tracts in the unoccupied Crown lands were finally opened to free labor, and employment opportunities for that class were greatly expanded by an ambitious program of public works. Moreover, many in Trinidad who were in accord with the reform goal of ending the privileged status of the plantocracy saw changing economic conditions on the international level as more likely than local political action to alter the balance of interests in the Crown Colony. The new system of free trade for British West Indies sugar was expected to act jointly with the depression in that industry to limit the prestige and influence of the planter interests in the public life of Trinidad—and in imperial affairs generally.

When the drive for reform finally quickened in the early 1880s, the Legislative Reform Committee was no longer in the vanguard. The initiative had shifted to the local press, in particular to the *Gazette* and *Public Opinion* in Port-of-Spain. Each of these newspapers had spearheaded a campaign against the administration of Sir Henry Irving, governor of Trinidad from 1874 to 1880. His administration had been scored by many in the colony for its alleged overcentralization and for following the old practice of appointing mostly foreign-born officials to high posts in the public service. Harsh allegations had also been leveled against it for tending to favor the plantocracy over other local interests and for its inefficiency and high expenditures, especially in the construction and maintenance of roads and waterworks by the colony's Department of Public Works.

These attacks on the former governor were not without irony and pointed symbolism. Irving had been recognized by supporters and foes alike as an unusually energetic and capable administrator, a break in the long line of colonial governors in Trinidad who had been resented for their alleged incompetence and lack of constructive imagination. But he had been charged by numerous critics with consistently failing to heed local sensibilities. His determined leadership and his major policies (which included opening unoccupied Crown lands to free labor and providing employment in a public works program) had been seen by his critics as excesses in the system of Crown Colony government based on a philosophy of trusteeship.[26] Because that form of government was generally regarded by the politically active segment of the population as a symbol of the harsh reality of imperial rule from London, not the foundation upon which a genuine Trinidadian identity and interest might be constructed, Irving suffered opposition for both his impressive achievements and his shortcomings.

Inspired by the newspaper campaign against Governor Irving, the reform movement prepared to take on his successor. In 1883, more than eight hundred residents of the Crown Colony, many notables among them, formally petitioned the governor, Sir Sanford Freeling, to curtail sharply expenditures on public works and public services. They were joined in their effort by the sugar plantocracy, which also assailed the economic burden associated with growing public expenditures in Trinidad. A similar petition was laid before the Colonial Office by the planters' representative in London, the West India Committee. Turning their attention specifically to the matter of political reform, several newspapers in Trinidad began to agitate for moderate constitutional change, calling, for example, for an Executive Council with the same powers as that in Barbados and for an elected minority in the Legislative Council to represent the most affluent classes.[27]

But it was soon evident that there was divisiveness in this generation of Trinidad reformers also. In a pattern firmly established in the reform movement, no force or leader emerged to bind together its various disparate, frequently contentious, and geographically dispersed elements. (Reformers in San Fernando, the second major town in Trinidad, were often at loggerheads with reformers in Port-of-Spain over economics and politics. The two seaports were rivals in domestic and international commerce, and San Fernando resented the overrepresentation of Port-of-Spain on the Legislative Council.

When the Gorrie affair [see below] erupted in the mid-1880s over the administration of justice by the chief justice in the Crown Colony, the San Fernando reformers rallied to his defense; in Port-of-Spain, the reformers were bitterly divided over the question of his suitability for judicial office.) A curious paradox seemed to overtake the reform movement in Trinidad: As enthusiasm for reform grew, its prime movers found themselves locked ever tighter in the throes of internal division and dissent.

Occupying a position to the "left" of the "moderate" faction in the reform pantheon in late-nineteenth-century Trinidad were the "liberals" and "radicals." Among the leading liberals of the period was Philip Rostant, the French creole publisher of the Port-of-Spain newspaper *Public Opinion.* He and his supporters were vociferous in their call for a substantial elected minority, or even a majority, in the Legislative Council, for a wider franchise in the colony, and for official action to encourage the growth of a peasant landowning class as the backbone of the economy. The most prominent radical reformer was Robert Guppy, a British-born lawyer and onetime mayor of San Fernando. Condemning the immigration policy for indentured Indians as costly and inhumane, he proposed in its stead a policy of free immigration, preferably from Europe. (Immigration of indentured laborers from India was not abolished in the British West Indies until 1917, the system of indentured labor five years later.) Guppy and his fellow radicals in San Fernando were bitter foes of the sugar plantocracy.

To the "right" of the "moderates" were the "conservatives," who brought to the reform cause a profound skepticism—for example, the French creole Louis de Verteuil.[28] Fearing the possibly radical implications of Rostant's call to "democratize" the Legislative Council, and concerned also with the growing strength of radicalism in San Fernando, the conservative Verteuil took the position that changes ought indeed to be made in the legislature but without undoing its traditional framework. He proposed that a Finance Committee be established in the Legislative Council, composed of all the unofficial members of the legislature and a minority of its official members, and that it be empowered to discuss the annual estimates before they were deliberated upon by the full chamber. Throwing its considerable weight behind the proposal for such a committee was the *Gazette* of Port-of-Spain, a newspaper owned by French creole interests. The *Gazette* raised high the standard of conservative reform, stressing the great risks posed by radical constitutional change in a heterogeneous society beset by economic difficulties and playing upon the theme of the unpreparedness of the masses for an active role in public life. In the latter vein, it noted the widespread political apathy in Trinidad (attributed to the backwardness of the masses and to the commitment of the Crown Colony government to real progress in economic and political affairs) and the failure of most eligible voters in the main towns to exercise their franchise in municipal elections.[29]

The various alignments—the fractures in the reform movement—pointed up differences between individuals and among class, ethnic, and religious cohorts. The affluent French Catholic creoles Rostant and Verteuil were far apart politically, as were other reformers of their social background. Similar differences could also be found in the Crown Colony among reform-minded British merchants and lawyers and among colored professionals.

The reform camp continued to divide over public policy and over personalities, as evidenced, for example, by the immigration issue and the so-called Gorrie affair. Because the future of the indenture system for Indian immigrants was tied to the larger struggle that pitted labor against capital and management, the immigration question remained for a long time the most significant among an array of deeply divisive issues. The campaign launched by liberals and radicals to force the abolition of the indenture system met with stiff resistance from conservative reformers in the propertied class, who feared, with reason, that their privileged status would be in jeopardy if free labor ever gained the upper hand.

A sharp clash among the reformers was precipitated by the appointment in 1885 of Sir John Gorrie as chief justice of Trinidad. Gorrie's evident humaneness in seeking to promote from the bench the interests of the creole and Indian peasants of Trinidad and Tobago appealed particularly to Rostant and his followers. (The Crown Colony of Tobago was merged with the Crown Colony of Trinidad in 1888 to form the Crown Colony of Trinidad and Tobago.) But other leading reformers, including Stephen Gatty and the distinguished barrister Henry Alcazar, bitterly criticized the bilious chief justice for serious breaches of judicial temperament and decorum. While Gorrie managed during his stormy seven-year term to acquire a substantial following in some reform circles and in the public generally, many other reformers (especially in Port-of-Spain) came to regard his highhanded administration of justice as a harbinger of radical change or, worse still, of socialism.[30] (As a result of the report of a commission established to inquire into his actions on the bench, the chief justice was removed from office in 1892.) Fearing the long-term implications of a "political" judiciary under Gorrie, Gatty broke with the reform movement. As chairman of the Royal Franchise Commission, sitting in 1888, he led a successful campaign against the proposal to elect unofficial members of the Legislative Council.[31]

VI

The cautious, gradual approach to constitutional change that a divided reform movement had been forced to adopt in the period 1856–95 was mirrored in the attitude of the imperial government in London. Few political concessions had been granted the Crown Colony in the four decades after the establishment of the Legislative Reform Committee in 1856. Among the important ones had been the reluctant decision of 1886, following Verteuil's proposal, to create a Finance Committee in the Legislative Council. By this action, which gave a greater voice to the nominated unofficial majority in preparing the annual estimates, the Colonial Office hoped to check the influence of the liberal and radical reformers, especially those who were pressing hard for the popular election of legislators and for home rule. In time, the Finance Committee managed to acquire a larger, albeit informal, role in the policy process. This development was given impetus when, in addition to the annual estimates, supplementary votes came increasingly to be submitted to the committee. Official members usually abstained from voting on those occasions, allowing resolutions to be carried by their unofficial colleagues. Governors often, in turn, regarded the resolutions as binding. Concerned lest government business in Trinidad be obstructed by the growing influence of the unofficial members in the Finance Committee, some senior officials at the Colonial Office continued to urge that the committee be abolished as quickly as political circumstances would allow.[32]

An opportunity to weaken the unofficial side in the Legislative Council, without formally abolishing the Finance Committee, soon presented itself. In 1888, on the occasion of the unification of Trinidad and Tobago in a single Crown Colony, the Colonial Office decided to terminate the unofficial members' narrow majority by creating a new position in the colony's administration, that of receiver-general. The original and decisive casting vote of the governor coupled with the votes of the receiver-general and seven other official members would henceforth virtually assure the government a legislative majority over the nine unofficial members.[33] However, the new official majority proved to be short lived. In late 1889, the unofficial members strongly opposed their having been relegated to a minority status in the legislature. On receiving their protest, along with conflicting advice from his senior officials in the Colonial Office, Lord Knutsford, secretary of state for the colonies, reluctantly decided to restore the unofficial majority by appointing another unofficial member in the legislature. Drawing on the main argument that Colonial Office officials had made against restoring the unofficial majority—that it might someday form a unified opposition—Knutsford sternly warned that the official majority would be restored if ever the unofficial members adopted the practice of voting en bloc against the government.[34] Four years later, in 1893, his successor as secretary of state, Lord Ripon, reaffirmed the intention of the Colonial Office to retain at least temporarily the unofficial majority in Trinidad's legislature.[35]

These actions of the imperial government in London in the late 1880s and early 1890s, together with internal memoranda at the Colonial Office, affirm the slow evolution of a strategy, the main object of which was to strengthen the hand of Trinidad's government as a means of retaining the status quo in the Crown Colony. For that purpose, the Colonial Office would employ several tactics. First, it would continue to deny to the unofficial members of the Legislative Council what their counterparts throughout most of the British West Indies colonies had already acquired or would probably soon acquire, formal membership in the governor's Executive Council and therewith a major role in the policy process. Second, the Finance Committee and the unofficial majority would be abolished in the legislature. Of these tactics, the least dangerous politically for the Colonial Office and the Crown Colony government was that having to do with the Executive Council; that move posed no open challenge to whatever prestige and influence the unofficial members had accrued. However, the sweeping proposal to abolish the Finance Committee and restore the official majority was fraught with considerable risk. The delicacy of that situation had been pointed up as recently as 1889, when the unofficial members had protested the loss of their majority status in the Legislative Council. In light of their success on that occasion, the Colonial Office felt that it had to maneuver cautiously on that issue lest it provoke great agitation in

Trinidad. How to pursue its larger purpose yet avert exciting public opinion against constituted authority? In exchange for abolishing the Finance Committee and restoring the official majority in the legislature, the Colonial Office would concede a change in Trinidad's constitution that had long been sought by liberal and radical reformers: the elective principle for unofficial members of the legislature. Moved far more by expediency at this late hour than by any consideration of principle—little risk appeared now to attend a course of action whose inevitability was in any event widely assumed—Lord Rosebery's Liberal government was preparing to grant that change when it fell in June 1895. A final—and, as it turned out, negative— resolution of the question had perforce to wait upon the new secretary of state for the colonies, Joseph Chamberlain, in Lord Salisbury's Conservative-Unionist government.[36]

VII

Dominated by a tiny, fractious middle-class element in the minority white population, the reform movement in Trinidad had had little success as it tried periodically in the nineteenth century to force the issue of constitutional change. Successive governments in London had all determined to proceed by small steps in the British West Indies.[37] Even the Liberal government, which by 1895 had been preparing to grant the elective principle in Trinidad, had no wish to abandon the traditional course. As seen, the Rosebery cabinet had intended this concession not as an earnest of its commitment to major reforms but as part of its scheme to deny to the unofficial members of the Legislative Council their growing influence as a majority caucus. (The Liberal government had made only two other concessions to reform opinion in the Crown Colony—each political, not constitutional. In 1892, the secretary of state for the colonies, Lord Ripon, appointed two creole reformers, George Garcia and the colored Vincent Brown, as, respectively, attorney-general and solicitor-general. Stunning as this action was, it did not signal that the Colonial Office had finally abandoned its practice of appointing only foreigners to high office in the colony; they continued to be appointed to most such offices. Discerning no political risk in appointing more reformers as unofficials in the Legislative Council, in 1893 Ripon suggested to Governor Sir Napier Broome that he do so as the next five vacancies occurred. In the period 1893–95, Broome named to the legislature a "balanced ticket" of four leading reformers—two French creoles, conservative Louis de Verteuil and moderate E. L. Guppy, and liberals Henry Alcazar and Eugene Lange.)[38] With the accession in 1895 of Joseph Chamberlain to the Colonial Office in a new Conservative-Unionist government, the Trinidad reform movement had to contend with a politician who would be influenced by considerations of background, personality, and evolving imperial interest to slow further—even to arrest—the pace of constitutional evolution in that colony.

Born in London in 1836 of middle-class, Nonconformist parents, Joseph Chamberlain was linked to the municipality of Birmingham from his late teenage years until his death in 1914.[39] At the age of eighteen, he joined the business of his uncle, a screw manufacturer. Successful in the firm, Chamberlain was able to conclude his active business career two decades later with a substantial fortune.

During his years as a businessman, Chamberlain was active in the public affairs of Birmingham. From 1873 to 1875 he served as its mayor. A strong advocate of local government, and of its reform, Chamberlain encouraged the municipality to purchase various public utilities and to undertake ambitious schemes for slum clearance and housing development. With the same vigor he also oversaw the establishment by the local authority of art galleries and free libraries. Bent on further reforms that local government could not achieve, Chamberlain decided to seek a seat in Parliament. Defeated in his first attempt in the general election of 1874, the young Liberal reformer was returned two years later in a Birmingham by-election. He quickly set about reorganizing the constituency's Liberal Associations on a representative basis, a move that enlarged his own political base, especially in the Midlands, and helped William Gladstone's Liberal Party come to power in 1880. Barely fours years after entering Parliament, Chamberlain joined the Gladstone cabinet as president of the Board of Trade.

During his presidency, Chamberlain continued in the role of a reformer, seeking especially to promote reorganization and modernization in the shipping industry. He also began to probe to find out why the economic boom that had coincided with his earlier years in Birmingham had, by the last quarter of the nineteenth century, given way to a deepening depression. Reluctant at first to join the rising chorus of protectionism, Chamberlain eventually helped spearhead the campaign for a system of imperial preference modeled upon the German *zollverein*.

Chamberlain also emerged in the 1880s as a leading advocate of national social reform. His program, which formed the basis for his reelection campaign in 1885, included free primary education, reorganization of rural government on an elective basis, tax reform (intended partly to pay for social reforms, including urban slum clearance), land reform (to encourage the formation of a class of yeoman farmers), disestablishment of the state church in England, Scotland, and Wales, manhood suffrage, and salaries for members of Parliament. Because they feared the radical implications of these proposals and the political ambition of their author, Chamberlain was opposed both by the Conservatives and by Gladstone and other leading Liberals. All of this opposition together helped weaken the impact of Chamberlain's program in the general election of 1885.

Following the Liberal victory that year, Gladstone declared his conversion to the principle of home rule in Ireland. Chamberlain was outraged. The Birmingham politician had already embraced home rule for Ireland and for other parts of the United Kingdom— conditional on unity being preserved and the imperial Parliament remaining in composition and authority the supreme lawmaking body. When Gladstone, intent on ridding Parliament of its contentious Irish faction, agreed to endorse full home rule, Chamberlain, claiming that it was tantamount to recognition of Ireland as a separate nation, broke with him and immediately launched a sharp attack on his home rule bill. Chamberlain managed to gather sufficient support within Liberal ranks to defeat the bill, thereby splitting the Liberal Party and ensuring its defeat in the next election.

Throughout his political career in Birmingham and as a Liberal parliamentarian, Chamberlain had displayed the key attributes of his personality and his political style.[40] Possessed of a formidable will, he was diligent in pursuing a wide range of interests. Skilled in conversation and oratory, he could evoke great sympathy and support from individuals and large gatherings. But he had no dearth of critics and detractors. Many upper-class Britons disdained his abrasive style, his irritability, his vulgarity, his unbridled egotism and frequent discourtesy, and, not least, his appeals to the masses with simple, radical solutions to their problems. Others in the upper class were attracted to him by his loyalty and his decisive, confident manner.

Chamberlain remained out of public office for nine years following his break with Gladstone in 1886. But it was not a quiet time in his life. Traveling in North America and the Middle East—sometimes to consult with foreign governments, on one occasion to head up a delegation appointed by Lord Salisbury to mediate a fishing dispute between the United States and Canada—Chamberlain soon shifted his gaze from issues of reform, national and local, in the United Kingdom to matters of wider imperial concern. During this period he began to lay great stress upon the genius of the Anglo-Saxon race in imperial affairs, upon the need to keep South Africa tied to the United Kingdom (especially after the discovery of Transvaal gold in 1886), and upon Canadian federalism as a model for eventual federation in the British Empire. He became convinced, too, that the major social and economic problems besetting the metropole could be remedied only within an imperial framework bound tightly by a system of preferential trade. In his view, such a framework required strengthening not merely to defend British interests in Ireland and South Africa but also to counter the growing challenge elsewhere of European and Japanese imperialism and, to a lesser extent perhaps, of U. S. expansionism.[41] Chamberlain's interest in the economics of imperialism was not dampened by his several misadventures as an investor and businessman in South America and the Caribbean.

With the Liberals having been routed in the general election of 1895, the Conservative Lord Salisbury had no difficulty persuading the Liberal Unionist leaders, whose number included Chamberlain, to join his government. Chamberlain selected the Colonial Office.

VIII

As secretary of state for the colonies, Joseph Chamberlain adopted a policy for Trinidad that did not accord with his reputation as a reformer in British public life. Even as he lent encouragement to municipal reform in that Crown Colony, particularly in its capital, overall the onetime reform mayor of Birmingham pursued an essentially retrogressive policy in Trinidad; and, as shall be seen, his reformist position on the municipal issue in Port-of-Spain was in fact integral to his strategy for blocking constitutional advance in the colony.[42] Pursuing that strategy, he also moved swiftly to deny an important concession in the constitution of Trinidad that the Liberal government had been preparing to grant, the elective principle in the Legislative Council. In evolving his policy for Trinidad, Chamberlain was influenced principally by considerations of race and culture, by conditions in the Crown Colony, and, most important perhaps, by broad imperial interests.

Even before joining the Salisbury cabinet in 1895, Chamberlain had been drawn to the idea that nonwhite, non-British communities were ill suited for representative institutions. Like many British imperialists in the late nineteenth century, he regarded the philosophy of trusteeship as the core of Crown Colony government in the West Indies and elsewhere in the empire. For these imperialists, the philosophy of trusteeship in force would be a check upon both the white oligarchy and the incompetent rule of color. They feared, in the first instance, that a white minority left to its own devices would lord it over the powerless majority of color among whom it dwelt; theirs was the same fear that, as seen, partly animated the original decision by Parliament to establish a Crown Colony government in slaveholding Trinidad. The expectation that a white oligarchy would wax against the majority interest of color was pointed out by Charles Lucas, the assistant undersecretary at the Colonial Office who was responsible for the West Indies between 1897 and 1907: "Again and again the history of colonization has shown that the safeguard of coloured races consists in a strong Home government outside and beyond local influences, and that Home rule for a dependency, where the white men are few and the coloured many, has in past times meant for the majority of its inhabitants not so much the gift of local freedom as the withdrawal of Imperial protection."[43]

The need to shield the colored majority from a white oligarchy had as its corollary the need to prevent rule by inept men of color and to frustrate the majority's abuse of the minority in its midst. Most proponents of Crown Colony government regarded the colored man as inferior, racially and culturally, to the white, and as unqualified by race or by training for representative government along the lines of the metropole. The majority could therefore be expected, if granted representative institutions, to mismanage public affairs or to impose a regime of oppression on the white minority. These two justifications for Crown Colony government in multiracial societies inhabited by groups that differed greatly in size, education, and, allegedly, innate abilities are reflected in observations by, respectively, the British historian James Froude and his frequent companion, Joseph Chamberlain: "The whites cannot be trusted to rule the blacks, but for the blacks to rule the whites is a yet grosser anomaly"; "Local government (falsely so-called) is the curse of the West Indies. In many islands it means only the rule of a local oligarchy of whites and half-breeds—always incapable and frequently corrupt. In other cases it is the rule of Negroes—totally unfit for representative institutions and the dupes of unscrupulous adventurers."[44]

Trusteeship predicated control of public affairs in the Crown Colony by the metropolitan power. Crown and Parliament together, represented by the secretary of state and his officials at the Colonial Office and throughout the empire, would have ultimate responsibility for all governmental business in the colony and for its security and general well-being.

Consistent with this view, as secretary of state for the colonies, Chamberlain held that the question of constitutional advance in the British West Indies always had to be addressed not with regard to the representative principle as such but as a matter of practical expediency. Was a particular advance compatible with the security of the colony? Would it enhance the efficiency of administration and the interests of all classes in the population? Chamberlain determined that conceding the elective principle in Trinidad would require either a high qualification for the franchise, thereby encouraging the formation of a white oligarchy based on planter interests, or a lower qualification favorable to the nonwhite majority.[45] Influenced particularly by James Froude, the Negrophobic critic of West Indies societies, Chamberlain as secretary of state rejected both alternatives.

On the matter of local conditions in Trinidad, Chamberlain allowed himself to be persuaded by insubstantial evidence that low voter turnout in municipal and rural road board elections was proof of the unsuitability of the elective principle in that Crown Colony. He persisted in this view despite the refusal of many Trinidad reformers to concede popular apathy and the admission by Governor Sir Napier Broome in 1895 that the elected road boards were performing a useful function in accordance with their legal mandate.[46] Having recourse again to questionable evidence, the secretary of state also contended that the reform movement had been divided on the *principle* of reform and that the reformers would doubtless seize upon the elective principle, if granted, to agitate for further change.[47]

Of special concern to Chamberlain was the effect that granting representative institutions in Trinidad might have upon other major crown colonies in the British Empire. Fearing that this concession in the West Indies would likely precipitate a clamor for similar change in strategic Hong Kong and Ceylon, he resolved to hold the line on the issue.[48]

Throughout his eight years as secretary of state for the colonies, Chamberlain granted only one minor, temporary concession in the constitution of Trinidad. Seizing upon an issue that had provoked little interest in the Crown Colony, district representation in the Legislative Council, he directed Governor Broome in 1895 henceforth to appoint as unofficial members only those who lived or owned property in the district they represented. But this "reform" had no significant effect upon the public life of Trinidad, and Chamberlain decided to withdraw it in November 1898.[49]

Several months before, Chamberlain had been presented with an opportunity to strike a blow to the prestige and influence of the unofficial majority in the Legislative Council. A former secretary of state for the colonies, Lord Knutsford, had threatened to end the unofficial majority if it ever adopted the practice of unifying against the Trinidad government. In June 1898, Sir Clement Courtenay Knollys, the colonial secretary in Trinidad who was acting at the time as officer administering the government, reported a growing tendency among some unofficial members to form an organized opposition in the legislature.[50] Without carefully examining Knollys's meager evidence, various senior officials at the Colonial Office advised Chamberlain to move with dispatch to restore the official majority.[51] Accepting their advice, Chamberlain designated the commander of Local Military Forces in the Crown Colony as an official member of the Legislative Council, thus raising the number of officials in that body to eleven, including the governor. By this action, the official majority was reinstituted, conditional on the governor's vote.[52]

Chamberlain displayed his mettle on that occasion, distinguishing himself from his cautious predecessor. Apprehensive that public opinion in Trinidad might be agitated by a precipitous move to end the unofficial majority, Lord Ripon was preparing shortly before the fall of Rosebery's Liberal government in 1895 to concede the elective principle as a quid pro quo. Three years later, a confident Chamberlain felt no need to barter for the same objective. Acting decisively on the pretext of Knollys's evidence, he restored the official majority as the Liberals were intending to do but without granting a concession to the weakened unofficial side or to reform opinion in the Crown Colony. Whether this bold action bore also the mark of sagacity would become known only in time.

IX

Chamberlain had lost no time "tightening the screws" on Trinidad. His actions were only partly in response to conditions there, however; they were also an affirmation of the negative, pessimistic attitude that he (and most of his senior officials at the Colonial Office) harbored toward all the impoverished Negro colonies in the British West Indies. That attitude was conveyed with great force in the Colonial Office's reaction to the Report of the West India Royal Commission in 1897.[53]

In late 1896, Chamberlain had arranged for a Royal Commission, under the chairmanship of Sir Henry Norman, a former governor of Jamaica, to investigate conditions in the British West Indies and to make recommendations for future policies. A year later, the commission advised that, while the depressed West Indies sugar industry was threatened with extinction, it should not be protected by imposing a duty on imported, subsidized beet sugar. (Dissenting from the majority recommendation, Norman himself called for the imposition of countervailing duties to protect the ailing industry.) Impressed with the commission's analysis, Chamberlain nevertheless rejected its recommendation and tried unsuccessfully to persuade the Salisbury cabinet to impose such a duty.[54]

The commission also recommended that imperial economic assistance be extended annually to the West Indies colonies but only if their constitutions were modified to improve administrative efficiency. Supported by the Treasury Department, Chamberlain succeeded in obtaining from the cabinet its pledge to ask Parliament to appropriate £500,000 to assist the West Indies colonies with free grants—conditional on their accepting imperial control of the administration.[55]

Chamberlain and his senior officials at the Colonial Office had seen in the Royal Commission recommendation on imperial assistance an opportunity to press for the restoration of pure crown colonies in the West Indies. In their view, the Negro colonies should be governed by strong, fiscally responsible administrations. Because those dependencies were regarded as poor candidates for eventual responsible government, the representative principle was deemed inappropriate in their governance.[56]

But the official attitude evaded an important development in the

West Indies: the growing political consciousness of colored and black peoples in the second half of the nineteenth century and their increasing participation in public life. In Trinidad, for example, those groups emerged in public life in the 1890s, and their participation grew rapidly after the turn of the century. In 1892, the reform-minded colored barrister Vincent Brown was appointed solicitor-general of the Crown Colony; eleven years later, he was elevated to the post of attorney-general.[57] At about the time that Brown took up his first post in the colony government, a new group, the Reform Committee, made its appearance. Although weakened, as the Legislative Reform Committee had always been, by internecine conflicts, it proved to be an important vehicle for a number of blacks who were destined to achieve great prominence—including C. Prudhomme David, a future member of the Legislative Council, who was secretary of the fledgling committee, and J. S. de Bourg, who headed its minority radical faction. In 1897, the Trinidad Workingmen's Association was founded; as seen, it pressed for various reforms in the Crown Colony and for a political alliance between black workers and colored professionals. Other blacks, while reluctant to align themselves openly with the reform movement, did nevertheless display a reformist zeal. Edgar Maresse-Smith, for example, a barrister who had earlier gained attention by publicly defending beleaguered Chief Justice Sir John Gorrie, would gain notoriety for his leading role in the bloody water riot in Port-of-Spain in March 1903 which resulted in the burning of the government center. At that time there would be many ordinary blacks among the rioters, marking both the political emergence of that element in the population and the provocation of a rigid, retrogressive imperial policy.[58]

X

Throughout most of the nineteenth century the more important political grievances held by Trinidadians were usually bound up with colonywide issues—tariff and immigration policies, restrictions on the franchise, control by officials of the legislative process, selection of public works projects, and so forth. All such issues were tied directly or indirectly to periodic attempts by political dissidents in Trinidad to force the issue of Crown Colony government, an artifact of British imperialism that, in place of responsible government in local hands, designed an administration carried on mainly by foreign officials under the control of the secretary of state for the colonies in London.

Having made little direct headway with the issue of Crown Colony government, many reformers began to channel their energies into an issue that had long been festering in Trinidad, local government reform. Interest in this matter was especially intense in Port-of-Spain in the mid-1890s, inaugurating what I refer to as the period of urban nationalism.

Two aspects of the urban reform issue—the responsibilities of local governments and the central government and the delivery of public services locally—had special significance in the capital, where a deteriorating situation could be traced back to the inception of its governing Borough Council in 1853. The attention of liberal and radical reformers in particular was fixed upon the Borough Council and upon the municipality's costly and inefficient waterworks in the hope that these two items on the reform agenda would be projected at once as local and national issues, that is, as a corollary of the larger issue of representative government in the Crown Colony. The reformers hoped that the residents of Port-of-Spain, recognizing the urgency of municipal reform, would be more attracted to that issue than they had been in the past to the more abstruse issue of Crown Colony government; they hoped, too, that the characteristic hardness that Joseph Chamberlain, the secretary of state for the colonies, was expected to display in Port-of-Spain affairs would fan popular discontent generally with the constitutional and political status quo.

The reformers' hopes were destined to be fulfilled. By the mid-1890s, the central government's approach to persistent financial and water supply problems besetting the capital seemed to many Trinidadians to exemplify the heavy-handedness of Crown Colony government based on a powerful administration and, correlatively, the ineptitude of its leading officials. The issue of municipal reform in Port-of-Spain remained at the forefront of the colony's political life in the period of urban nationalism, from 1895 to 1914, during which it was widely regarded as integral to the issue of Crown Colony government itself.

Public agitation over the financial straits of the Borough Council reached a high intensity near the end of the century when, with Chamberlain's strong encouragement, the council was abolished in favor of a dominant role for the central government in Port-of-

Spain's affairs. It was soon channeled to the even more explosive water issue, culminating on March 23, 1903, in widespread violence and destruction in central Port-of-Spain. Venting their grievances over the state of municipal affairs, thousands of demonstrators struck violently at the seat of Trinidad's colonial government; watching Red House burn, they could feel the reverberation of political change in Chamberlain's eighth and final year at the Colonial Office.

Some of the leading dissidents and their followers who were associated with either or both of these municipal issues in the capital had doubtless been motivated by a wish to challenge imperial rule in Trinidad and to assert the goal of eventual self-determination. But other protesters in Port-of-Spain saw themselves as responding more immediately to particular imperial measures that seemed to them unjust or oppressive.

Many middle-class whites in the municipality, impelled by their perception of class interest, were seeking to check the erosion of local control over municipal affairs. Laying even greater emphasis on the class factor in pluralist Trinidad, many poor blacks and whites were reacting against a proposed water rate scheme, one they regarded not merely as unnecessary but as a discriminatory measure inimical to their interests.

The popular resentment and rancor produced by these two municipal issues in Port-of-Spain and channeled in the period of urban nationalism into street demonstrations and violence did much to intensify the already deep distrust of imperial motives in Trinidad and of leading officials in its Crown Colony government. I shall examine in chapters 5 and 6 the Borough Council and water issues that crystallized as urban nationalism against the backdrop of the rise and fall of reform politics in nineteenth-century Trinidad. First, however, it is necessary to highlight the social and political evolution specifically in Port-of-Spain during that first century of British rule.

4

Port-of-Spain: The Strains of Growth in a Nineteenth-Century Colonial Capital

I

LOCATED OFF THE NORTHEAST COAST of South America, Trinidad seemed to many in the nineteenth century to hold great promise as a trading partner for the continent. The vast interior of its southern neighbor would someday be opened, by direct and by transshipment trade with Trinidad, via the Orinoco River near whose mouth the British Crown Colony lay. Port-of-Spain was the key to this hope. Endowed with a magnificent natural harbor that could accommodate the leading commercial fleets in the world, Port-of-Spain was a likely major depot in international commerce;[1] optimists pointed also to its heterogeneous and expanding population and to a cosmopolitan atmosphere without equal in the West Indies.

But these dreams were fulfilled neither for the colony nor for its capital. While better off than its generally impoverished neighbors in the West Indies, Trinidad was never able during the first century of British rule to cast off the shackles of an economy tied closely to the sugar plantocracy. The economic fortunes of the colony and its municipalities reflected the vicissitudes of cane sugar in the world market. Colony and capital had, therefore, to settle for more modest economic development in the nineteenth century than had been anticipated by the enthusiastic proponents of a great trading partnership with South America.

II

Trinidad and Port-of-Spain each experienced a spectacular demographic transformation in the first century after the British conquest (see table 4.1).[2] In the period 1797–1891, the island's population increased more than tenfold (by 1,030 percent), from 17,718 to 200,028. By 1901, its population was 255,148, more than a thirteenfold increase (1,341.4 percent) in little more than a century. The population of the unified Crown Colony of Trinidad and Tobago, established in 1888, was 218,381 in 1891, more than an elevenfold increase (1,133.7 percent) over the level for Trinidad alone in 1797. By 1901, there were 273,899 inhabitants in the two islands, representing more than a fourteenfold increase (1,447.4 percent) over the level for Trinidad in the last year of Spanish rule.

The population of Trinidad increased 107.9 percent in the first four decades of British rule, 1797–1838, fueled mostly by French immigration and the importation of African slaves. After manumission in 1834, a scramble began for new sources of cheap labor for the British West Indies, culminating in 1845 in the establishment of an indenture system based on immigration from India. Largely as a result of that immigration and of the soaring birth rate in the Indian community,[3] the population of Trinidad continued to increase dramatically in the second half of the nineteenth century, between 21.5 percent and 39.8 percent.

The magnitude of the transformation wrought in nineteenth-century Trinidad could be seen also in Port-of-Spain. In the period 1791–1891, the population in the capital increased more than sixfold (by 636 percent), from 4,525 to 33,273. By 1901, it had 54,100 inhabitants; its population had increased nearly elevenfold (1,096.7 percent) in little more than a century. In the last year of Spanish rule, 25.6 percent of the population of Trinidad lived in the capital; four decades later, in 1838, the proportion had risen to 42.7 percent. Overall, the capital's population grew 224.5 percent in the period 1797–1838, fueled mostly by French immigration and the influx of former slaves after manumission. Its growth continued to soar,

Table 4.1. Population of Trinidad and its three major towns, 1797–1901

	Trinidad		Port-of-Spain			San Fernando			Arima		
	Population	% increase for bracketed period	Population	% increase for bracketed period	% of Trinidad population	Population	% increase for bracketed period	% of Trinidad population	Population	% increase for bracketed period	% of Trinidad population
1797	17,718		4,525		25.6						
1838	36,655	107.9	14,670	224.5	42.7						
1851	69,609										
1861	84,438	21.5									
1871	109,638	29.9									
1881	153,128	39.8									
1891[a]	200,028	30.7	33,273		16.6	6,570		3.2	3,653		1.8
1901[a]	255,148	27.6	54,100	62.7	21.2	7,613	15.9	2.9	4,076	11.6	1.5

a. The figures in these two years are for Trinidad alone. Because the Crown Colonies of Trinidad and Tobago were merged in 1888, the discussion in the text explicates also the demographic changes down to 1891 and 1901 that were based on the unified Crown Colony of Trinidad and Tobago.

rendering its inhabitants a sizable minority in the island. For example, 16.6 percent of the population of Trinidad lived there in 1891 and 21.2 percent ten years later. The capital's population rose sharply in the decade 1891–1901, by 62.7 percent; by that time, many young men in the rural Indian community could no longer resist the lure of the town.

The phenomenal growth of population in and around Port-of-Spain can be discerned in two other sets of data. By 1851, a metropolitan area of sorts was emerging around the capital. Among the eight counties in Trinidad, St. George (which included the towns of Port-of-Spain and Arima) had 38,600 inhabitants, or 55.4 percent of the colony's population. Most of the inhabitants of St. George County that year lived in the capital or in the suburbs and villages that were springing up around it. Officials and the propertied classes usually reacted with helpless anger at the sight of squatter communities rising in the town and outside its jurisdiction, on private and Crown lands.[4] Over the next century, Port-of-Spain would develop, on the base of that suburban growth, into the modern hub of a sprawling, densely populated metropolitan area in northernmost Trinidad.[5]

Each of the other two main towns in Trinidad, San Fernando and Arima, had a small population in the nineteenth century compared to Port-of-Spain. As table 4.1 indicates, in 1891 and 1901 the inhabitants of San Fernando, thirty miles south of the capital, comprised 3.2 percent and 2.9 percent, respectively, of the island's population; in those two years, Arima, twelve miles east of Port-of-Spain, contained only 1.8 percent and 1.5 percent of the island's population. (The proportions of the population of the unified Crown Colony of Trinidad and Tobago that lived in the three main towns in 1891 and 1901 were in Port-of-Spain, 15.2 percent and 19.8 percent; in San Fernando, 3 percent and 2.7 percent; and in Arima, 1.6 percent and 1.4 percent.) San Fernando and Arima experienced population growth of 15.9 percent and 11.6 percent, respectively, in the decade 1891–1901—modest levels compared to the 62.7 percent increase in Port-of-Spain.

III

By the end of the nineteenth century, Port-of-Spain had annexed many of the neighboring communities—Belmont, Chaguaramas,

Diego Martin, Laventille, St. Ann's, St. Clair, Woodbrook, areas outside the town that had been under sugar cultivation during the last
generation of Spanish rule. Once nestled with its two streets against
the Gulf of Paria, the town had expanded inland and along the coast
in the first century of British rule, on a network of new roads and
pathways. But town development based mainly on periodic annexation posed problems. Enlarging its physical space to accommodate a
growing population put the municipality in a spiral of annexation
and population growth. With limited financial resources and a rapidly mounting public debt after mid-century, the municipal government in the capital found it difficult to manage the delivery of public
services. The general frustration over the distressed condition of
Port-of-Spain merged in the mid-1890s with the frustration of the
Trinidad reform movement over the issue of representative government in the Crown Colony. The result in the ensuing two decades of
urban nationalism was growing political instability and violence.

A motley population inhabited the capital and its environs: whites,
predominantly Roman Catholics of French, Spanish, and British descent; Trinidadian blacks; people of mixed race, in different hues;
runaway slaves and free blacks from the United States; Portuguese,
Chinese, and West Africans, immigrants in the first generation after
manumission in 1834; venturesome and upwardly mobile West Indians from Grenada, Barbados, St. Vincent, and St. Lucia; Venezuelan refugees from the political wars in Caracas, and their compatriots who had abandoned seasonal labor for a settled residence in
the island; Indians, Hindu and Moslem (and eventually Christian,
too); even a few native Amerindians, their presence in the town a
wistful evocation of a doomed race.[6] The social fabric of Port-of-
Spain, as of the colony, was a collage of peoples and cultures.

The affluent class of planters, merchants, and professionals based
in the capital laid claim to privilege, including access to the governing class of foreign-born officials appointed by the imperial government in London. The mass of the population at or near the bottom of
the economic ladder in the capital (and colony) was left to live as
best it could. Long before the end of the nineteenth century, most of
the larger estates, factories, and businesses in Trinidad were owned
by members of the British, French, and Spanish communities—with
large proprietorships in the British community based predominantly
on a nonresident class.[7] Few barriers were raised in the colony
against sexual contact across racial lines, accounting for the rapid
growth of the mixed-race element in the population, but the barriers

raised by wealth and privilege were decidedly more limiting. For example, the Trinidad census of 1851 revealed that among the 69,609 inhabitants of the island, 26,989 were without visible means of support: one-fourth and one-half of the adult population in the colony and in Port-of-Spain, respectively, mostly former black slaves and their descendants.[8] The alternating cycle of economic depression and modest upturn in nineteenth-century Trinidad ensured a persistently high level of under- and unemployment, particularly in the main towns.

And always there were resentments: by the politically conscious middle class in the colony against the governing class[9] and by the lower and laboring classes against the foreigners, even those on the lower rungs of the government service. For example, in the mid-1880s only two native-born creoles were members of the Trinidad constabulary; among the 430 policemen comprising the force, the majority were Barbadians of color who, like the governing class in the Crown Colony, were widely resented for their arrogance and condescension.[10] Notwithstanding, after mid-century, as seen, the colony's government could take comfort from the weakness of a reform movement based on a tiny, fractious middle-class element in the population. Officials appeared not to apprehend fully the explosive potential in the prevailing arrangement of wealth, power, and privilege in Trinidad or the depth of alienation, especially among the inhabitants of Port-of-Spain.[11] In the early and mid-1880s, as we shall see, two popular festivals culminated in mass rioting in the capital and elsewhere; the riots, the latest in a series of public disturbances stemming from the annual festivals, were directed mainly against the Trinidad constabulary, a body that symbolized for many the system of Crown Colony government based on a remote authority in London. The recurrence of such disturbances over several decades was an augury of the role that violence would play in the public life of the colony and the capital in the next generation and beyond.

IV

From the outset of British rule in Trinidad, the imperial government in London had two major concerns: foreign invasion and internal security, specifically, in the latter case, apprehension about rebellion by the French and Spanish communities or by the majority slave population. The decision to establish a Crown Colony government in Trinidad directly responsible to London and based on Spanish law was taken, as seen, partly to check the French and Spanish communities; the imperial government had calculated that by this action it would allay the fears in those communities of a colonial regime based on a small British population fortified by English law and a British constitution.

Yet another gauge of imperial concern with security in Trinidad can be seen in the pattern of gubernatorial appointments in the first half century of British rule. The first civilian governor was not appointed until 1813, sixteen years after the British conquest; before the appointment of Sir Ralph Woodford that year, the office was occupied by a succession of military officers, three of whom served together briefly in 1803 as a Council of Commissioners for the colony. Three governors came after Woodford in the period 1829–46, two military officers and a civilian. All told, in the period 1797–1846, eight military officers served a total of twenty-seven years as chief executive in Trinidad, two civilians a total of twenty-three years.[12] Whatever its character, the executive authority in Trinidad, if it were deemed necessary for the maintenance of peace and order, could enlist the aid of military forces in the island and in neighboring colonies in the British West Indies.

The first evidence of a possible major slave rebellion in the Crown Colony surfaced in 1805, near the end of the first decade of British rule. Rumors swept the capital of a plot among the slaves—who numbered about 20,000 in the island—to rise up against the minority white and free colored population in Trinidad on Christmas Day. The government, headed by Brigadier-General Sir Thomas Hislop, moved swiftly to apprehend the leaders, who, with most of their followers, were attached to the estates of French planters near Port-of-Spain. Eschewing judicial proprieties, the principals were quickly tried under a strict Spanish law against insurrectionary conspiracy and were hung; lesser figures in the conspiracy were punished by mutilation, flogging, and banishment from the colony. The revolt was stillborn. In the ensuing three decades, down to manumission in 1834, periodic slave insurrections, usually small scale, were suppressed by the authorities in Trinidad. But anxiety over a possible widespread rebellion was omnipresent; fears intensified especially when a major slave insurrection elsewhere—as in Jamaica in 1831—invoked the prospect of a chain reaction throughout the slave colonies in the British West Indies.

The first serious breach of public order in British Trinidad occurred on October 1, 1849, in Port-of-Spain, more than a half century after the conquest. Shortly before, prison regulations had been enacted to provide that during their confinement, debtors would receive a food ration and clothing in exchange for their labor and that they would have their hair closely cropped (to ensure cleanliness and prevent disease).[13]

A public meeting convened on October 1 to protest the new regulations for debtors, mostly black, and to select six persons to remonstrate with the governor, Lord Harris, and his Executive Council. The deputation walked to Government House, followed by a crowd estimated at three thousand.[14] During the committee's meeting with the governor and his officials, the crowd milling outside began to hurl stones and other debris at the meeting room. Despite pleas by Harris and the attorney-general, the throng refused to disperse. When it grew more menacing, three hundred special constables were sworn in and a company of the West India Regiment was called to the scene. The Riot Act was read, but the crowd hurled another volley of stones. A general melee ensued, during which several policemen and soldiers were wounded. Finally, the soldiers fired into the crowd, wounding three women and a child; one woman and the child died soon after. Hours later, in the evening, houses of several government officials were stoned, along with the prison.[15]

The next day, thousands marched into Port-of-Spain to show solidarity with those who had rioted the day before. Encountering a wall of resistance mounted by the soldiers, the marchers had to settle for burning a few houses in the capital and some sugar estates nearby. Fearing that Government House itself would be assaulted, Governor Harris had earlier sent for more troops from Barbados. Upon their arrival in Port-of-Spain on October 3, the situation in the capital returned to normal and the new prison regulations were put into effect.[16]

The principal instigators were tried and convicted, then pardoned by Governor Harris after they had served a part of their sentences. Despite the gravity of the episode, the governor evinced no anger or alarm. After the rioting crowd was finally dispersed on October 1, he collected in a tray all the stones that had been hurled into his office; on the tray he had inscribed, "A Memorial from the Inhabitants."[17]

Not everyone shared Harris's equanimity. From London the *Times* discerned in the episode an augury of future unrest: "The mania for revolution [was] spreading itself." It insisted that more soldiers be dispatched to Trinidad to restrain the black population, many of whose idle and laboring members, impoverished or nearly so, had joined the affray, and it urged that the Crown Colony exercise greater control over the French refugees from Martiniqu? and Guadaloupe, some of whom were found to have been principals in the disturbance.[18]

V

Over the next thirty-five years, there occurred in Port-of-Spain, San Fernando, and other communities a succession of public disturbances accompanied by a rising level of serious violence. These outbreaks were based on two popular festivals, Carnival and Hosein (the latter sometimes called "Hose" or "Hosea").

Carnival and Hosein shared a common origin as annual rites of religious observance that eventually lost that significance. In time, Protestants and even non-Christians became active participants in the black-dominated, pre-Lenten rite of Carnival, with syncretistic roots in medieval Catholic Europe and the bacchanal of the ancient Roman masquerade.

Hosein, which began in the Crown Colony in the 1850s, had its roots in an ancient martyrology, the Shi'ite Moslem festival of Mohurram, which commemorates the seventh-century murder of Hosein, the grandson of the Prophet Mohammed. In Trinidad the Shi'ites, a minority sect within the minority Moslem population in the Indian community, mounted a large procession based on lavish displays of models of the martyr's tomb (taziyahs), which were thrown into a body of water when the daylong march was concluded. In time, the festival was virtually taken over from the Shi'ites in the Indian community by the larger Hindu group. By the late 1850s, the participants in the festival included black Christians, who were hired for the occasion to beat the drums and to carry the taziyahs. The extent to which the Shi'ite commemoration had been transformed in only a few years can be seen in another development. Even the Sunnis, the majority of the Moslem population in the Indian community, eventually participated, notwithstanding their traditional rejection of the Shi'ite claim that Hosein's descendants alone were the true heirs of the Prophet. In 1881, deeply wounded by what they regarded as a profanation of their faith, more than a hundred Shi'ites tried unsuccessfully to persuade the governor, Sir Sanford Freeling, to prohibit the commemoration of Hosein on religious grounds.[19] As with Carnival, the festival of Hosein had taken on a significance in the colony that bore scant resemblance to its origin.

Carnival in Trinidad was marked by slave traditions in the West Indies. Its two-day torchlight procession evoked "Canboulay" (patois for the French *cannes brûlées*), where black slaves in the French islands commemorated plantation fires by parading in the fields with torches made from cane stalks. The practice of bearing torches and sticks was adapted by former slaves in Trinidad to symbolize their release from bondage.

"Canboulay" appears to have been absorbed into Carnival in the Crown Colony in the 1840s, causing the pre-Lenten festival to shed the polite demeanor of an upper-class Roman Catholic amusement. From then on, Carnival was based on a new syncretism, merging the style of ancient Roman revelry with African traditions in music (especially drumming), dance, and mask culture. Under those influences, the annual festival organized around a torchlight procession was the occasion for the mostly lower-class black participants to vent emotions pent up over the year. A key element in Carnival was satire, usually directed against the pretensions of the upper class but sometimes, with political pointedness, also against the arrogance and condescension of high officials and other leading figures in the Crown Colony. Competing against each other—in music, in dance, and in the donning of fantastic masks and costumes—the revelers could pretend for a while that they had stepped into the role of their "betters" in society. This merriment was usually accompanied by drunkenness and rowdyism. Exhausted physically and emotionally, the participants hoped to be better prepared to face the manifold strains of their low status in Trinidad's economy and society.

The low-caste Hindus, "coolies" in the disdainful parlance of the time,[20] derived a similar gratification from the festival of Hosein. For them, the annual rite was an occasion to mark symbolically the boundaries of their collective identity in Trinidad vis-à-vis all other groups—Europeans, blacks, and even non-Hindu Indians—and to gain the emotional strength they needed to cope with the daily strains of low social status. The festival also provided an opportunity to symbolize the need they felt to soften certain rigid aspects of the caste system that Hindus had brought to Trinidad from India—high-caste attitudes regarding, for example, marriage, employment after the five-year period of indenture service, caste roles in ritual life, and the allocation of temporal power among the castes.

Carnival and Hosein, dominated respectively by blacks and Hindus of low social status, were strikingly similar in nineteenth-century Trinidad. Both evinced an uninhibited recreational style that was at once noisy, rowdy, and competitive: the black revelers sought to impress with music, dance, and displays of masks and dress; the Hindus had rival groups of workers from different estates construct models of the martyred Hosein's tomb and then race to throw the taziyahs into a nearby lake or river or into the sea.

But there were also important differences. While the origins of Carnival are generally known, it is not known why the Hindus in Trinidad chose to base their festival on a Shi'ite Moslem commemoration of the revered Hosein. It must suffice here to recall that in India, Hindus and Moslems sometimes drew on the other community for their ritual practices in a kind of cultural transference between intrinsically antagonistic groups. "Hindu Hosein" also differed from Carnival in that participants shunned masking, role playing, and satirizing upper-class pretensions.

For the small European community in nineteenth-century Trinidad, what distinguished Carnival from Hosein was less important than the behavior common to the two festivals. Especially in the middle and upper classes, the Christian European sensibility was disturbed by what it regarded as a renewal of paganism—a barbarism that seemed to menace not only the moral and political order but also the inhabitants' property and safety. The ofttimes riotous torchlight procession at Carnival time aroused an especial fear in the European community—that by carelessness or design the "niggers" (or "darkies," as the blacks were then disdainfully called) might cause a recurrence of the great fires that had in past years laid waste Port-of-Spain and other settlements in the island.[21] Even before the 1880s, the nerves and patience of the Europeans had been sorely tried by the festivals of Carnival and Hosein and by the practice among the blacks of holding boisterous nighttime socials and funeral vigils based on the African tradition of music, dancing, and drinking.[22]

VI

Soon after "Canboulay" torchbearing was merged with Carnival, the Crown Colony government moved to assert control over the festival. Fearing that an outbreak of incendiarism in Port-of-Spain in early 1846 might be exacerbated by anonymous masked revelers in the upcoming Carnival torchlight procession, the authorities banned outdoor masking.[23] Three years later, an ordinance passed in the Legislative Council reduced the festival from seven days to a two-day period before Ash Wednesday.[24]

But because masking in public had only been reduced, not wholly eliminated, a new governor, Sir Robert Keate, resolved in 1858 to try to effectuate the ban by sending a detachment of police to arrest violators; encountering but a few masked figures in Carnival that year in Port-of-Spain, the policemen seized mostly revelers who had donned showy, expensive garments.[25] Popular anger was aroused by the heavy-handedness and severity of the police action. In the next Carnival season, the governor tried again to end masking in public, this time by authorizing a police raid in the section of the capital where violations of the ban were expected to occur—the so-called French streets, east of the Dry River. When the policemen began to confiscate an array of personal belongings, the proceedings quickly turned into a melee.[26]

Tempers had begun to rise over Governor Keate's aggressive opposition to public masquerade; the next provocation was a rumor in January 1860 that the governor was preparing to ban Carnival altogether. Fearing that such action would bring a violent response, some leading groups in Port-of-Spain urged Keate to reconsider. The *Free Press* advised that Carnival be allowed to die an inevitable natural death.[27] The governor solicited the views of the merchants in the town; having long profited from selling expensive imported paraphernalia to the Carnival revelers, the business community advised that the festival be allowed to proceed. The colony government decided not to prosecute a ban on Carnival, and it continued to flourish each year thereafter in the pre-Lenten season.

The revelers grew bolder in the 1860s and early 1870s, in two ways. First, to give expression to the West African tradition of satire singing, many more prominent men and public events were ridiculed in burlesque, including several governors, the attorney-general, the chief justice, and leading clergymen, physicians, and newspaper editors—the upper-class professional establishment in Trinidad.[28] In 1866, the revelers lampooned a recent murder trial; several years later they directed their barbs against what they regarded as miscarriages of justice in the colony.[29] By mocking the status and behavior of their "betters," the black revelers in particular could express their protest against and resistance to the prevailing sociopolitical arrangement. In that way, the artistic creation that was Carnival came to have, in the words of Abner Cohen, "a *bivocal* form, an *ambiguous unity* of cultural and political significance."[30]

Second, while criminal elements, young delinquents, and prostitutes had long ago found their niche in Carnival, they began to play a more assertive role in the 1860s. Thievery and street fighting reached new limits, and bands of prostitutes marched along the main streets in the capital brazenly calling attention to themselves with obscene language and gestures. Offended by this turn of events, the Roman Catholic archbishop of Port-of-Spain withdrew his tacit endorsement of Carnival by discontinuing his practice of driving through the streets to observe the festivities.[31] In 1868, the Legislative Council passed an ordinance increasing the regulatory powers of the police over the festival and prohibiting the bearing of lighted torches if ever they were deemed a public nuisance.[32] For three-quarters of a century thereafter, Carnival bore the stigmata in polite society of a perverse and lawless event. Not until after the Second World War, when the creole bacchanal came to be regarded by the middle and upper classes as an excellent symbol of a national identity, did the festival gain a new respectability. A historic irony marked this development: Where Carnival once underscored the division of colonial Trinidad by class and by race, in the era of nationalist struggle and decolonization it symbolized a transcendent nationhood enriched by social pluralism.

Generally less flamboyant than Carnival, Hosein nevertheless acquired a similar notoriety for reckless abandon and lawlessness. Public disturbances were associated with the festival almost from its beginnings in the 1850s. In 1859, an unruly procession marked Hosein in Port-of-Spain and a procession degenerated into a riot in St. Joseph;[33] a year later, a large detachment of police had to be sent to the onetime capital of Spanish Trinidad to keep a close watch on the festival there. Disturbances were also reported in 1860 in festivals of Hosein throughout the colony, aggravated, some thought, by the Indian Mutiny of 1857 in the subcontinent. In 1865, at the festival in Chaguanas, a large-scale riot broke out between rival groups of workers from two estates; one "coolie" was killed in the affray, a Chinese who had tried to assist his Hindu mates.[34] Other Hosein riots had to be put down by the police in 1872.

The incidence of violence during the two festivals increased sharply in the 1880s. Fearing a new outbreak of incendiarism, in

1880 the commandant of police invoked the ordinance of 1868 and banned the bearing of lighted torches by masked revelers.[35] No protest was lodged against this action until the Carnival season of 1881, when some inhabitants of Port-of-Spain mounted a placard campaign urging Governor Freeling to rescind the ban on torch bearing. The governor told the colonial secretary in Port-of-Spain to instruct the commandant of police not to invoke the ban without receiving specific authorization to do so. Apparently the commandant never received this message, and he instructed his force to begin to extinguish torches when Carnival began. (As a preventive measure in the charged atmosphere of the time, several dozen soldiers from the West India Regiment were mobilized for standby duty.) When 150 policemen tried to enforce the ban, rioting and street fighting broke out in the east Dry River section of the capital. Thirty-eight policemen were injured, eight seriously, and twenty-one rioters were brought to trial.[36]

At the behest of the Port-of-Spain Borough Council, Governor Freeling ordered the police to remain out of sight while he addressed the agitated crowd. He explained that torchbearing had been banned only because of the imminent danger of fire and that he would withdraw the police if a peaceful procession were instituted. When the marchers shouted their assent, the policemen were ordered back to their barracks; except for the stoning of some private residences and street lamps, and a mock funeral of the commandant of police, Carnival proceeded that year without further serious disturbance. Five days later, fifty-eight policemen tendered their resignations but withdrew them at the urging of the commandant. Upon returning to duty, the policemen were mocked and stoned. Even with the gradual return to normalcy, it was evident that the lower classes in Port-of-Spain had delivered a damaging blow to the Trinidad constabulary. A commission was subsequently appointed by Lord Kimberley, secretary of state for the colonies, to investigate and report on the recent disturbance. Its report stressed that there was no evidence of an organized opposition to authority; it pointed, rather, to a transitory feeling of ill will against the police. The commission advised that the Crown Colony government, even while it pursued a conciliatory policy, should take precautionary measures for the future, among them restricting torchlight processions at Carnival time to one area in Port-of-Spain.[37] With the issuance of the commission report, public opinion in the capital was mollified. But the constabulary remained a prime target for the disaffected. In 1883, for example, a bloody encounter took place at Princes Town between the police and a band of creoles; two creoles were killed and several wounded.[38]

Another major public disturbance occurred in 1884, this one precipitated by Hindus on the occasion of a Hosein festival. Three years before, a Hindu worker had been killed when an argument erupted over which of the rival groups of workers would have precedence in the procession. Having that incident in mind, in July 1882 the Legislative Council in the Crown Colony passed an ordinance authorizing the governor to promulgate regulations for the Hosein processions. Governor Freeling demurred. Not until the riotous Carnival of 1884 did he resolve to enact strict rules for controlling the Hosein crowds. Based upon his consultations with key planters and officials, he drew up a list of regulations and submitted them to Lord Derby, the new secretary of state for the colonies. Upon receiving Derby's approval, Freeling announced the new regulations on July 30, 1884, three months before the Hosein festival. The principal prohibitions were against processions entering Port-of-Spain and San Fernando or moving along public roads without obtaining approval in advance from the district magistrate. The regulations were posted on all large estates in the Crown Colony, and agents were dispatched by the protector of immigrants to publicize the ordinance in Hindi.[39]

Notwithstanding, early in October rumors began to circulate in Port-of-Spain that a large body of Hindus was preparing a Hosein procession through San Fernando, en route to the sea. The protector of immigrants issued new warnings that the marchers from the neighboring Naparima district (in which there lived more than 20,000 "coolies") should not move on the town. A force of fifty-three policemen was dispatched with twenty soldiers to block roadways leading into San Fernando. As two thousand Hindus approached the town from the east, the district magistrate began to read the Riot Act to them. The commandant of police ordered the procession to halt, but the marchers continued to push forward, whereupon the police were ordered to fire on the crowd. Most of the marchers dispersed at the sound of gunfire, leaving many wounded and dying Hindus in the road. The same kind of incident occurred at the northern approach to the town. All told, twelve marchers were killed and 110 wounded.[40]

The events at San Fernando attracted much attention in Great Britain. A spate of letters appeared in the London *Times,* reflecting a broad range of views on the issue.[41] Lord Derby moved quickly to dampen the fires; on December 16, 1884, he announced that Sir Henry Norman (who would serve as governor of Jamaica in the period 1884–88) would go to Trinidad to investigate the disturbance. Taking testimony during a one-week investigation from thirty-four persons of varied background, Norman heard it alleged that, in the period 1881–84, the attitude of Indian workers in the Crown Colony had changed radically from docile to insubordinate. In his report, he exonerated the colony's government and the constabulary, ascribing the disturbance instead to four causes: the economic depression then engulfing the West Indies; the regimen of increased work imposed on the Indian estate workers without a commensurate increase in compensation; the growing consciousness in the Indian community of its size and strength; and the recent bankruptcy of an Anglican clergyman who had received $350,000 on deposit from Indian workers over a thirteen-year period. The Norman report recommended that the regulations issued and enforced in 1884 be continued in force.[42]

VII

The principal causes of strain in nineteenth-century Trinidad and in its capital were seen to be associated with the process of growth. (1) The persistence of significant political influence in the sugar plantocracy combined with recurrent economic distress in the colony to thwart the development of a great trading partnership with South America. (2) The Crown lands policy, by its restrictiveness until the 1870s, encouraged the flight of free blacks to the towns and blocked the emergence of a viable rural yeoman class between the top and bottom of Trinidad's society. (3) The indenture system based on Indian immigration and the high birth rate in that community fueled the flight of blacks to the towns and the depression of wages in the free labor market. (4) The population explosion, particularly in and around Port-of-Spain, was accompanied by annexation and "metropolizing" in the area of the capital. (5) The dismissal of the chief justice in the Gorrie affair and the refusal of the Royal Franchise Commission in 1888 to endorse the elective principle in the Legislative Council both exacerbated the divisions in Trinidad's reform movement. (6) The reform movement was ineffectual and, correlatively, the pace of constitutional advance slow in the colony. (7) The white minority population was divided, mainly along lines of nationality, religion, and economic interest. (8) The colony's population was divided, mainly along lines of race, class, nationality, and religion, as exemplified by the chronic high unemployment particularly among blacks in Port-of-Spain and the other main towns, by the prison riot in the capital in October 1849, and by Carnival and Hosein and the growing violence that attended them. One other principal cause of strain has not yet been discussed, the evolution of municipal government in Port-of-Spain in the first century of British rule. With that, the groundwork will have been laid for an examination in chapters 5 and 6 of the issues of public policy that cut across the colony and its capital at the end of the nineteenth century, in the period of urban nationalism.

The establishment of Crown Colony government in Trinidad continued the process of weakening the municipal authority in Port-of-Spain that had been started, as we saw, in the last half century of Spanish rule. The decision was made in London to retain the cabildo, albeit without the extensive governmental and ecclesiastical functions and privileges that had once made the council a powerful rival to the Spanish governor and his royal officials. In due course, the traditionally self-elected body was constituted on the elective principle, with a restrictive franchise based on property and residence qualifications. By the end of the Napoleonic Wars, the practice was discontinued whereby the cabildo in Port-of-Spain appointed the first and second alcaldes ordinarios to act as chief judges, with jurisdiction in criminal and civil matters. Henceforth the cabildo would have responsibility only within Port-of-Spain for the delivery of public services (including poor relief, sewage disposal, and street repair), the raising of a town constabulary, and the maintenance of a hospital, a leper asylum, two schools, and (until 1837) the royal jail. Moreover, the cabildo was weakened by the creation of the governor's Council of Advice and had to vie for influence over the chief executive. Finally, under the new dispensation the governor could expect to dominate the cabildo by continuing the old Spanish practice of presiding over its deliberations.

Spanish law having ended in the island several years before, the cabildo was replaced in 1840 by the Port-of-Spain Town Council; an elective body, the council was based on a similarly restrictive franchise and had essentially the same limited powers. By that action, the last institutional vestige of Spanish rule was eliminated in Trinidad.[43]

Under the new system of municipal government in the capital, the Town Council set the rules for its deliberations, and it could pass resolutions, enactments, by-laws, and regulations—all valid only when expressly approved by its presiding officer, the governor.[44]

Notwithstanding these constraints upon their authority, the cabildo and the Town Council in Port-of-Spain were both able to act with some effectiveness as focal points of opposition to a powerful Crown Colony government. The cabildo even managed occasionally to resist further encroachments by the governor upon its municipal role by skillfully garnering political support among leading officials in the colony.[45] The opposition role of successive municipal authorities in the capital, a legacy of Spanish rule, was reinforced throughout the nineteenth century by several factors: (1) the status of Port-of-Spain as the center of government and of economic, educational, and cultural life in the colony; (2) the presence within the capital and its suburban ring of the largest concentration of population in the island;[46] (3) the continuing efforts of the imperial government in London to strengthen the system of Crown Colony government in Trinidad by making its base mostly foreign officials; and (4) the appointment of many reformist members of the elective municipal authority in Port-of-Spain, particularly in the second half of the century, to serve concurrently as members of the Trinidad Legislative Council. Prestige and influence accrued to both the individual councillor/legislator and the municipal authority in this two-tiered political arrangement. (The number of reform-minded unofficial members of the legislature was increased when, based on the precedent of Port-of-Spain, municipal councils with limited powers were established also in San Fernando [1845] and in Arima [1888].)

The Town Council was destined to be short lived in Port-of-Spain. In 1853, the municipal authority in the capital (and in San Fernando) was constituted around a new body, the Borough Council. Ordinance 10 passed that year by the legislature[47] provided that there be fifteen members of the Port-of-Spain Borough Council and that they be elected in five wards for staggered three-year terms. A restrictive franchise based on property and residence qualifications was adopted for the municipality; in the first election under the new system, there were only 809 eligible voters (burgesses), that number constituting less than 5 percent of the more than 15,000 inhabitants of the capital. For the purpose of defining voter eligibility, Ordinance 10 stipulated that a burgess was a male person of at least twenty-one years of age who lived within three miles of Port-of-Spain. That broad conception of the "political space" of the capital, exceeding its territorial limits, was inherited from the old Town Council system; the notion of an expanding political space encouraged the capital's gradual annexation of what were regarded as "its own suburbs." As under the Town Council system, Ordinance 10 set strict limits on officeholding, stipulating, for example, that leading officials of church and state in the colony could not serve on the municipal council. Provision was made for a salaried mayor to be elected to a one-year term by the Borough Council from among its own members. The mayor (who replaced the governor as presiding officer of the council), the town clerk, and other officials of the municipality were to be remunerated from council funds.[48]

Like its predecessors under British rule, the cabildo and the Town Council, the Borough Council was assigned responsibility for the delivery of public services in the capital but with wider responsibility than had earlier been given. The council was charged under Ordinance 10 with organizing police and fire services in the town and with maintaining and repairing much of the municipal infrastructure, including schools, cemeteries, streets and pedestrian walks, markets, squares, and alms-houses and asylums for infirm and indigent residents of Port-of-Spain. It was assigned financial responsibility (as were its predecessors) also for indigents from elsewhere in the colony admitted to any public hospital in the capital. (In 1875, Port-of-Spain was empowered henceforth to make a fixed annual contribution of £750 in lieu of its paying a fee for each person admitted into a government hospital in the town; it was authorized, moreover, to make a fixed annual contribution of £500 toward public education in the capital, thereby relieving it of the responsibility to maintain schools.) Finally, the Borough Council was obliged to meet any and all expenses not provided for in the ordinance that might be incurred in executing the numerous provisions of the law.

To carry out its legal responsibilities, the Borough Council was empowered by ordinance to levy a 5 percent rate on houses in the municipality, excluding properties owned or leased by the Crown Colony government. The government was further exempted from paying the Port-of-Spain water rate. The ordinance provided other major sources of revenue: rents on municipal houses and lands; license fees collected on meat shops, carts, markets, and porters and hucksters; and various tolls and dues. (This arrangement for municipal revenues was carried over from the old cabildo and Town Council systems.)

From its inception, the Borough Council faced staggering problems. Besides inefficiencies associated with its diffuse committee structure and a weak mayoralty, it had to contend with other major problems. Municipal revenues were strained by the annexation of neighboring suburbs and by the influx of rural Trinidadians and of immigrants from other islands in the West Indies and from Europe, North America, Africa, and the northern arc of South America. Intergovernmental relations were worsened by the ambiguity surrounding limits of municipal responsibility where functions overlapped with the Crown Colony government.

The municipality had always to operate on the brink of insolvency. The nub of the problem of overlapping jurisdictions was the failure of municipal and central governments in the Crown Colony to resolve the confusion over expenditures for local and for general purposes. Many residents of Port-of-Spain felt, for example, that the colony's government, not the Borough Council, should have principal or even sole responsibility for hospitals and asylums and for other general services in the populous capital. Throughout the second half of the nineteenth century, Port-of-Spain (and later San Fernando and Arima) were assigned ever greater responsibilities without a commensurate increase in council powers or in sources of revenue.

Unable to meet its growing obligations from annual revenues, the Borough Council had perforce to resort to heavy borrowing. Its mounting public debt became a major strain between the municipality and the imperial government in London. Several months before the appointment in 1895 of Joseph Chamberlain as secretary of state for the colonies, the Borough Council petitioned Trinidad's government for permission to introduce a bill in the Legislative Council authorizing the municipality to borrow £25,000 for essential services: the construction of a slaughterhouse to ensure adequate inspection of meat, the acquisition of a mechanical device for sewage disposal, and the repair and improvement of pedestrian walks. When a year later Port-of-Spain's debt soared to £48,000, the stage was set for a dramatic confrontation between the strong-willed Chamberlain and the hard-pressed municipal council. Early in the period of urban nationalism, from 1895 to 1898, the backdrop of the emerging confrontation was formed, interrelatedly, of the deepening fiscal crisis in Port-of-Spain and the frustrated drive by the Trinidad reform movement for constitutional advance in the Crown Colony.

5

Urban Nationalism I: The Colony, the Capital, and the Politics of Municipal Governance in Port-of-Spain

I

WITH THE APPOINTMENT of Joseph Chamberlain to the Colonial Office in July 1895, the reform movement based principally in Port-of-Spain could be cautiously optimistic about its future and that of reformism in the Crown Colony. In the four years from 1892 to 1895, Liberal governments headed successively by William Gladstone and Lord Rosebery had appeared willing to give impetus to reform in the public life of the colony. In 1892, two creole reformers, George Garcia and the colored Vincent Brown, had been appointed as the principal law officers in Trinidad—as attorney-general and solicitor-general, respectively. In the three years following, four prominent reformers, including the liberals Henry Alcazar and Eugene Lange, had taken their seats as unofficial members of the Legislative Council. And in the twilight of the Rosebery ministry, the Liberals had been preparing to concede an important change in the constitution of Trinidad—the adoption of a quasi-representative principle in the colony's legislature for the election of its unofficial members. But the appointments of Garcia, Brown, and the four reform legislators had produced no formal change in the constitution of Trinidad. And before it fell in June 1895 the Rosebery ministry had been intending to concede such a change in the Legislative Council only as part of its strategy for disciplining the unofficial members in that body: The elective principle would be instituted concurrently with the restoration of the official majority in the colony's legislature and with the abolition of the Finance Committee on which the unofficials had built their prestige and influence. But because the Crown Colony had suffered a "constitutional drought" for most of the first century of British rule, even the mixed signals by the Liberals could be read by many reformers in Trinidad as an augury of better times.

Nor was there reason yet to despair over the appointment of Chamberlain as secretary of state for the colonies. He had after all pursued his public career until 1886 principally as a reformer—in his native Birmingham, then at the center in London. There was cause for hope that upon taking up public office again in 1895, after a nine-year respite precipitated by the break with Gladstone over home rule in Ireland, the Liberal imperialist would still be animated by the idea of reform—this time in the colonies, especially in their municipalities. A year before coming to the Colonial Office, Chamberlain had indeed underscored in the *New Review* his continuing strong interest in municipal affairs.[1] His remarks there on municipal institutions in England and the United States can be read in perspective as an omen of his stern, bullying policy in Port-of-Spain, but that is less important perhaps than what appeared at the time to be a reaffirmation of his principled commitment to municipal reform.

But the optimism that inspirited the Trinidad reform movement in mid-1895 quickly drained away. By the end of 1898, the imperialist Chamberlain would severely discipline reformists in that Crown Colony by refusing to concede the elective principle for unofficial members of the Legislative Council and by ending the unofficial majority in the legislature. The latter action was, among other things, a blow to the prestige of the unofficials and to their influence on the Finance Committee. Early in 1899, Chamberlain struck yet another blow to reform by orchestrating the abolition of the major legislative institution in the colony based on the elective principle, the Port-of-Spain Borough Council. A retrogressive disposition marked imperial policy in the Chamberlain Colonial Office and its actions in Trinidad. In consequence, urban nationalism crystallized in Port-of-Spain as anticolonialism based on issues of municipal public policy that affected the colony and its principal municipality— issues of constitutional advance in Trinidad and of municipal reform in its financially straitened capital.

The integrating of anticolonialism in its urban and its wider territorial expressions in Trinidad in the period 1895–1914 was based on those issues, and the dramatic struggle over them began soon after the new Conservative-Unionist government took office with Chamberlain as its secretary of state for the colonies.

II

Municipal government in Port-of-Spain began to falter early in the era of British rule in Trinidad.[2] Administrative conditions in the municipality continued to worsen throughout the nineteenth century, fueled by the confusion between Port-of-Spain and the Crown Colony government over expenditures for local and for general purposes and by chronically insufficient revenue to meet municipal obligations. Predictably, the deterioration in town services intensified public discontent—as exemplified by the low voter turnout in elections for the municipal council.[3] (Ordinarily, no more than 5 percent of the inhabitants of the capital were listed as town burgesses eligible to vote; usually fewer than one-fourth of them turned out for municipal elections.)

Unable to meet the rising costs even of its original responsibilities, the Borough Council found itself more burdened still by additional obligations laid upon it by the Trinidad government over the next four decades. In 1868, the municipal council was required to pay one-half of the cost incurred by the inhabitants of Port-of-Spain who constructed pavements in front of their dwellings; the municipality had no control over these undertakings, since the inhabitants received permission directly from the surveyor-general in the colony.[4] After 1872, the council was obliged to pay for the registration of vaccinations in the capital.[5] Three years later, as seen, it was relieved of the obligation to maintain schools and hospitals but still had to make a fixed annual contribution for these services in the municipality.[6] Nearing the period of urban nationalism, ever more costly responsibilities were laid upon the municipality by the colony's government. In 1893, the Borough Council was required to pay two-thirds of the cost of improving the Dry River that ran through a large part of the town; the government paid only one-third, despite the fact that it retained full control over the project, including its financing.[7] A year before Joseph Chamberlain came to the Colonial Office, Port-of-Spain was required (along with the boroughs of San Fernando and Arima) to pay one-third of the cost of maintaining the municipal fire brigades, but, as with the Dry River project, the government retained administrative control over fire services.[8] Faced with a debt of £48,333[9] and with a continuing slide in public confidence, the council decided to press its case before the government.

On January 24, 1896, the Port-of-Spain Borough Council communicated to the colonial secretary in Trinidad, Sir Clement Courtenay Knollys, its bitter resentment over what it regarded as a long record of unfair treatment of the municipality by the Crown Colony government.[10] The council proposed that the government help it to manage the municipal deficit by relieving it of all financial responsibilities for hospitals and schools and for the registration of vaccinations, births, and deaths. The council claimed, moreover, that the municipality, not the government, should collect and retain the fees obtained from certain licenses issued in the capital. The government was scored for drawing heavily for the past two decades upon the municipal waterworks to supply its buildings in Port-of-Spain along with areas outside the municipality; it was asked henceforth to pay for its supply of municipal water. Because the government was paying neither municipal rates for its buildings in the capital nor license fees for its carts plying the town, the council pressed it to contribute to the maintenance of municipal roadways and drains.

Upon receiving the Borough Council's communication from Knollys, Governor Sir Napier Broome appointed a commission to investigate the matter and make recommendations.[11] He loaded it with officials and supporters of the government: Among the nine commissioners, only two were publicly identified with the reform movement, the liberals Henry Alcazar and Eugene Lange, both unofficial members of the Legislative Council.

Because of a lack of consensus, in September 1896 the commission delivered its findings and recommendations in three separate reports.[12] The majority report was framed by six members, two minority reports by Commissioners Alcazar and Lange. The ninth commissioner, J. C. Newbold, the English creole mayor of Port-of-Spain, had resigned from the commission soon after it had begun to deliberate.[13] At about the same time, Alcazar departed the colony for medical reasons but not before preparing a memorandum that detailed his own—and the Borough Council's—position.

In its report, the majority rejected nearly every proposal put forth by the municipal council in January 1896.[14] In its view, the council's fixed annual contributions for hospitals and schools were appropriate because they were only a small portion of the total budget for those institutions. Port-of-Spain should have financial responsibility for vaccinations and for registering births and deaths because those were ordinarily municipal functions. Transferring license and other fees from the government to the municipality would be inexpedient and inappropriate, especially as the government balanced the loss of revenue to Port-of-Spain from those sources by maintaining the police and judicial establishments in the capital. Because the government had long borne responsibility for maintaining, improving, and expanding the municipal waterworks, the majority saw no reason for it to pay the water rate. Government buildings in the capital should not be subject to municipal taxation; it would violate a precedent established in England. Because the government was maintaining public roadways and wharves in the capital, Port-of-Spain had no right to tax government carts plying the municipality.

The only concession made by the commission's majority was that the Borough Council be relieved of all financial obligations in the matter of hospitals, schools, vaccinations, births, and deaths—conditional on its raising the house rate in the municipality from 5 percent to 7.5 percent; the latter rate applied throughout the colony except for Port-of-Spain and Arima.

On the minority side, Alcazar contended that the root cause of the dispute between Port-of-Spain and the Crown Colony government was the persistent confusion between them over funding for local and for general purposes.[15] He observed that under the borough system established for municipal government in 1853, Port-of-Spain's revenues were used as indirect subsidies for deficits incurred by the rural wards in the colony; ward deficits, he said, were routinely defrayed by the colony's treasury, to which the municipality was contributing by its payments of license and other fees. While Alcazar preferred that all revenues derived from the municipality should be paid to it, he conceded that it might be necessary to compromise on the matter—especially as the government was helping to maintain the municipal waterworks and to put sanitation services in the capital on a sound footing. Accordingly, he proposed that the government share equally with Port-of-Spain all fees generated within the municipality. (The majority explicitly rejected this proposal, partly because it regarded as inapposite the Alcazar rationale based on government financing of ward deficits.)

Alcazar attacked the system of block payments made by Port-of-Spain for schools on the ground that it contravened the Education Act of 1890. According to him, because it lodged control over the schools in a new Education Board, not in the municipality, the act required that education be funded exclusively from the general revenue of the colony. He insisted, moreover, that the government had owed water rates to the municipality for over two decades, and he presented his reasons. In 1851, the old Town Council in Port-of-Spain had raised a loan of £20,000 to construct the municipal waterworks. At the time, each property owner in the town had been assessed an additional rate in order to repay the loan. In 1875, the government had ended interest payments on the loan by Port-of-Spain because the principal had been repaid and because it intended to continue drawing on the municipal waterworks free of charge for its buildings in the capital and for certain areas outside the municipality. As promised in 1851, the water rate in Port-of-Spain had been reduced with repayment of the loan. Alcazar discerned in this record of the last quarter century solid evidence that the Borough Council owned the waterworks and that by forgoing the further payment of interest by the municipality in 1875, the government had conceded its own obligation to pay the municipal water rate. The government had failed to pay the rate since that year, and Alcazar proposed that the matter be settled with the municipal council "on a fair and equitable basis." The minority report submitted by Eugene Lange mirrored that prepared by Alcazar.[16]

The Crown Colony government accepted the majority position with one qualification: It would defer a decision on the claim that the government should be taxed for its buildings and carts in Port-of-Spain pending the resolution of questions concerning the proposed extension of the municipal water and sewerage works.[17] Finding the majority position in the commission too favorable to the government's interests and therefore unacceptable, the Borough Council informed the government that it would soon petition the secretary of state for the colonies on the matter. Colonial Secretary Knollys, the officer administering the government, then advised Chamberlain that because municipal government in Port-of-Spain had long been mismanaged, he should endorse the recommendations of the commission's majority.[18]

From that point on, the calendar by which the principals maneuvered on the municipal question in Port-of-Spain assumed importance along with the substantive issues over which they contended. The Borough Council had promised to deliver its petition in December 1896 but delayed doing so until after the arrival in the colony of the next governor, Sir Hubert Jerningham. It hoped that the new chief executive would be more sympathetic to municipal interests than his predecessor, Broome, and the incumbent colonial secretary, Knollys. Jerningham took up his office in January 1897, but the petition was not delivered to him until July 10. Without informing the Colonial Office of its delivery, the governor established his own commission to weigh the petition.[19] In the meantime, with the Broome commission's reports and Knollys's hardline assessment of the municipality already in hand, an impatient Colonial Office decided to move against Port-of-Spain without further delay.[20]

The Colonial Office view was that the municipality wished to shirk its responsibilities. According to this view, the Borough Council had skimped on capital investment; too much of the municipal debt had been used to defray operating costs. It proposed the following correctives: that the municipal rate be raised from 5 percent to 7.5 percent in lieu of the contributions made by Port-of-Spain to hospitals, schools, and the registration of vaccinations, births, and deaths; that, to the extent possible, license fees be transferred to the municipality; that the government pay the municipal rate for its buildings in the capital; that the municipality make a fixed annual contribution to the government to support the police force in Port-of-Spain; and that the government receive the municipal budget annually for its assent. With that last proposal, the Colonial Office had signaled its wish to strengthen the hand of the Crown Colony government in municipal affairs in Port-of-Spain.

The Borough Council petition finally arrived in London in September 1897, after the Colonial Office had begun to stake out its own hardline position. According to the council, because Port-of-Spain was already too heavily taxed, it should not be pressured to raise the house rate. It observed that, unlike their counterparts in the country districts, various categories of vendors in the capital were burdened with license fees. The water rate was an additional burden, as was the tax on the sale of spirits. The Borough Council preferred an alternative strategy to increased taxation as the basis for municipal reform in Port-of-Spain: Jurisdictional boundaries should be clarified between the municipality and the colony government, thereby allowing them to dispel the confusion over expenditures for local and for general purposes. (Left unstated in the petition was the councillors' fear that, without a reciprocal resolution of the basic problem of intergovernmental relations, increased taxation would cause a further weakening of public confidence in the municipal authority.) Annexation of various suburban areas was proposed as a more appropriate way to increase municipal revenues than raising taxes. Partly to appease a secretary of state for the colonies who from his early days in Birmingham had been a staunch foe of municipal government by oligarchy,[21] the council proposed that the franchise be widened in Port-of-Spain.

The commission established by Governor Jerningham to assess the position of the Borough Council on the municipal question in Port-of-Spain differed markedly in its composition from that established by his predecessor. It had only four members, at least two of whom could be expected to favor municipal interests, in contrast to the nine-man Broome commission, which had had a two-thirds majority of officials and others favorable to the government. Jerningham had asked the council to appoint two of its members to form the commission with two representatives of the government.

The council selected Henry Alcazar and Leon Agostini, both prominent reformers. They were joined by George Gordon, a reform-minded unofficial member of the Legislative Council, and H. C. Bourne, the registrar-general in the Crown Colony, who was designated commission chairman.

The Jerningham commission proved to be a strong advocate of municipal interests. Echoing the Borough Council, it recommended with one voice that Port-of-Spain be relieved of its responsibility to fund hospitals, schools and the registration of vaccinations, births, and deaths, and that the Crown Colony government pay the municipal house rate for government buildings and lands in the capital, pay license fees for its carts plying the municipality, and purchase Ariapita Asylum from the municipality and maintain it. It proposed, moreover, that the government transfer to Port-of-Spain 10 percent of the spirit taxes it collected in the capital. Monies credited to the government waterworks account were also to be transferred to the municipality, along with title to the existing waterworks, but it was proposed that these facilities continue to be maintained and controlled by the government. The commission calculated that its recommendations, if adopted, would save Port-of-Spain more than £19,000 annually, an amount sufficient to retire the municipal debt and restore sound management. Finally, the commission recommended that the municipality have greater flexibility in establishing the house rate—in the range of 5–10 percent—and that the Borough Council immediately raise the rate from 5 percent to 7.5 percent, as it was in both the suburbs and the municipality of San Fernando.[22] In a separate memorandum, Registrar-General Bourne offered the acute observation that because the colony government had long condoned the actions of the municipal council, it must share the responsibility for council policy over the years.[23]

Impressed with the commissioners' unanimous support for the various recommendations, Governor Jerningham proposed to the Colonial Office in August 1897 that the Crown Colony government assist the municipality "to carry out, without incurring further debt, the ordinary work which is its duty to perform."[24] He endorsed the view of the commission that the municipality had legitimate claims to lay before the government, but he did register his dissatisfaction with particular recommendations. For example, he did not want to establish the precedent of relieving Port-of-Spain of all responsibility for asylums, hospitals, and schools, lest a growing population in the capital someday increase to unreasonable levels the burden of government expenditures for social services. Similar reservations were expressed by Jerningham regarding the house rate on government buildings and lands in Port-of-Spain. He advised, too, that the waterworks proposal be reconsidered. Eschewing a line-item approach, Jerningham proposed instead that the municipality be granted an annual subsidy of £5,000—approximately the operating deficit of the Borough Council in 1897—for about ten years and that it be empowered to levy a house rate in the range of 5–10 percent. He took no position on the commission's recommendation that the house rate be raised immediately to 7.5 percent. In subsequent dispatches to the Colonial Office, he recommended that the municipality be allowed to annex various suburbs[25] and that, if necessary, there be enacted in the colony a general stamp tax to help relieve Port-of-Spain's deficit.[26]

Despite his reservations, Governor Jerningham had proven himself a partisan of the municipality. He had had to stake out his own position on the municipal question under the pressure of time and with the knowledge that the Colonial Office would soon have a broad range of policy options before it. In January 1897, Colonial Secretary Knollys had lent strong support to the pro-government report of the majority element on the Broome commission. Later that month, the Colonial Office had signaled its desire that the colony's government play a more active role in the public life of Port-of-Spain. Jerningham's endorsement of municipal interests would be transmitted to the Colonial Office in August 1897 along with the even stronger endorsement delivered to him several days earlier by his four-man commission. A month later, there would arrive in London the Borough Council petition against the strong pro-government line on the municipal question adopted by the Broome commission and by Knollys. If the secretary of state for the colonies should prove willing to "reopen the file" on Port-of-Spain, he would find there these options originating in the colony: a stern posture toward the municipality (espoused by the Broome commission and by Knollys); a strong endorsement of municipal interests (registered by Jerningham); and a strong endorsement of the municipal authority (advocated by the Jerningham commission and by the Borough Council itself).

But the passage of time had not softened the attitude of officials at the Colonial Office toward Port-of-Spain. On the contrary, the arrival in London of divergent policy recommendations seemed only to strengthen their resolve to discipline the municipality. One official at the Colonial Office recommended against the Crown Colony government extending any assistance until the municipal rate had been raised to 7.5 percent;[27] a colleague wrote biliously that "the Borough Council of Port-of-Spain is the most disgraceful Municipal Body in the W. Indies—probably in the world. . . . [I]t is despised by the inhabitants who take no interest in the elections. The first thing to be done is to reform it and widely increase its franchise."[28] The augury was of an even sterner course of action against the municipality than had been proposed by the Colonial Office in January 1897.

III

In February 1898, Chamberlain staked out his own position on the municipal question in Port-of-Spain—far to the right of the Borough Council, the Jerningham commission, and even the governor himself.[29] The secretary of state rejected the contention of Registrar-General Bourne that the Crown Colony government had been a major factor contributing to the financial distress of Port-of-Spain. Rather, he emphasized his belief that even if the Borough Council had some "ostensible reasons" for claiming relief from the various charges about which it complained, it was still largely responsible for its own plight. He rebuked the municipal council for having raised its indebtedness by borrowing, when it might have remained solvent by seeking the approval of the government to raise the house rate to 7.5 percent. (Interestingly, his rebuke did not extend to the government, which had lent easy approval whenever the Borough Council petitioned it to raise municipal loans.) He recalled that his intention expressed soon after taking office in 1895 was to encourage the development of municipal institutions as the basis for a slow constitutional evolution in the Negro colonies in the British West Indies—conditional on the municipalities supporting themselves.[30] Finding this condition unmet in Port-of-Spain, Chamberlain observed that he had perforce to reject Governor Jerningham's proposal that a £5,000 subsidy be appropriated annually for ten years from the general revenue of the colony.

But the secretary of state was not content merely to level his indictment against the municipality. Pursuing the larger goal of strengthening the hand of the Crown Colony government in the municipality, Chamberlain set a trap for the Borough Council, baiting it with an apparently conciliatory gesture. He offered to relieve Port-of-Spain of its payments to the colony government for asylums, hospitals, schools, and the registration of vaccinations, births, and deaths and to make government buildings, lands, and carts in the capital subject to the municipal rates. He calculated that these concessions would provide relief amounting to about £2,400 annually—slightly more than the average yearly deficit incurred by the municipality over the last two decades. The offer was sharply hedged, however.

The Royal Commission established to investigate conditions in the British West Indies had proposed in 1897 that imperial assistance be extended annually to the Negro Crown Colonies conditional on the amendment of their constitutions to improve administration, i.e., on their accepting tighter imperial control.[31] Consistent with that recommendation, Chamberlain offered now to extend financial assistance to Port-of-Spain conditional on the establishment of "better and sounder finance in the municipality." In this regard, he proposed that a wider franchise be instituted in the capital to create a more efficient Borough Council and to provide more intelligent management of municipal affairs—or, alternatively, that a high official in the Crown Colony government be appointed mayor or council chairman. (He cited as precedents for the latter some recent developments in Bombay and Colombo.) The first proposal struck squarely at the white oligarchy in Port-of-Spain and, by extension, in the colony.[32] It was intended by Chamberlain partly to promote a cardinal principle of municipal reform[33] and partly to drive a deep wedge between the political leadership in Port-of-Spain and the mass of the population. The second proposal was a thinly disguised attempt to ensure virtual control of the municipality by a powerful colony government by disregarding the requirement in Ordinance 10 of 1853 that no government official should serve on the municipal body. Chamberlain had calculated that an entrenched white minority in the capital, based on a restrictive franchise, might seek to defend its privileges against an increasingly restive nonwhite majority by opting for tighter control by the imperial power over public life in Port-of-Spain.[34] To ensure that the colony's government would in any event have the upper hand in the municipality, the secretary of state proposed that the Borough Council henceforth submit its annual budget to the governor for his assent and that the municipal accounts be audited annually by the colony's auditor-general. Chamberlain also proposed that Port-of-Spain raise at least £5,000 annually by increasing the house rate. He concluded with the statement that all these matters would soon be addressed by yet another commission, on whose report he would then comment.

Threatened by a hostile Colonial Office, the Borough Council maneuvered cautiously now to drive a wedge between Governor Jerningham and Chamberlain by registering, in the words of Henry Alcazar, its disappointment over Chamberlain's failure to endorse the "able, liberal, and generous spirit" with which its "most sincere friend," the governor, had chosen to deal with Port-of-Spain. Speaking for his fellow councillors, Alcazar observed further that it would be inappropriate to discuss Chamberlain's proposals before the new commission had had an opportunity to review them.[35]

But others in Port-of-Spain preferred more aggressive opposition to the Colonial Office. Spearheading that element was the press. For example, the *Gazette,* the leading newspaper in the capital, accused the secretary of state of having been too much influenced in municipal and other matters by antagonistic forces: by "entrenched interests" in the Crown Colony which "anathematize Municipal Institutional Reform, Minor Industries, and Popular Representation," and by the former governor, Sir Napier Broome, who had been widely regarded as a foe of the Borough Council. It also hinted broadly that the views of Chamberlain and his supporters in the colony were racially motivated. It remarked upon the reluctance of the secretary of state to accept the governor's recommendation that the colored solicitor-general, Vincent Brown, be the next attorney-general. The *Gazette* discerned in the Brown case further evidence of opposition to the "development of [the Crown Colony] in new directions." In that event, it concluded, the colony might have to bypass the Colonial Office and take its case directly to Parliament.[36] The press campaign against the secretary of state and his adherents grew more strident as the day approached for the governor to release the report of the commission he had established to review Chamberlain's proposals.

The new four-man commission mirrored the reformist hue of its predecessor.[37] Its members included the auditor-general in the Crown Colony and three leading reformers: George Garcia, the outgoing attorney-general; Vincent Brown, the solicitor-general; and Henry Alcazar, who was serving concurrently as mayor of Port-of-Spain and as an unofficial member of the Legislative Council. In light of its composition, the commission's analysis and recommendations were hardly surprising. Its only concession to Chamberlain was the recommendation that property qualifications should be lowered for voters in Port-of-Spain elections and that they should be removed for candidates for the Borough Council. The commission rejected his proposal that a high official in the Crown Colony government be appointed mayor or council chairman because such an official would, at the least, be an irritant in the council; worse, he would feel obliged to the governor who had appointed him, not to the municipal authority. The commission also rejected Chamberlain's proposal that the colony's government conduct an annual review of the municipal budget. In its opinion, such a proposal, if adopted, would lodge ultimate responsibility in the governor; the commission would concede the right of the government merely to insist that the Port-of-Spain budget be "technically correct" and balanced from the local rates. Finally, the commission rejected Chamberlain's proposal that the municipal house rate be raised to 7.5 percent; it pointed out that future annexation of various suburbs would enable the municipality to meet the requirement that it raise an additional £5,000 annually. The commission stressed that Port-of-Spain differed in at least one important respect from a similar community in England: Already burdened by having to pay too large a percentage of their personal income for rent, the ratepayers of Port-of-Spain could not now bear a sharp rise in the regressive rate.

Governor Jerningham lined up solidly behind the unanimous report of the commission—indeed even more solidly than he had in the case of his first commission's report. Perceiving that the existence of the Borough Council was at stake, he appealed to the Colonial Office to accept the "very able report of my four luminaries."[38] But an impatient Colonial Office refused to yield ground,[39] and Chamberlain resolved to "try and indoctrinate" Jerningham when the governor arrived in London in June 1898 for consultations.[40]

The Borough Council met in special session on April 5, 1898, to consider the intransigence of the secretary of state and to weigh its options.[41] Its mood was one of frustration and foreboding. Hearing concern about the future of the council, the mayor, Henry Alcazar, tried to steer his colleagues to accept what he thought would be a workable compromise on the municipal question in Port-of-Spain.

Alcazar proposed that the council endorse passage by the colony's legislature of a new Ballot Act that would lower requirements for the municipal franchise and eliminate the property qualification for borough councillors. The council should also agree to annex various suburbs, to submit the annual estimates and accounts of the municipality respectively to the governor and the auditor-general (subject in both cases to the municipal authority retaining its initiative and discretionary powers in financial affairs), and to levy a uniform house rate of 7.5 percent in order to raise sufficient annual revenues to meet expenses and liabilities (such rate to include and be in lieu of all other rates levied by the municipality). Alcazar's motion proposed as a quid pro quo that the municipality be relieved of the obligation to make payments to the government for hospitals, schools, and vaccinations, that government buildings and lands in Port-of-Spain be subject to the municipal rates, that government carts plying the capital be licensed by the municipality, and that a joint committee of government and municipal representatives be appointed to assess government buildings in Port-of-Spain for the purpose of fixing their rates.

Despite the position that he himself had recently adopted as a member of the second Jerningham commission, Alcazar advised the Borough Council at its April 5 meeting that the inhabitants of the capital were in fact lightly taxed in relation to other cities in the British Empire, hence his proposal that the house rate be raised to 7.5 percent. Near the end of the four-hour session, amendments were carried calling for a joint committee of government and municipal representatives (not, as Alcazar had proposed, for the government alone) to audit the municipal accounts and for the retention of a property qualification for borough councillors in Port-of-Spain but one lowered from £50 to £25. The Alcazar motion, as amended, was then passed by a three-fourths majority in the council—an outcome that seemed to mirror the growing clamor in the capital for a moderate, compromise resolution of the municipal question.[42] Many inhabitants of Port-of-Spain hoped that Governor Jerningham would be able to negotiate such an arrangement for the municipality when he met with Chamberlain several months later.

But the Borough Council meeting of April 5 had also pointed up the potential for increasing rifts should the governor fail to reach an accord with Chamberlain—within the Borough Council, between the municipal authority and the secretary of state, and between that official and a mercurial public opinion in Port-of-Spain. The three-man radical faction, whose leading members were Councillors Ignacio Bodu and Robert J. Nanco, had voted against the Alcazar motion, as amended, chiefly to express their outrage over Chamberlain's insistence on higher rates in the capital. Ironically, the secretary of state would soon prove an "ally" of the radicals against moderate, conciliatory opinion in the council and among the population of Port-of-Spain.

When they met at the Colonial Office in June 1898, Chamberlain impressed on Governor Jerningham that the Borough Council must become self-supporting by raising the rate or it must relinquish its privileges. The Crown Colony would not be taxed to aid the municipality, he insisted. He evinced no sympathy for the fact that municipal interests had even been espoused by five members of the Executive Council in the colony's government—by Jerningham himself and by the attorney-general, the solicitor-general, the registrar-general, and the auditor-general. The governor failed to persuade his superior to accept Henry Alcazar's compromise formula or any facsimile of it. Chamberlain would agree only to consider an application for a loan by Port-of-Spain, albeit on stringent terms. He stressed his intention not to yield on the municipal question.[43]

Two months later, the Borough Council received Chamberlain's ultimatum: The council must be fully responsible for the management of its affairs if it wanted to retain full control of them, but if it insisted on handing over any of its responsibilities to a higher authority in the Crown Colony it must also hand over its control.[44] The secretary of state would not countenance a subsidy for the municipality from the general revenue, as it would place an unfair burden on the ratepayers in the colony. To achieve financial relief, the council would have to accept four conditions: The municipal budget must be submitted annually to the governor for his approval; the auditor-general in the colony must conduct an annual audit of municipal accounts, with power to levy a surcharge on the municipality for "unauthorized or irregular expenditure"; the municipal council in Port-of-Spain would be empowered to raise the house rate to any level necessary to balance its budget; and the council must agree to have its status evaluated by an official appointed by the colony's government. In a confidential dispatch to Governor Jerningham, Chamberlain underlined his impatience with the Borough Council. It had to accept his four conditions or the governor would be instructed to introduce a motion in the Legislative Council replacing the elective Borough Council with an appointed Board of Town Commissioners.[45]

Two meetings were held by the Borough Council in October 1898 to deal with Chamberlain's ultimatum. At the first one, the council registered its "surprise and indignation" at the turn of events, observing that to acquiesce in these "extraordinary demands" would be tantamount to conceding that "there would no longer be any further need of its existence."[46] Later that month, the council reaffirmed its refusal to accept Chamberlain's proposals. That meeting began with a last-ditch effort by Deputy Mayor Leon Agostini to reach a compromise solution. He moved that, while regretting the conditions imposed upon it, the council should acquiesce as an act of self-preservation and should ask the governor to petition the secretary of state to grant it a consultative role with regard to those responsibilities soon to be transferred to the colony's government. The new mayor, J. A. Rapsey, moved to scuttle the Agostini motion with an amendment that expressed strong opposition to the ultimatum. After heated discussion, Rapsey's amendment was carried by a vote of seven to five.[47] Significantly, the council had divided only over the question of an appropriate response to the secretary of state. No councillor came forward to defend Chamberlain on that occasion.

Public opinion in the capital was similarly divided over the action taken by the Borough Council. For example, while generally applauding the conscientiousness with which the council had approached its difficult task, the Port-of-Spain *Gazette* believed that the control that Chamberlain intended the Crown Colony government to have over municipal affairs would prove "very slight" and "neither irksome nor humiliating."[48] Accordingly, it scored the council for not pursuing the course of "compromise and expediency."[49] By this action, the *Gazette* had executed an abrupt about-face in its assessment of the secretary of state. No longer did it regard Chamberlain as an ally of entrenched interests antipathetic to popular representation in the Legislative Council and the Borough Council. According to its editorial writer, the secretary of state had all along perceived that neither the appointed unofficials in the colony legislature nor the borough councillors whose election was based on a highly restricted franchise could validly claim to represent some larger constituency. Conceding the accuracy of Chamberlain's perception, the writer expressed the hope that in the upcoming elections for the Borough Council a strong popular mandate would establish the representativeness of the municipal institution.[50] The leading newspaper in Port-of-Spain pointed up the need to elect to the municipal council five new members who would favor reconsidering the vote against the secretary of state.[51] But the moderate element in the capital was by then outnumbered and on the defensive. Public opinion in the municipality had begun to harden against an obdurate secretary of state in London. A rally held in Prince's Building on October 29, 1898, voiced strong support for the "no surrender party" in the council, and municipal elections held early in November returned five anti-Chamberlain members to the council, affirming the considerable strength of "no surrender" sentiment in Port-of-Spain.[52] On November 21, the council met again to register its unwillingness to submit to the secretary of state.

Governor Jerningham began to waver in his support of the Borough Council. He reported to Chamberlain that the moderate element in the council and the municipality would soon petition the Colonial Office not to regard the "no surrender" councillors as representatives of public opinion.[53] He emphasized to the council that it must own up to its record of financial mismanagement and resolve to mend its ways; he also advised the council that he had informed the legislature of the confidential instruction given him by Chamberlain to abolish the Borough Council if it did not accept the four conditions imposed on it.[54] Caught between the Colonial Office and the council, Jerningham sought to defend his role in the conflict by retreating to a legalist position: He declared that "the Secretary of State whose absolute authority over us cannot possibly be denied by any sensible being, has given what he considered a just and proper reply."[55] (Soon after retiring from the Crown Colony in 1900, Jerningham wrote in *The Empire Review* that "A prudent mother gradually loosens the strings of the apron and thereby strengthens the ties of affection." As evidence of an imprudent, provocative imperial policy in Trinidad, he cited the Crown's exercise of too strict control over financial affairs, its decision to abolish the unofficial majority in the Legislative Council, and its failure to add unofficials to the Executive Council.)[56]

The denouement was at hand. Having failed to produce a reconciliation, Governor Jerningham proceeded on December 19 and 20 to move through all its stages in the Legislative Council the ordinance abolishing the municipality of Port-of-Spain.[57] In place of the elective Borough Council, there would be an appointed Board of Town Commissioners. According to Ordinance 1 of 1899,[58] the new municipal authority in the capital would assume all the powers, responsibilities, assets, and liabilities of its predecessor. The board chairman would be the chief commissioner, a post the governor would fill with a high civil servant in the colony. The other commissioners, whose number the governor was to fix, would be appointed by him from among those government officials who were ratepayers in Port-of-Spain. Commissioners could be dismissed by the governor during their initial three-year term of appointment.

Ordinance 1 provided that the Board of Town Commissioners would be relieved of payments toward hospitals, schools, and the registration of vaccinations, births, and deaths. An annual grant of £1,750 would be made by the Crown Colony government to the new municipal authority in Port-of-Spain in lieu of any rate or tax on the government by the municipality. The ordinance authorized the colony government to grant assistance from general revenue toward the board's purchase of houses and lands for municipal use. The board was also empowered to raise the house rate. Finally, the ordinance stipulated that the governor would annually check, approve, and amend the municipal estimates and that the auditor-general in the colony would conduct an annual audit of the municipal accounts.

The long struggle over the municipal question in Port-of-Spain had produced bitter animosities, personal and political. At the final meeting of the Borough Council on January 17, 1899, the majority "no surrender party" turned on Governor Jerningham, accusing him of having conspired all along with the secretary of state against the municipal interest. Whereupon Henry Alcazar, the onetime mayor, denounced that party for having "strain[ed] every nerve to destroy." In ironic contrast, the liberal reformer observed, the most conservative elements in the community, rallying around the Port-of-Spain *Gazette,* had paid a "magnificent tribute" to representative institutions by working tirelessly to save the Borough Council.[59]

Mistrust and recrimination became norms of political life in Port-of-Spain upon the abolition of the Borough Council. The principal beneficiaries of that development were leading radicals and militants in the reform movement. Those elements were buoyed by the emergence in the municipality of the "no surrender party" and of a radicalized public opinion. Radicals and militants, especially in Port-of-Spain, anticipated renewed confrontation with the Colonial Office headed by the hardliner Joseph Chamberlain and with the Crown Colony government in Trinidad. Their expectations would soon be fulfilled, catalyzed by yet another municipal issue affecting the public life of the colony and its capital: the administration of the waterworks in Port-of-Spain.

IV

Shortly before Chamberlain became secretary of state for the colonies in 1895, his predecessor, Lord Ripon, had been advised by Governor Broome that because the Liberal government intended to establish the representative principle, its concession was not a pressing issue in Trinidad. Broome had further advised Ripon that "the desire for a political change in Trinidad is not based . . . on any indictment, which can be sustained, of misgovernment in the present constitution." The governor concluded that a moderate reform would therefore suffice, perhaps reconstituting the colony's legislature to include seven appointed official, seven appointed unofficial, and seven elected unofficial members.[60] Convinced by the Broome report that Trinidad was a well-managed colony with an ineffectual reform movement, Chamberlain confidently set about denying the representative principle in the Legislative Council and, in 1898, abolishing the unofficial majority in that body.[61] (Consistent with those actions, in 1902 he would deny the unofficials' petition that they be granted more than an advisory role in the Finance Committee of the colony's legislature.)

In 1899, after nearly four years at the Colonial Office, Chamberlain could feel the same confidence about his handling of the municipal question in Port-of-Spain. Controlled by a tiny fragment of the small middle-class element in the capital, and beset by administrative and financial problems, the Borough Council could mount no effective resistance to the strong-willed secretary of state. He had moved with dispatch to tighten the imperial grip on municipal affairs in Port-of-Spain, all the while professing to favor piecemeal constitutional advance in the colony, beginning with municipal reform. Critics assailed the essentially retrogressive policy that the secretary of state had adopted for the colony and the capital, pointing up its basic contradiction: "Trinidad has prospered wonderfully materially, but politically is a child at school. We are constantly told that we are not sufficiently educated in political matters to be entrusted with representative Government and it may be so. It is a question needless to discuss, but if it be true, at whose door lies the fault? If a parent not only neglects to send his child to school, but actively interferes to prevent him from acquiring knowledge, is the incapacity of that child when he becomes a man to be reproached to him or to the father? Questions such as these carry their own answers."[62] But Chamberlain would not be diverted from his course.[63]

Yet on close examination we discover that Chamberlain's critics in the Trinidad reform movement had been defeated only partly by his designs. Reformism in Trinidad had long borne the stigmata of political isolation and ineptitude, never having organized effectively around an animating idea. The appointed unofficial members of the Legislative Council were indeed unrepresentative,[64] as, to a lesser extent, were the elected members of the Port-of-Spain Borough Council. (The Colonial Office had always interpreted the low voter turnout among the small electorate in Port-of-Spain and San Fernando as proof that representative institutions were not highly prized in the colony.)[65] The "no surrender party" had emerged as the radicalized majority faction in the twilight of the municipal council, albeit without establishing a firm hold on reform opinion in the capital. Its critics continued to point up the radicals' failure to secure a sweeping mandate, either electorally or in the street. Viewing all of this, Chamberlain could be confident that, whatever its connection with the larger issue of Crown Colony government based on the principle of trusteeship, the municipal question in Port-of-Spain was not widely regarded in Trinidad as a rallying point for the disaffected. The "no surrender party" had garnered only weak support among the reformers in San Fernando and Arima, despite the administrative and financial problems that those two small municipalities shared with Port-of-Spain.[66] Issues that had long divided the reform movement geographically[67] could not be subordinated now to common concerns over the growth of imperial power in Trinidad. Chamberlain could be confident, too, that the issue of representative government would continue to have limited appeal to the general population of the colony. In the past, that cause had been embraced principally by the urban middle class, many of whose members were themselves deeply distrustful of a liberal franchise in heterogeneous Trinidad. The great majority in the colony, formed of hard-pressed urban laborers, mostly black, and of indentured Indians in the country districts, had not been drawn to the cause of legislative reform based on the representative principle. Indeed, their growing alienation, expressed, as seen, in the symbolism and violence of the Carnival and Hosein festivals, had yet to be organized politically. The Trinidad Workingmen's Association, founded in 1897, had failed to achieve its goal of spearheading a politics of protest based on the alliance of black workers and colored professionals in the main towns. And the Legislative Reform Committee, small and elitist from its inception in 1856, had refused for nearly a half century to conceive a strategy of politics with mass appeal.[68] By the end of the nineteenth century, then, no political principle or issue or organization had captured the imagination or allegiance of the mass of the population in Trinidad or its capital.[69]

All of these developments in Trinidad's affairs had worked together to dull Chamberlain's sensitivity to a shifting popular mood in the Crown Colony—particularly in Port-of-Spain, where an amorphous feeling of discontent was spreading through the largely nonwhite population. His disposition to be dismissive of Trinidad and other nettlesome small colonies in the backwaters of the British Empire was doubtless reinforced by the press of imperial business elsewhere—in South Africa, for example, where tensions in the white community would soon erupt in war between Briton and Boer. Dependent on his officials in Trinidad, themselves apt to be insensitive to changing currents in the popular mood, the secretary of state would shortly face an ominous issue in the public life of the colony. Chamberlain and the Crown Colony officials were unprepared for the broad-based opposition that that issue would inspire in Port-of-Spain and for the violence it would engender. Unlike the municipal question in Port-of-Spain and the larger issue of representative government in the colony, the water issue in the capital would galvanize public opinion across lines of class, race, religion, and nationality, its urgency keenly felt by leading and ordinary citizens. Ostensibly a parochial issue in Port-of-Spain, in fact it would raise fundamental questions about the capacity and integrity of Crown Colony government based on the principle of paternalistic trusteeship.

6

Urban Nationalism II: The Colony, the Capital, and the Politics of Water in Port-of-Spain

I

LIKE THE MUNICIPAL QUESTION in Port-of-Spain, the water issue had been long evolving before it came to a climax after 1895 in the period of urban nationalism. There had been a problem of water supply in the town since the early days of Spanish rule, but it had not attained serious proportions until the second half of the nineteenth century when Port-of-Spain's population growth accelerated because of a high birth rate, the annexation of suburban areas, and migration from the country districts and from outside the colony.[1]

In 1874, each of the 25,000 inhabitants of the capital was using, on average, more than twice the per capita allocation of water in London.[2] Various conservation measures were proposed at the time, including the installation of water meters, but they were not adopted and the problem worsened. In 1881, a commission established by the Crown Colony government to investigate the matter found that, despite some conservation measures contained in Ordinance 3 (Water

Works) of 1880, fully one-third of the daily supply was being wasted through carelessness. Accordingly, it recommended that conservation be promoted by reducing the diameter of pipes. Enacted in 1883, that measure merely encouraged greater waste. Taps were left open longer because of the slower delivery of water through the conduits.

By 1892, the population of Port-of-Spain had swelled to 50,000, the increase based partly on the recent annexation of the large suburb of Belmont. Still more anticipated annexations threatened the municipality with untenable demands on the available water supply.[3] In that year, the colony's government decided henceforth to cut the supply twice daily for several hours during the dry season, in order to permit the main reservoir at Maraval to be replenished. A special commission established by the government proposed that even sterner measures be adopted to halt waste and that an auxiliary reservoir be constructed to store an extra supply. But, notwithstanding mounting public pressure to act decisively in the matter, the government continued to resist formulating a coherent policy for the waterworks in Port-of-Spain.[4]

Finally, in 1895, the basis for such a policy was conceived by Osbert Chadwick, a government engineer. Chadwick proposed that the water supply in the capital be augmented by 1.5 million gallons daily and that the level of supply in the dry season be increased to the level of 3 million gallons enjoyed daily in the wet season. The increased supply would be made possible by developing facilities at three sites, one in the Diego Martin Valley, at the mouth of the Maraval River in suburban St. Clair, and one on each of two estates (whose acquisition he recommended) through which the Maraval flowed. He urged also that conservation be pursued aggressively by close inspection and repair of pipes and taps and, as in most European cities, by the installation of water meters. Chadwick stressed the equitability of meters, noting that their use would make it possible to levy higher charges on those who traditionally had been most wasteful, especially on the more affluent classes.[5] (Instead of using regular-size baths containing up to eighty gallons, for years the wealthy residents of Port-of-Spain had enjoyed baths whose capacity ranged up to two thousand gallons; the oversized baths would usually be filled by allowing taps to remain open throughout the day and often into the night.)

But the proposed stringencies met stiff resistance from all sectors of the population in Port-of-Spain. In 1896, a bill was introduced in the Legislative Council requiring that meters be installed in oversized baths and pools and that the water rate be raised sharply. Only two unofficial members of the legislature balked, and the bill was quickly enacted into law. A public outcry in the capital caused Governor Sir Napier Broome to withdraw the ordinance. He advised Secretary of State for the Colonies Joseph Chamberlain that under the circumstances it would be more prudent to push ahead with the new waterworks scheme at Diego Martin and other sites and, to the extent possible, to enforce existing laws for the conservation of water.[6] But this concession failed to restore public confidence in a government that many had come to regard as chronically indecisive and overbearing in its handling of the water issue in Port-of-Spain.

The perception of official arrogance in the matter of water supply was a legacy from the preceding generation, when an unusually imaginative and resourceful administration had been criticized for being authoritarian. Governor Sir Henry Irving (1874–80) had launched an ambitious public works program for water and roads, but his administration was chastised for being overcentralized, inefficient, costly, and dominated by foreign-born officials. Local sensibilities were also offended when Irving decided to follow the long-time practice of calling on Crown Agents, not merchants in Trinidad, to supply materials to the colony's Department of Public Works.[7] Succeeding administrations lacked the energy and zeal that had marked the Irving administration, and by the 1890s the population of Port-of-Spain thought that the government was pursuing a "dilly-dally policy," as the *Gazette* put it, in the matter of the municipal water supply.[8]

Alternately permissive and stern in its administration of the Port-of-Spain waterworks before 1895, the Crown Colony government brought contempt on itself. Experiencing ever greater frustration as it tried to cope with the worsening problem of supplying water, the government became increasingly heavy-handed and insensitive in its approach. In response, the popular mood in the capital became more embittered. Chamberlain had expressed conditionally his willingness to have the colony's government pay the municipality for the use of water by certain government institutions in Port-of-Spain but the matter was deferred while tension escalated between the secretary of state and the Borough Council over the municipal question.[9] The inhabitants of the capital grew impatient because they were still subsidizing the government's use of the overburdened municipal waterworks.

Tension increased over the conservation measures adopted by the

Crown Colony government. Proclamations posted throughout Port-of-Spain informed the public that the water supply would be suspended twice daily, from noon to 3:00 P.M. and from 10:00 P.M. to 4:00 A.M., but cutoffs were sometimes instituted as early as 8:30 A.M. The government was criticized for this "sharp practice." [10]

Yet another measure that aroused public indignation allowed great latitude in official inspection for waste. This policy, adopted in September 1901 by Walsh Wrightson, director of public works in the colony, allowed department inspectors to go to local residences at any hour without prior notice to check for waste of water. On encountering waste, often caused by pipes and fixtures in disrepair, the inspectors would cut off household taps until fines had been paid. These inspections and cutoffs were regarded by the public as invasions of privacy by a government too little concerned with civil liberties. [11] By 1903, an additional supply of 1.6 million gallons daily was acquired by developing the facilities proposed by Osbert Chadwick; it became possible for a time to end cutoffs of the household water supply in the capital and almost to double the pressure of the water flow. Believing that the problem of supply had finally been overcome, the population in Port-of-Spain turned even more sour when Wrightson decided in February to cut off water used to flush street gutters. A public outcry ensued over the necessity of sweeping dry gutters, forcing Wrightson to renew the flow of water. But it was too late to mollify the angry inhabitants. Wrightson had made the decision to cut off the supply for flushing just as a new waterworks bill was being prepared in the Legislative Council. By late February 1903, the popular mood had become feverish over the prospect of the installation of water meters and a sharp increase in the water rate.

Finally, popular discontent was fueled by evidence of corruption and venality among officials in the Department of Public Works. The department had been periodically scandalized by revelations of bribery and sharp practices in the letting of contracts. In the 1890s, the generally low esteem in which it was held by the public was reinforced by criticisms directed specifically at its foreign-born director, Walsh Wrightson. He was assailed for receiving a lucrative salary when local-born officials in the Crown Colony government were being denied salary increases[12] and for taking leave with pay to serve briefly in neighboring Venezuela as a private consultant on harbor engineering. Public anger escalated when it was disclosed that Wrightson had hired an assistant to oversee the Port-of-Spain harbor works during his absence from the colony.[13] He was bitterly criticized also for his inspection policy and for the slow progress of the new waterworks scheme at Diego Martin and other sites. Many inhabitants of the capital charged further that an unhurried construction schedule for the waterworks had been responsible for the failure to prevent several fires from spreading in the town and that the numerous delays had endangered public health. (Most buildings in Port-of-Spain were constructed of wood. Major fires occurred in the capital in 1895 and 1901, causing fire insurance companies to raise their premiums by more than 100 percent in that period. Public indignation was also aroused when, early in March 1903, an epidemic of eruptive fever, possibly smallpox, raged through Port-of-Spain; many inhabitants blamed this menace to public health on an insufficiency of water to flush streets and dispose of sewage.) In the public mind, Wrightson had come to symbolize a government indifferent to human needs. Popular hostility to him and to the government increased sharply as public officials rallied to the defense of the director of public works.

II

In the first three years of the twentieth century, the political atmosphere of urban nationalism in Port-of-Spain was charged by three issues of public policy: constitutional advance, the municipal question, and the water issue. Disaffection had grown particularly among the reformist middle-class element in Port-of-Spain over the adoption by Chamberlain of a retrogressive policy on representative institutions. After denying the elective principle in the Legislative Council, in 1898 he had moved to strengthen the system of Crown Colony government in Trinidad by restoring the official majority.[14] He delivered more blows to reform sentiment by refusing four years later to enlarge the role of the unofficial members of the Finance Committee in the colony's legislature[15] and by abolishing the elective Borough Council in Port-of-Spain in 1899 and replacing it with an appointive Board of Town Commissioners stacked with officials of the Crown Colony government.

Finally, disaffection grew among all sectors of the population in Port-of-Spain over the decisions in September 1901 and February 1903 to promote water conservation, first by official inspections and household cutoffs, then by sweeping dry street gutters. By late February 1903, public consternation was pushed nearly to the breaking point by impending legislation to establish water meters and a higher water rate in Port-of-Spain.

All of these developments helped to focus radical political sentiment in the capital. After the turn of the century, official provocation and radical politicization would be locked in a dangerous spiral. It would culminate in death and destruction on March 23, 1903, in the Port-of-Spain water riot.

There emerged in Port-of-Spain in the period 1895–1903 several radical protest groups and a radical newspaper destined to play roles of varying importance in urban nationalism. Two of the protest groups have been noted: the Trinidad Workingmen's Association,[16] founded in 1897, and the "no surrender party,"[17] which appeared in 1898 as the majority faction in the Borough Council. At its founding, the association had about fifty members, mostly black creole artisans and laborers and a few immigrants from other islands in the West Indies. It set an ambitious agenda for improving the lot of workers, especially of black workers. Among its goals for the colony were the abolition of the indenture system for Indian labor, the improvement of living and employment conditions for workers, lower taxes particularly on foodstuffs and work tools, the development of public transportation, the establishment of minor industries and savings banks, and the opening of more Crown lands to small proprietors. It also had three explicitly political goals: municipal reform in Port-of-Spain, establishment of the elective principle in the Legislative Council, and the end of expatriate control of the only electricity company in Trinidad.[18] As seen, the small, loosely knit organization was largely ineffectual in the period of urban nationalism: It achieved none of its goals, nor did it succeed in building a political alliance between black workers and colored professionals in Port-of-Spain and other towns. Notwithstanding, the association can be seen in perspective as having earned a niche in the history of nationalism in Trinidad—as a stimulus to black political consciousness and as the harbinger of a strategy of mass politics on which would be based the nationalist struggle against colonial rule in the half century after the First World War.[19]

Like the Trinidad Workingmen's Association, the "no surrender party" in the Port-of-Spain Borough Council symbolized a challenge to the nineteenth-century tradition of reformism based on a gradual evolution in the constitution of Trinidad. Among the principal figures in the party were Ignacio Bodu, a Spanish creole, Robert J. Nanco, an English creole, and Edgar Maresse-Smith, a black barrister; all three evinced great impatience with a conventional pressure-group strategy which, early in the period of urban nationalism, had lent encouragement to the retrogressive imperialism of Joseph Chamberlain. While the association and the party had only small formal memberships, together they managed to attract a large following in the capital. Often the same people would appear at meetings and rallies of each group.

Doubtless the most important protest group to form in Port-of-Spain in the period of urban nationalism was the Ratepayers' Association. Founded in September 1901, it was concerned with protecting the interests of ratepayers and property owners after the abolition of the Borough Council.[20] Recognizing the limited political appeal of its narrow social base, a month later the association began to accept as members people who were neither ratepayers nor property owners. Acting with caution lest the ratepayer interest eventually be submerged in a large, heterogeneous organization, the founders decided to create two categories of membership, ratepayers and associates. The subordinate status of the latter group was established in the rule that only ratepayers would be allowed to vote on matters of finance and governance in the organization.[21] Anticipating a flood of new members despite this discriminatory arrangement, the association provided also for the election of a twelve-man Executive Committee, including the president and vice-president of the association, and for the appointment of a paid secretary. But a year after its founding it had attracted only eighty-four members,[22] mostly white and colored lawyers and merchants. (By 1903, the membership had grown to 185.)[23] The ratepaying members comprised less than 3 percent of the ratepayers in Port-of-Spain.[24]

Little was heard from the Ratepayers' Association until March 1902, when Emmanuel Lazare, a radical black solicitor, joined its ranks. Motivated by a strong social consciousness and by personal ambition, Lazare decided to become a member soon after resigning from another protest group, the Pan-African Association. That association had been founded in Port-of-Spain in July 1901 as a branch of the African Association, which had been established in 1897 in London by several blacks, including the barrister H. S. Williams, a Trinidadian. Regarding itself as the voice of a collective black interest spanning Africa and the diaspora,[25] the African Association took up the cause of numerous peoples and places: It lobbied against the maltreatment of tribal groups in Africa and of poor blacks in the American South and for aid to the depressed Negro sugar colonies in the British West Indies. Williams's work on behalf of Pan-Africanism made him popular in Trinidad. On a tour of the Crown Colony in 1901, he was received with great fanfare by the black and colored population.[26] That July the first Trinidad branch of the African Association was founded in Port-of-Spain, taking as its name the Pan-African Association. By the end of 1901 at least eight more branches had been established throughout the island. Upon his election as chairman of the Executive Committee of the Trinidad Pan-African Association, Lazare moved swiftly to assert his credentials as a political radical.[27] Claiming to speak for all the branches in the colony, he pressed for a British West Indies Pan-African Association and for political liberty based on a new West Indies confederation within the British Empire.[28] This proposal for constitutional advance within a larger regional framework was shrewdly couched by Lazare to appeal to a hostile secretary of state for the colonies who aspired eventually to reorganize the empire as a federation based upon the Canadian model.[29] But Lazare's scheme impressed neither Chamberlain nor the array of contentious factions and persons forming the Trinidad Pan-African Association. As the association foundered, Lazare and his followers withdrew to the Ratepayers' Association.

Emmanuel Lazare quickly rose to a position of leadership in the Ratepayers' Association. Despite its small membership, under his tutelage it gained stature rapidly. Members and supporters of both the Trinidad Workingmen's Association and the "no surrender party" rallied around the ratepayers' organization. Even black workers and black women in Port-of-Spain embraced its newly adopted goals: establishment of the elective principle in the Legislative Council, restoration of the Borough Council in the capital, and, somewhat more ambiguously, an enlarged role in public life for the politically powerless. The call that the Trinidad Workingmen's Association had earlier made for a broad-based alliance between black workers and colored professionals had impressed Lazare.[30] On joining the Ratepayers' Association, he quickly set about radicalizing the organization and pushing it to the forefront of political agitation in Port-of-Spain.

Throughout the nineteenth century, various newspapers in Port-of-Spain had been identified with one or another current in the Trinidad reform movement—for example, the *Gazette* with conservative reformism based on French creole cocoa interests, *Public Opinion* with the cause of liberal reform. Not until the period of urban nationalism did there appear in the capital an influential newspaper with a radical orientation. The *Mirror* was launched in 1898 by Richard Mole, an English journalist who had emigrated to Trinidad twelve years earlier. Soon after arriving in the Crown Colony, Mole secured a position with *Public Opinion,* owned by the liberal reformer Philip Rostant, a French creole. From that vantage point, he could observe the internecine conflicts in the reform movement and the interplay of reform politics with imperial policy based on the Colonial Office and the colony's government. Mole founded his own newspaper at the height of the crisis over the Borough Council.[31] He regarded the *Mirror* as the organ of the English community (foreign-born and creole) and of radical reformism in the colony. The *Mirror* lashed out against three principal targets: the *Gazette,* its French-owned conservative archrival; the system of Crown Colony government based on the principle of paternalistic trusteeship; and the colony's government, which Mole accused of mismanaging the public affairs of the colony and the capital, particularly the issues of the water supply and the Borough Council. His keen journalistic sense and tactics would prove a major factor in the growing popularity of the Ratepayers' Association in Port-of-Spain. For example, on March 10, 1902, there appeared in the *Mirror* a story reporting that a downturn in the French-dominated cocoa industry had left thousands of laborers without wages; the story was published coincidentally with the decision taken by Emmanuel Lazare and his followers to bolt the Pan-African Association for the Ratepayers' Association.[32] The newspaper laid the blame for the economic woes of Trinidad—a chronically ailing sugar industry and a downturn in the cocoa industry—squarely with the colony's government; the charge helped the ratepayers' organization to attract strong support among the laboring classes in the capital. Intensely political and ambitious, Mole did not shrink from misrepresentation or fabrication when his interest or that of the radicalized Ratepayers' Association was at stake.[33] For example, on September 10, 1902, the *Mirror* falsely reported that Walsh Wrightson, the controversial director of public works in the colony, had proposed raising the municipal water rate to 7.5 percent at least. An outraged public in Port-of-Spain responded by rallying behind the association. Mole's firebrand journalism helped to radicalize political sentiment in the capital. Under his direction, the *Mirror* spoke for those in and around the association who, despairing of a conventional pressure-group approach, would seek to influence public policy through the tactic of political agitation.[34]

III

Even after publicly rejecting Joseph Chamberlain's ultimatum of August 1898 that the Borough Council must accede to his four conditions or face abolition, the majority "no surrender party" sought to strike a deal with the Colonial Office. Anticipating that the radical faction in the municipal council would take such an initiative, the governor, Sir Hubert Jerningham, advised Chamberlain that the group would soon try to arrange "a dignified retreat" for itself.[35] The decision had been made by the colony's government to enact on January 18, 1899, the ordinance replacing the elective Borough Council with an appointive Board of Town Commissioners.[36] Just two weeks before that date, the "no surrender party" dispatched a telegram to the secretary of state for the colonies urging him to put off implementing Ordinance 1 pending a further petition in the matter.[37] But by now Jerningham himself was impatient for a resolution of the deeply divisive municipal question in Port-of-Spain. Expecting that the moderate minority faction in the Borough Council would shortly petition the secretary of state to deny the radicals' request for a delay, the governor urged Chamberlain to ignore the telegram.[38] Herein lay the basis for the vituperative charge leveled by the "no surrender party" that the governor had all along conspired with the Colonial Office against the municipal interest.[39]

Several weeks after the abolition of the Borough Council, the "no surrender party" dispatched its petition to the Colonial Office. Signed by thirty-six prominent burgesses in Port-of-Spain, the document denounced the decision to establish an appointive Board of Town Commissioners as "a retrograde step."[40] But seeking to strike a conciliatory note, the petitioners agreed that the municipal house rate should be raised to 7.5 percent.

They informed the Colonial Office that a committee would soon be appointed to travel to England to seek the reestablishment of the Borough of Port-of-Spain "on a fair and independent basis." While implying a willingness to continue to negotiate over the municipal question, the petitioners' plan to send a committee evoked the threat made by the Port-of-Spain *Gazette* in March 1898 that the colony might appeal directly to Parliament.[41]

Chamberlain made clear now his unwillingness to reopen the matter. Speaking before the House of Commons on March 20, 1899, he observed that a committee had recently arrived in London from the Crown Colony to ask certain members of Parliament "for an extension of representative government in Trinidad." He described the "hopeless disorder" that had characterized municipal finances in Port-of-Spain and the unwillingness of the Borough Council to meet his four conditions for relieving the situation, and he concluded on a dismissive note: "They refused to do that. ... [Accordingly] it has been necessary to abolish the municipality and carry on the work by a Commission. That is the experience of a representative government of which these gentlemen desire an extension—an experience which does not encourage us to go further."[42]

Chamberlain's speech brought to a close the political fireworks over the municipal question in Port-of-Spain and sealed the fate of the "no surrender party." Nearly thirty months passed before the issue of the defunct Borough Council surfaced again in the Crown Colony. During that time, the party found itself without an effective voice in the cause of radical reform. It made no serious effort to build an organizational structure around its seven members who had comprised the majority faction in the twilight of the old municipal council. Without its political base in the council, the tiny party was too weak to constitute a powerful force either for reestablishing the Borough of Port-of-Spain or for radical change in the colony. Moreover, as time passed it fell prey to internal divisions not unlike those that had long weakened the reform movement in Trinidad. Radical sentiment in Port-of-Spain, growing but diffuse down to the middle of 1901, had yet to gather its strength around an effective spearhead organization.

The reform pantheon in nineteenth-century Trinidad was filled with many individuals and political groupings—and with a handful of influential newspapers, mostly based in Port-of-Spain. Periodically, one or more of those newspapers would move to bolster the flagging reform movement, or some grouping in it, by adopting a vanguard role for itself. In the second half of the 1870s, it will be recalled, the *Gazette* and *Public Opinion* launched a strident campaign against the administration of Governor Sir Henry Irving that was to galvanize reformism over the next two decades.[43] In August 1901, the *Mirror* sought to promote radical interests with its own major initiative: it launched an attack against both Chamberlain and the governor of Trinidad, Sir Alfred Moloney, who had succeeded Sir Hubert Jerningham in December 1900. Its campaign against the Colonial Office and the colony's government was calibrated with its effort to help launch a new organization on which radicalism might be based, the Ratepayers' Association in Port-of-Spain.

The *Mirror* began its campaign on August 10, 1901, with an editorial broadside that sought to reopen the municipal question. Quoting selectively from the speech delivered by Chamberlain in Commons on March 20, 1899, the editor rebutted the charge of financial mismanagement that had been laid against the old Borough Council and demanded that that institution be restored. Drawing a parallel between Trinidad and South Africa in the British Empire, the *Mirror* proclaimed the rights for which free men were then struggling—the burgesses in Port-of-Spain, the warring Uitlanders on the South African veldt.[44] The editorial precipitated no immediate reaction in any quarter.

On August 14, the *Mirror* tried again to whip up radical sentiment in the capital—this time by exciting anxiety among the inhabitants over official intentions in the water issue. Its editorial writer alleged that a plan was afoot to raise the water and sewerage rates at least to 10 percent in Port-of-Spain. The increase was "fully anticipated," he wrote, adding that "Whether this dismal prognostication is to be fulfilled we know not." The tactic of sowing confusion was calculated to cause distress especially among the mass of renters in the town, mostly blacks in the laboring class. According to the editorial writer, property owners would doubtless follow the traditional practice of passing along the higher levy to their "already overtaxed" tenants. The *Mirror* proposed that all the inhabitants of the capital lay aside their differences now and join together to form a Ratepayers' Association that would "watch over their interests and see to it that their rates are not made unnecessarily high."[45] Curiously, no effort was made by officials to counter the false rumor of an impending sharp increase in the rates. The colony's government and the Board of Town Commissioners stood silently by as the *Mirror* set about raising the political temperature in Port-of-Spain.

Three weeks later, the *Mirror* carried an announcement that twenty-five leading merchants had founded an organization "to protect the interests of the people of Port-of-Spain by watching over the expenditure of the Town Commissioners and protecting against unnecessary increase in the rates either by the Commissioners or government."[46] The newspaper was ebullient, predicting that the new Ratepayers' Association it had helped spawn would be "most successful." It lent assurance that, despite a small membership based on ratepayers and property owners, the organization would gather support among the mass of people who feared higher rents resulting from sharp increases in the rates.[47]

Despite the fanfare with which the *Mirror* had heralded its founding, the Ratepayers' Association got off to a slow, inauspicious start. At its inception, it evoked those nineteenth-century reformist political organizations whose middle-class members generally preferred to pursue their goals by constitutional means, not by mass action; the Legislative Reform Committee had been the exemplar in Trinidad.[48] Unlike most such organizations, the association hoped to excite popular support, but the ineffectiveness of its principal tactics was quickly revealed: Petitions addressed to officials and letters printed in the *Mirror* both failed to move the government or the populace. For example, soon after its establishment, the association petitioned Walsh Wrightson, director of public works, to stop using unannounced inspections and cutoffs to discourage the waste of water.[49] Wrightson refused to accede to the association's proposal that offenders be granted twenty-four-hour notice before cutoffs were effected.[50] Its ineffectiveness underscored by Wrightson's rebuff, the association failed to gain political credit even as public indignation over the inspection policy intensified.

Over the next six months, the Ratepayers' Association would take heart from the patronage of the *Mirror* and from the rising chorus of criticism directed at the Colonial Office and the Trinidad government. Editorials attacking Joseph Chamberlain and the administration of Governor Sir Alfred Moloney appeared regularly in that newspaper, among others. Leading radicals in the colony came forward to question the prevailing imperial arrangement—C. Prudhomme David, for example, who pointed out what he perceived to be the basis for the West Indies' weak loyalty to the British Crown.[51] And there was similar criticism in Great Britain from which the Trinidad radicals might draw strength. In its issue of April 24, 1902, for example, the *Mirror* played up a recent article in the London *Daily Telegraph* which had scored the onetime "uncompromising radical" Chamberlain for not "under[standing] what the interests of the West Indies are . . . [and for] his obstinate, dictatorial character."[52]

But the charged rhetoric failed to move the Colonial Office or the Trinidad government—either on the municipal question or the water issue or on the larger issue of Crown Colony government. Unable to influence policy by itself, the Ratepayers' Association reached out to powerful groups representing moderate opinion in Port-of-Spain—

for example, the Trinidad Chamber of Commerce and various Christian churches. But these efforts were unavailing. The chamber refused to join the association in convening a public meeting to discuss the water issue. Citing the recent pledge by Governor Moloney to issue a statement on the matter, the merchants' group concluded that the proposed meeting would be premature.[53] Frustrated in its attempt to gather strength across the political spectrum, and fearing isolation as yet another ineffectual pressure group, the association decided to adopt political agitation as its principal weapon. The driving force behind that fateful decision was Emmanuel Lazare, who in March 1902 led his followers—mostly black laborers who were renters in Port-of-Spain—from the Pan-African Association to the Ratepayers' Association.

In June 1902, the Ratepayers' Association convened the first in a series of mass meetings in Port-of-Spain—ostensibly to protest the recent decision of the colony's government to effect economies by canceling a gala ball celebrating the coronation of Edward VII. Well attended by a cross section of the population, the meeting voiced sharp criticism of what was widely regarded as yet another instance of official highhandedness. Lazare was cheered loudly when he proposed that a telegram be dispatched to the Colonial Office denouncing the cancellation of the celebration.[54] Lazare had acted with impressive skill on that occasion to help propel the association onto the center stage of radical politics in Port-of-Spain and to reaffirm his own bona fides as a loyal, if radical, subject of the Crown.

Three months later, the Crown Colony government promulgated a new water policy for Port-of-Spain. Drawing upon the Chadwick Report of 1895, it proposed to enact a comprehensive ordinance superseding nearly a dozen statutes then in effect; the ordinance would establish an ambitious program of conservation based on a system of water meters. A bitterly hostile popular reaction was not long in coming. After falsely reporting that the government intended to raise the water rate at least to 7.5 percent, and that the Legislative Council would be denied a voice in the matter, the *Mirror* urged the residents of Port-of-Spain to resist the impending "calamity."[55] On October 17, 1902, the Ratepayers' Association convened its second mass meeting in the capital—this one to deal specifically with the water issue. Inflammatory speeches were delivered by several radicals, among them Ignacio Bodu, Edgar Maresse-Smith, and the colored creole Dr. George Masson. The large crowd roared its approval as association leaders moved resolutions objecting to the proposed consolidated water ordinance and to the installation of water meters.[56]

Emmanuel Lazare and the other leaders of the Ratepayers' Association had acted with great skill at the October mass meeting, fashioning a rationale for their radical opposition that would gather wide support in the municipality. Taking their cue from the *Mirror,* Lazare and his colleagues succeeded in exacerbating the antipathy that many inhabitants of Port-of-Spain felt toward Joseph Chamberlain and the system of crown colonies that he advocated for the British West Indies: They contended that the unofficial members of the Legislative Council, who in 1898 had been stripped by Chamberlain of their majority status in the legislature, were about to lose their remaining advisory and financial powers over water policy in the colony.[57] Association leaders claimed, moreover, that the installation of water meters would pose a major threat to public health in the municipality by encouraging the poorer classes—the great majority—to sacrifice cleanliness to minimize expense. In one stroke, the association had managed to convey the force of urban nationalism, of anticolonialism based on issues of municipal public policy that affected both the colony and its capital. It had maneuvered brilliantly to establish in the public mind the connection between the parochial water issue in Port-of-Spain and the larger issue of Crown Colony government based on the idea of paternalistic trusteeship; and it had generated political support in all social classes by arousing their common fear with regard to public health. The meeting concluded by urging Governor Moloney to transmit the record of its deliberations to the secretary of state at the Colonial Office.[58]

Impressed by this mass public protest, Moloney moved with dispatch to withdraw the consolidated water ordinance. As in 1896, when Governor Sir Napier Broome had reacted to a public outcry by withdrawing another ordinance based on the Chadwick Report,[59] the colony's government appeared now to weaken in its resolve to enact a coherent water policy for Port-of-Spain. Wishing to show that he could be conciliatory, Moloney impressed a delegation from the Ratepayers' Association and the capital's inhabitants by promising to meet with them again to discuss the issue. The government seemed to recognize the association, not its own appointive Board of Town Commissioners in Port-of-Spain, as the chief representative of municipal interests. Thirteen months after its founding, the association proclaimed itself "the general body of the Municipal body," a "Vigilance Committee" established to check an overbearing administration.[60] The proclamation evoked an ancient legitimacy in Trinidad, its wellspring the cabildo under Spanish rule: the right—even the obligation—of the municipality of Port-of-Spain to array itself against the central authority in the colony.[61]

But in fact the Crown Colony government had merely executed a tactical retreat when it withdrew the consolidated water ordinance in late 1902 and expressed a willingness to deal with the Rate-payers' Association. On the latter, the governor had sought (in the words of Philip Selznick in another context) to "formally co-opt" the organization without sharing power with it.[62] The government continued to act vigorously on the administrative front as it laid plans for a renewed legislative effort. For example, stressing the need to curb waste, the director of public works proposed to the Legislative Council in January 1903 that it strengthen the enforcement provisions of the 1880 water ordinance. When the legislature balked, Wrightson increased sharply the number of household inspections to curb waste, but, following the conciliatory lead of Governor Moloney, he did issue warnings to households scheduled to be inspected.[63] This apparent concession to the association, which had earlier urged Wrightson to adopt a more felicitous inspection policy, was an important part of the effort by the colony's government to restore public confidence in its conservation program. But fueled by a press campaign against both Moloney and Wrightson, the popular mood was still skeptical and hostile. Despite the charged atmosphere, the government decided to move ahead on the legislative front.

A new bill, the Port-of-Spain Water Ordinance, 1903,[64] had its first reading in the Legislative Council on February 23. Hoping to avoid further delays in implementing its water policy for the municipality, the government adopted a tight schedule for legislative action: The bill was to be published in the official gazette on March 5, circulated in the legislature the next day, and enacted into law soon after its second reading on March 16.[65] Along with this tight timetable, the details of the proposed ordinance also produced public consternation: a Water Authority would be established with sweeping powers to construct, maintain, and administer the waterworks, to acquire by easement or purchase new lands for water supply and water rights, and to fix the general water rates along with special rates for large baths. The authority would be empowered, moreover, to promote conservation by installing water meters in households and commercial establishments and pursuing an aggressive inspection policy. To mollify public opinion, the bill stipulated that henceforth inspections must be conducted at reasonable times and at the discretion of a court, not the Department of Public Works or the Water Authority. Under the consolidated ordinance, the authority would consist of four officials—the director of public works, the surgeon-general, the receiver-general, and the chief commissioner of Port-of-Spain—and five other persons appointed by the governor. Individuals with grievances stemming from the administration of the new ordinance could seek redress in the courts. Recognizing that many people still believed that the affluent would persist in their profligate use of water even under this stringent policy, the government tried to reassure the skeptics by stressing its basic premises: that the water supply was not unlimited, that the money to retire loans made for construction and maintenance of the waterworks must be raised from users, and that the principle of equity must be instituted. Large users would pay more, small users less. Moving the bill in the Legislative Council on March 16, Acting Attorney-General Vincent Brown had emphasized the essential fairness of the stipulation on rates.

To many residents of the capital, the legislative agenda was proof that the government had determined to rush ahead in flagrant disregard of the Ratepayers' Association and of public opinion, for which that organization claimed to speak. The government had also resolved to initiate action without consulting the unofficial members of the Legislative Council, who had registered their strong opposition to the abortive 1902 water ordinance. In the aftermath of the water riot of 1903, an official Commission of Enquiry ruled that the government, acting unilaterally and in haste on the 1903 ordinance, "was very injudicious, and certainly calculated to give color to the view that [it] cared naught for public opinion."[66]

IV

Even before the proposed water ordinance had its first reading in the Legislative Council on February 23, 1903, radical elements in the capital had already begun to organize against its enactment. On November 13, 1902, the director of public works had submitted to the acting colonial secretary in Trinidad his assessment of the various resolutions adopted by the Ratepayers' Association at its mass meeting on October 17; the second part of his report contained an analysis of the water supply for Port-of-Spain and an outline of the probable scope of the bill to be laid before the legislature.[67] When the details of the report became available to the radicals, they set about planning a major campaign against the bill to begin after its first reading on February 23. Taking the lead when the campaign opened was the principal radical newspaper in the capital.

For several weeks beginning February 27, 1903, the *Mirror* denounced the proposed ordinance; it exhorted the Ratepayers' Association to mobilize public opinion against it and challenged the association to "justify its existence" on the water issue. On March 7, the *Pioneer,* a radical magazine in Port-of-Spain, joined the campaign. The *Mirror* published the draft ordinance in two parts on March 6 and 7,[68] and a week later the association swung its campaign into high gear. On March 14, its mass protest meeting in Queen's Park Savannah (north of the town center) attracted more than two thousand people.

The crowd was whipped into a frenzy by the speakers, among them J. C. Newbold, president of the association and a onetime mayor of Port-of-Spain. He accused Walsh Wrightson of exploiting the proposed ordinance to enhance his own power in the colony's government. Without having read the bill himself, he falsely alleged that it would allow the director of public works to deny water to the poorest classes in the capital—and, in the guise of conducting inspections for waste, to violate "the sanctity of your houses, . . . your wives and daughters [in] their baths." Presented with three proposals, the throng shouted its approval. The first one, moved by Robert J. Nanco, called upon the inhabitants of Port-of-Spain to protest the ordinance and "the present system of uncontrolled taxation" and to "assert their right to be consulted in the fixing of rates." The second resolution, put by Edgar Maresse-Smith, urged the secretary of state for the colonies to dispatch an independent commission, at the expense of the municipality, to investigate the "establishment by the government and their administration of the Waterworks of Port-of-Spain." Finally, it was resolved to name a delegation to present a record of the proceedings to Governor Moloney for transmission to the secretary of state.[69]

A delegation from the Ratepayers' Association met with the governor on March 16, only hours before the Legislative Council was to begin its second reading of the bill. Moloney promised that he would transmit the full record of the March 14 public meeting to both the legislature and the Colonial Office, and he assured the delegation that it need not fear hurried enactment of the ordinance.[70] Despite his assurances, the legislative session was in an uproar that day. Shouting and catcalls emanated from the packed visitors' gallery as Acting Attorney-General Vincent Brown, who had moved the bill, began to explain its rationale and details. More interruptions ensued as members of the Legislative Council tried to comment on the proposed ordinance. When the clamor reached fever pitch in the visitors' gallery and in the streets nearby, Governor Moloney adjourned the second reading until March 23.

Emboldened by its ability to force an adjournment of the Legislative Council, the Ratepayers' Association moved quickly to build on what the *Mirror* had termed only a "partial success." The organization called for another mass protest meeting on March 21. The association had gathered wide support in Port-of-Spain. Even the *Gazette,* the conservative nemesis of the *Mirror,* hailed the call for renewed protest. The *Gazette* helped stoke the political fires also by accusing Wrightson of allowing his vengeful antipathy toward the people of Port-of-Spain to blind him to any reasonable alternative on the water issue.[71] The radicals' hand was further strengthened when the Trinidad Chamber of Commerce met on the day of the protest meeting to endorse the association's proposal that the secretary of state appoint an independent commission to investigate the entire matter and that legislative proceedings on the ordinance be halted until the commission had concluded its work.[72] Moved both by their opposition to government handling of the water issue and by their fear of renewed public disorder, a wide array of reform interests had come to embrace the principal objectives, if not the strident rhetoric, of the radical agitators. The civic leadership and the population of Port-of-Spain were more united than ever on the issue of the waterworks.

In order to prevent a recurrence of disruption when the Legislative Council reconvened on March 23, the governor and his Executive Council decided that the public should be admitted only by ticket. According to their plan, tickets would be issued on a first-come-first-served basis until the visitors' gallery was filled. Publication of the ticket regulation precipitated an immediate challenge to its legality by several lawyers affiliated with the Ratepayers' Association.[73] (The measure was defended by the acting attorney-general and the acting chief justice in Trinidad and subsequently by law officers of the Crown in London.)

On March 21, a large crowd gathered in Brunswick (now Woodford) Square, the public park facing Red House, the government cen-

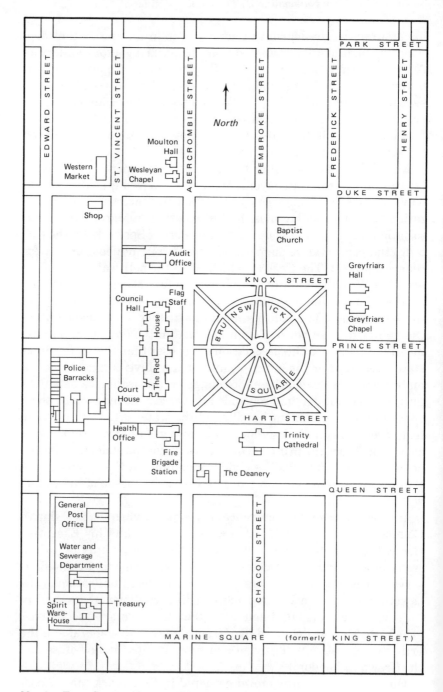

Map 3. *Town Center of Port-of-Spain, with Government District*

ter, which also housed the Legislative Council (see map 3). There they heard leaders of the Ratepayers' Association denounce the ticket regulation as illegal and impractical. Public opinion, already inflamed, was easily persuaded that on March 23 the Crown Colony government would contrive to pack the legislative chamber with its own supporters by issuing an undue proportion of the available tickets to government clerks. Edgar Maresse-Smith and Emmanuel Lazare both urged the crowd to ignore threats made by the government to imprison citizens who pushed their way into the visitors' gallery that day; Maresse-Smith pointed out that there was not sufficient space in the prisons to accommodate all those who would violate the ticket regulation. Lazare went on to attack the principle of taxation (i.e., fixing of water rates) without popular representation in the legislature. The meeting concluded with instructions to the crowd to gather early on March 23 in Brunswick Square, where, shouting their opposition to the proposed water ordinance, they would again force the governor to adjourn the second reading.[74]

Governor Moloney met with a delegation from the Ratepayers' Association on the evening of March 21 to try to compose his differences with the organization. J. C. Newbold, its president, lent his assurance that order would be maintained during the second reading of the bill—conditional on the government canceling its ticket regulation. The governor would not countenance the idea, citing his fear that disorder would reign if admission to the visitors' gallery were not regulated with tickets.[75] Whereupon the delegation withdrew, leaving the government to proceed with its own plans for maintaining public order on March 23. A violent denouement would cap that day's events.

V

Upon consulting with Lieutenant-Colonel H. E. Brake, inspector-general of police, who commanded local forces in Trinidad, Governor Moloney concluded that disruption on March 23 could best be deterred by a display of strength. Nearly three dozen heavily armed policemen would be posted inside Red House before dawn, and the constabulary would be bolstered with thirty-five additional men from the surrounding country stations. All told, some two hundred policemen would be available for duty that day, including sixty-four assigned to march with their long staves to the government center about an hour before the legislative session began at noon. The government was braced to deter a popular disturbance or, if necessary, to quell it with force.[76]

The March 23 issue of the *Mirror* carried a notice from the Ratepayers' Association exhorting the inhabitants of Port-of-Spain to march together from the office of the association's vice-president to the legislative chamber in Red House. Further exacerbating the popular mood that morning was a report in the *Mirror* that the acting chief justice, Nathaniel Nathan, had registered his strong disapproval of the ticket regulation. (Nathan would later deny this allegation.)[77] But even as the association's radical leaders and their allies in the press were arousing the public, they continued to caution it to act calmly and constitutionally. Few heard that plea, and on March 23 the public was dangerously inflamed; Port-of-Spain was poised for trouble.

That day's events quickly gathered momentum.[78] At about 11:20 A.M. several hundred people appeared at the main entrance of Red House seeking admission into the legislative chamber; at their head were J. C. Newbold, Emmanuel Lazare, Ignacio Bodu, Edgar Maresse-Smith, and other leaders of the Ratepayers' Association. The milling crowd was offered tickets by a policeman but refused to accept them, contending that people had a right to be admitted without tickets. An abortive attempt was made by some protesters to force their way into the building. Observing from a distance that the police cordon might be broken, the inspector-general, Colonel Brake, decided to intervene personally. Walking to the main entrance, he explained to the gathering that the ticket regulation would be strictly enforced and that he was prepared to accept the legal consequences of forcibly repelling any persons who might try to gain admission illegally. A brief exchange ensued. When some people challenged Brake to commit a "technical assault," he obliged them by touching several of the protesters; this precipitated threats to take him to court. Recognizing the dangers inherent in the situation, the association appeared to want to draw back. Three of its leaders began to press upon the crowd their versions of a prudently restrained course of action. But failing to state any common purpose, tactical or strategic, their conflicting counsel had the effect (probably unintended) of sowing confusion among their listeners. Newbold implored the throng to disperse and gather again at 7:00 P.M. "to come to Government House to protest." (Despite corroborative evidence, he later denied voicing that directive.) Henry N. Hall, publisher of the *Pioneer,* entreated the assemblage to sing the national anthem and, after the legislative proceedings began, to cheer each clause of the draft ordinance as it was being read in the Legislative Council. Finally, Emmanuel Lazare urged the crowd to follow him across Abercrombie Street to Brunswick Square to hold a meeting; according to one witness, he cautioned the gathering "to be constitutional, and keep quiet." Most of the crowd—whose number had swelled to more than a thousand—moved to the square, where they were addressed by Newbold, Maresse-Smith, and Nanco.[79] The government subsequently charged that the popular mood had been further inflamed by the meeting in the square.

Meanwhile, the legislative session began promptly at noon, albeit in an agitated state. Without waiting for the minutes to be read, the liberal reformer Henry Alcazar, an unofficial member, rose to denounce the ticket regulation as illegal. Upon being ruled out of order by Governor Moloney, Alcazar registered a further protest by moving that the session be adjourned. Seconded by George Goodwille, vice-president of the Trinidad Chamber of Commerce, another reform-minded unofficial, the motion was put to a vote and defeated fourteen to six; the majority included four unofficials and the solid bloc of ten official members. Alcazar left the legislative chamber, followed soon after by another unofficial member, George Gordon, president of the Chamber of Commerce. The minutes were then read and some minor business transacted before the governor addressed the Legislative Council on the proposed water ordinance, about to receive its second reading.

Developments inside Red House and without had already begun to merge in an ominous pattern. While speaking against the ticket regulation, Henry Alcazar had been repeatedly interrupted by a tumult outside the building. Even before noon, knots of men had begun to drift away from the meeting in Brunswick Square toward Red House, where, joined by many women and young boys, they hoped to disrupt the legislative proceedings with singing and shouting. Emmanuel Lazare and another man were observed waving flags at the head of a crowd circling the building. Just as Alcazar was leaving the Legislative Council, some of the protesters tried to force their way into Red House; they were repulsed by a body of unarmed policemen. In the meantime, Richard Mole, publisher of the *Mirror,* who was inside the building as a member of the press, shouted to the crowd that Alcazar had withdrawn from the legislative chamber. (Mole's participation in the events unfolding in Red

House had actually commenced a short time before. Standing on the verandah, he had dropped several pieces of paper to the crowd "with a view of keeping the people informed of what was going on.")[80]

What had been relatively orderly proceedings at Red House and in nearby Brunswick Square now took a violent turn. Protesters clustered near the entrance of the building started to hurl stones and other objects through the windows, continuing on and off for a brief period. Governor Moloney's carriage was vandalized, then dragged several blocks to the waterfront and thrown into the sea.

At about 1:30 P.M. the crowd—which had grown to more than five thousand—began to force its way into Red House. Once inside, it advanced on the legislative chamber hurling stones. Proceedings in the Legislative Council ended abruptly when Governor Moloney and various officials fled the chamber, seeking refuge in another part of the building. Moloney was determined to go out on the verandah to address the unruly crowd, but he was dissuaded. Colonel Brake signaled from the verandah for the police reserve to come to Red House. He then telephoned the deputy inspector-general, instructing him to bring up his men armed with staves; after some confusion and delay, this force arrived. Mounted police had also been summoned. Fearing full-scale riot, Brake telephoned St. James's police barracks (west of Red House, across St. Vincent Street) for volunteers from those in training there. Finally, he relayed a message to Captain Hope Robertson, R. N., commanding H. M. S. *Pallas,* anchored in Port-of-Spain's harbor, that he dispatch every available sailor to Red House. Robertson had begun to act before the message came. Observing fire in the vicinity of the government center and learning from the officer commanding H. M. S. *Rocket,* anchored nearby, that a "serious riot was in progress,"[81] *Pallas* had dispatched a landing party.

Immediately upon leaving St. James's barracks, the police reserve met with a volley of stones. Colonel Brake tried vainly to address the rioting crowd from the verandah of Red House. Shouted down, he dispatched a small party of armed policemen—estimates ranged between twelve and thirty—into nearby St. Vincent Street to force the crowd back with the butt ends of their rifles. They were foiled by an enraged crowd that continued to hurl stones at the approaching policemen. Intent on making a charge, the deputy inspector-general ordered his men to fix bayonets. But persuaded that nothing less than gunfire would affect the crowd, Brake ordered the men to fall back quickly into Red House to assist in its defense.

Surrounded by rioters, Emmanuel Lazare and another official of the Ratepayers' Association were working feverishly, but in vain, to calm the crowd. Occupying both the quadrangle on which Red House was situated and all but a few offices on the ground floor of the building, the rioters continued to vent their fury. Chaos reigned in and around the government center, and by about 2:30 P.M. Red House was ablaze. Unable to contact Governor Moloney, who was sequestered in the Education Office, Colonel Brake asked Colonial Secretary Knollys for permission "to authorize the reading of the Riot Act, and the subsequent dispersal of the crowd, if necessary by firing."[82] His petition was immediately granted. When the act was read from the east and west balconies of the building, the crowd hurled still more stones at one of the readers, A. S. Bowen, warden[83] of Diego Martin; he was brought down with severe cuts to the face. Brake then ordered his men to fire independently into the crowd. Quickly regaining his composure, Bowen countermanded the order in an attempt to protect a local merchant who was in the center of the crowd trying to restore calm. Departing with an armed contingent for another part of Red House, Brake ordered those men to fire independently on the throng. The stone throwing continued until several volleys had been fired. When the crowd finally broke and ran, the firing ceased.

As these first shots were being fired into the crowd, A. S. Bowen and several other civilians were making their way to the Fire Brigade Station (south of Red House, across Hart Street) to try to turn out the engines and hose. By order of Colonel Brake, three or four policemen were firing one round each into a group of rioters near the entrance of Red House. Other policemen, acting without orders, were firing in a southerly direction down St. Vincent Street. Shielded by all this firepower, Governor Moloney was able to make his way out of the flaming building to the relative safety of the police barracks. In due course, sailors from H. M. S. *Pallas* and H. M. S. *Rocket* and volunteers from St. James's barracks arrived to help disperse the crowd.

VI

The affray had taken a heavy toll of lives and property. Two hundred shots had been fired by policemen and troops; sixteen people had been killed at the riot scene or died later in hospital from their wounds, and forty-four had to be treated for their wounds at the

Port-of-Spain hospital. Red House had been destroyed by fire, as had all the records stored there except those in the fireproof vault of the registrar-general. But there was a further accounting to be made, and a difficult period lay ahead. Pitting many ordinary citizens against their government over issues of municipal public policy that affected the colony and the capital, urban nationalism had culminated in an orgy of *political violence*. Accordingly, there had still to be calculated the *political cost*—to men, in high places and low, and to institutions.

7

Urban Nationalism III: A Painful Stocktaking

I

THE PORT-OF-SPAIN WATER RIOT was a singular event. The tranquility of the island colony had sometimes been disturbed by invasion and rebellion,[1] by riot,[2] even by political agitation.[3] But the events of March 23, 1903, marked a turning point in the public life of Trinidad: For the first time popular discontent, played upon by an adroit campaign of political agitation, had vented itself in violence against constituted authority. Never before had thousands of citizens in the colony expressed a political grievance by assaulting the leading symbols, structures, and officials of a regime based on the principle of paternalistic trusteeship. In contrast to the water riot in Port-of-Spain, the riots associated with the festivals of Carnival and Hosein had been essentially unorganized, anomic reactions against lesser targets conceived only vaguely in political terms: offending regulations for the annual festivals harshly enforced by a lower officialdom, the Trinidad constabulary, which was dominated by mem-

bers of an unpopular immigrant group from Barbados.[4] Understand-
ably, among all these disorders the water riot alone was followed by a
period of intense political activity, within official circles and without.

In the early morning of March 24, Joseph Chamberlain learned
through the London newspapers of the calamity that had struck
Trinidad the day before.[5] A few hours later, he cabled Governor Moloney that he should "Send full particulars as to alleged riot by telegram."[6] With that communication, there began a weeklong exchange
of telegrams between key individuals and groups in London and in
Port-of-Spain. The telegraph played an ambivalent role in this phase
of the political crisis. It enabled the Colonial Office to monitor the
situation in Trinidad more closely by soliciting information, as
needed, and by swiftly issuing directives. But the flurry of telegrams
would exacerbate the crisis by underscoring its urgency,[7] and
heightened tension increased the risk of further violence.

Later in the day on March 24, Chamberlain received his first communication from the Crown Colony since the riot—a telegram from
the Ratepayers' Association[8] denouncing the "oppressive water ordinance" and pointing out that the whole community, including the
Trinidad Chamber of Commerce, was united in opposition to "increased taxation, restricted and arbitrary cutting off [of water] supply, failure new waterworks, exclusion ratepayers [from] Legislative
Chamber despite protest [by] members of council." Along with the
Mirror and other newspapers in Port-of-Spain,[9] the association
blamed the colony's government for the riot and its consequences
and requested an independent inquiry.

Before daybreak on March 25, Chamberlain received another
cable from Trinidad, this one from the Chamber of Commerce.[10] It
adopted an even harder line, urging the secretary of state to "immediate[ly] remov[e] . . . Governor and principal officials in whom public confidence has been entirely lost, so as to restore order and prevent further rioting and bloodshed pending appointment of Royal
Commission of Enquiry, most urgently needed."

Later that day, the secretary of state received his first communication from the governor—a telegram sent on March 24,[11] replying
to the request for "full particulars." The timing of the reply would
prove as significant as its contents; the two factors together would
form the basis for the forthcoming accusation by the Ratepayers' Association and others in Port-of-Spain that the governor had con-
trived to mislead the secretary of state as to the circumstances of the
riot. In light of that serious charge, it is important to clarify the

transmission of dispatches between the two officials, by cable and by post, during the two days following the riot.

Shortly before noon on March 24, the secretary of state had cabled the governor to send him "full particulars by telegram." Unknown to Chamberlain, Moloney had taken the initiative and had sent to London by post that day a long, detailed report, including pertinent documents;[12] it would not arrive at the Colonial Office until April 9. Probably because his report with "full particulars" was already en route to the secretary of state by post, the governor chose not to repeat himself when he replied by telegram on March 24 to the cable he had received earlier that day from Chamberlain. Instead, he cabled Chamberlain a brief description of the riot, the toll in lives and property, and what he deemed to be the principal causes: political agitation over the issue of representative government, toward which "the whole [public excitement] was turned," the excitement and misrepresentation surrounding the proposed water ordinance, the protest meeting of March 16 and the consequent legislative adjournment, and the public meeting on March 21 to protest the ticket regulation. The governor advised Chamberlain that two hundred Lancashire Fusiliers (whites) were en route from Barbados to help maintain public order and concluded his cable by adding his voice to the mounting public clamor in Trinidad for a Commission of Enquiry.

Moloney's telegram arrived at the Colonial Office at 8:00 A.M. on March 25. Nearly seven hours later, Chamberlain cabled the governor his "deep . . . regret" over the riot and its toll. He instructed Moloney to provide him with the "fullest possible particulars by post" and to inform the Ratepayers' Association and the Chamber of Commerce that a Commission of Enquiry would be appointed.[13] Chamberlain's second cable to Moloney may be taken as evidence that even by March 25 the secretary of state did not know that the governor had already sent him by post "the fullest possible particulars."

Clearly it would have been better for Governor Moloney had he complied with the original request to cable "full particulars"—or at least noted in his cabled reply of March 24 that he had sent a detailed report by post. By the time the report arrived at the Colonial Office, more than two weeks later, the governor's integrity had been impugned, along with his competence. On March 27, the secretary of state received yet another telegram from the Ratepayers' Association, this one protesting that the governor had cabled to Chamberlain an "entirely misleading" account of the riot and promising its own further details by post.[14] It is doubtful that the association knew yet that the governor had already posted a fuller report to the secretary of state. We can only speculate how the organization would have reacted by March 27 if it had had that information.

During the critical first week following the water riot, Chamberlain had taken care to point out to Governor Moloney his open-mindedness on the matter: he referred to the "alleged riot" in Port-of-Spain, conceded the need for an independent Commission of Enquiry, and on March 31 wrote the governor that "pending report [of] the commission, I will withhold judgment entirely on what has taken place."[15] There were several reasons for Chamberlain's wait-and-see attitude: he was preoccupied with larger, more proximate matters (notably the impending British elections, set against the background of political struggle over his proposal for a kind of imperial *zollverein* based on protectionism);[16] he wanted to distance himself and the Colonial Office from what looked to be a discredited government in Trinidad; and he wished to avoid being drawn into the eruptive politics of Port-of-Spain (as he had been earlier on the municipal question). Thus, interrogated on Trinidad affairs in the House of Commons in early May, the secretary of state struck a pose of detachment, stating that the proposed water ordinance was a purely local matter of which he had had no prior knowledge. He emphasized his dispassionate and fair-minded attitude by affirming that Governor Moloney would continue to administer the Trinidad government at least while the Commission of Enquiry was at work in Port-of-Spain.[17]

Notwithstanding his professing an unprejudiced attitude toward the riot, the secretary of state managed to reveal himself otherwise, albeit subtly: His dispatches to Governor Moloney in late March were also an evocation of Chamberlain the stern imperialist, impatient to have his way. On March 28, he cabled Moloney, "What steps are being taken to bring to justice leaders of riot?"[18] (The governor would quickly reply, "No leader has yet been arrested. Matter is in hands of Inspector-General of Police.")[19]

Writing to the governor three days later, the secretary of state did not try to conceal his dismay that such a "very serious disturbance . . . [had] taken place in a colony which holds a leading position in the West Indies; and whose conditions, as compared with those of His Majesty's other West Indian possessions, have been conspicuously prosperous."[20] That theme would be repeated many times by Chamberlain and his officials at the Colonial Office. In his letter, he informed Governor Moloney that three commissioners would probably be appointed to conduct the inquiry, the cost of which would be borne by the Trinidad treasury.

In the interim between April 1 and the first public sitting of the Commission of Enquiry on April 29, a fuller record of the water riot was developed by the Colonial Office with further exchanges between London and Port-of-Spain. Writing to Governor Moloney on April 6, Chamberlain noted that he had recently received from Sir Clement Courtenay Knollys, the colonial secretary in Trinidad, the dispatch of December 3, 1902, which contained these items: the several resolutions passed at the public meeting convened by the Ratepayers' Association on October 17 to denounce the proposed consolidated water ordinance; the critical appraisal that had later been made of those resolutions by Walsh Wrightson, director of public works; and Wrightson's proposals for a coherent water policy in Port-of-Spain based on a new Water Authority. Chamberlain also informed the governor that he had recently solicited the advice of Osbert Chadwick, the former government engineer in Trinidad, about the Wrightson proposals and report.[21] (Chadwick endorsed the case put forth by Wrightson, emphasizing especially the need to curb waste by installing water meters.)[22]

Much detail was added to the Colonial Office's record of the water riot from the lengthy report that Governor Moloney had sent to Chamberlain by post on March 24, which arrived on April 9. Recognizing early on that the riot could have grave consequences for the Crown Colony government in Trinidad and for his own career, the governor raised a strong defense. He tried to persuade the secretary of state, and later on (through Knollys's testimony) the Commission of Enquiry, that his administration had all along acted judiciously in the face of extreme provocation. His report stressed, among other things, his determination from the outset neither to hurry the draft ordinance through the Legislative Council on March 23 nor to withdraw it under the threat of public disorder. But apparently he had had second thoughts regarding the latter contingency: his report revealed that, fearing full-scale riot, he was preparing to announce his decision to defer the second reading and to place the whole matter before the secretary of state for resolution, when Red House became bedlam. In that circumstance, he wrote, firing on the rioters was "absolutely necessary" to protect the lives of policemen and many others in the building. The governor concluded, at length, that responsibility for the riot and the consequent toll of lives and property lay with those diverse interests that had coalesced in the rioting crowd:

27. The policy and action of the Government [in the matter of the proposed water ordinance] have been consistently misrepresented by the press and by many persons who excite the uneducated with inflammatory speeches.

28. The motives which I believe will be found to have influenced this course of conduct are, among the rate-payers generally, a simple desire to escape any augmentation of their water rates, and, in view of its extravagant use in the past, unwelcome restrictions on the waste of water; among the more respectable of the *political* agitators, the wish to put an end to the system of Crown Colony Government, and to obtain elective and representative institutions of their own, and naturally under their personal guidance, and, unfortunately, a small and less-respectable section have other ultimate objects which it is not expedient to particularise.

29. For the moment these three sections, all apparently well organized, seemed to have combined their efforts, with the results above described, and which I so sincerely deplore. The poor common people, who have had, and have, indeed, my sympathy and sincere regard, most densely ignorant, have no general ill-feeling and when unexcited are docile and kindly. But they are terribly subject to be excited into acts of violence, and are ready to accept as true, and without the slightest consideration to act on, any statement made in language intelligible to them, spoken or, still more, printed.[23]

In leveling that charge, Governor Moloney had sought to exculpate his administration by cleverly playing on the twin fears that had long animated proponents of the system of Crown Colony government—that in a heterogeneous society like Trinidad the probable alternative to government based on the principle of paternalistic trusteeship was rule by a white oligarchy or by inept men of color forming the majority of the population.[24] According to the governor, the "uneducated ... densely ignorant" masses, largely nonwhite, had been provoked into violence on March 23 by a group of journalists and political agitators, white and black, greedy for power in the guise of representative government. His analysis of the origins of the water riot struck a responsive chord at the Colonial Office:

The secretary of state was himself disposed to regard Crown Colony government in the West Indies as the only alternative to rule by "a local oligarchy of whites and half-breeds—always incapable and frequently corrupt" or by "Negroes—totally unfit for representative institutions and the dupes of unscrupulous adventurers." [25]

Moloney's analysis would not fail to harden other leading officials at the Colonial Office against the rioters and their leaders. For example, on reading Moloney's report, Charles Lucas, the assistant undersecretary responsible for the West Indies, wrote that prosperous Trinidad had "least cause for riot," adding that responsibility for the violence must perforce lay with "the white creole population" which was, in Lucas's view, "an unsound one with its French and Spanish blood . . . [in league in] . . . Port-of-Spain [with] . . . colored men from all parts of the West Indies." [26]

Two other dispatches arrived at the Colonial Office from Trinidad by post on April 9—from the Chamber of Commerce and the Ratepayers' Association. The chamber's dispatch had been composed in two parts on March 25 and 27 and sent on the latter date. [27] Its contents were a confirmation of the telegram the chamber had earlier sent to the secretary of state and a protest against certain misstatements of fact and alleged errors of omission in the cable transmitted by Governor Moloney to Chamberlain on March 25. The association had posted a lengthy dispatch on some unspecified date in late March, [28] as it had promised to do in the telegram it sent to Chamberlain on March 27. This dispatch was, in effect, a rebuttal to the governor's report which had outlined the circumstances surrounding the water riot on March 23 and had defended the actions of his administration on and before that date.

On April 9, the secretary of state wrote to Governor Moloney that three commissioners had been appointed to conduct the inquiry. [29] That action elicited an expression of gratitude from the Chamber of Commerce, whose cable also included the proposal that an independent water engineer be allowed to accompany the commission; [30] two days later the Ratepayers' Association cabled the Colonial Office its endorsement of the proposal. [31] On April 14, Chamberlain wrote to Moloney to inform him of the receipt of the report with "full particulars" that the governor had posted on March 24 and to affirm that he would not remark upon it until the Commission of Enquiry had submitted its own report. Moloney was instructed in the letter (and in another sent by Chamberlain on April 24) [32] to inform the chamber and the association that there would be no need for a water engineer to assist the commission in its work. On April 15, the secretary of state sent the governor by post extracts from a letter that Captain Hope Robertson, R. N., had written to the Admiralty regarding the actions on March 23 of the landing party from H. M. S. *Pallas*.[33] Between April 24 and the first public sitting of the commission five days later, there was no further significant communication between Chamberlain and Moloney on the circumstances of the water riot.

II

Tension remained high in Port-of-Spain for many weeks following the riot, and its effects were keenly felt elsewhere in the colony. On learning of the riot, a small group of agitators paraded along two main thoroughfares in San Fernando, shouting, "Let us kill the white people."[34] But their protest was quickly halted when a detachment of armed policemen from Port-of-Spain arrived to help maintain order in the town.

Inspired by the strong antigovernment feeling on which the water riot had been based, more protest groups formed in the capital and throughout the colony—a development that Henry Alcazar had predicted moments before he withdrew from the Legislative Council on March 23.[35] The United Trinidad Committee was born five days later in Port-of-Spain, its stated purpose to gather reliable information on the causes of the riot and to prevent a recurrence.[36] But the committee had the potential to move swiftly into political agitation. Its leaders were drawn from the leadership of the Ratepayers' Association, who were resolved now to broaden their base of political support by opening the ranks of the committee to everyone in the colony on an equal basis. The inhabitants of Arima were soon after invited to join the new umbrella organization, as were the islanders on Tobago. Over the next five weeks, several other organizations were founded throughout the colony, and they quickly affiliated with the committee. A new Tenants' Association appeared in Port-of-Spain by the end of March, its purpose to cooperate with the United Trinidad Committee and the Ratepayers' Association in representing the interests of renters in the capital.[37] Groups modeled upon the Ratepayers' Association had formed in Tunapuna and Couva by the end of April.[38]

But the radicals' main target for political mobilization was San Fernando, the second largest town in the Crown Colony. Despite its reputation in nineteenth-century Trinidad as a hotbed of reform, the southern town had never lent strong support to the reformers in Port-of-Spain.[39] In the aftermath of the water riot, the *Mirror* made clear its disappointment that only a small group of agitators had come forward in San Fernando to support the rioters' cause. The radical newspaper now implored the San Fernando Borough Council, "the premier representative institution" in Trinidad after the abolition of its counterpart in Port-of-Spain, to join a cause that affected all the inhabitants of the colony. Galvanized by this plea, a handful of burgesses in San Fernando petitioned the mayor to convene a public meeting "to express our appreciation of the action of the Port-of-Spain Ratepayers' Association and desire to co-operate with them and the United Trinidad Committee."[40]

When the mayor did not accede to the request, agitators in the town convened their own protest meeting.[41] The turnout was disappointingly low, apparently because of a rumor that the government had secretly dispatched armed policemen to take up positions near the meeting place.[42] Another protest meeting was convened in Princes Town, this one attended by a large crowd. Speakers praised the efforts of the Ratepayers' Association and the Trinidad Chamber of Commerce to make known to the secretary of state the political grievances of the population; it also expressed sympathy with the relatives of those who had been killed or wounded in the water riot and, as a token of its support for the United Trinidad Committee, offered to collect funds for the committee.[43]

All of this political activity alarmed Governor Moloney. Five days before the Commission of Enquiry was to begin its proceedings, he requested that a man-of-war be dispatched to Port-of-Spain along with two hundred more Lancashire Fusiliers from Barbados to help maintain public order.[44] (H. M. S. *Pallas* was still anchored in Port-of-Spain harbor; H. M. S. *Rocket* had left the colony.) He justified his request for additional military support by claiming that plans were being laid for a major insurrection in Trinidad.[45] While no such uprising occurred, terrorism had spread in the colony by early May, and there had been a significant increase in the importation of arms and ammunition. The governor was deeply concerned also with the unrelenting campaign in the press against his administration.[46]

III

The Royal Mail Steamer *Trent* dropped anchor in Port-of-Spain harbor after daybreak on April 28, 1903. Among the passengers were the three commissioners who had come to the Crown Colony to "enquire into the origin and character of the recent disturbances at Port-of-Spain, into the nature and sufficiency of the steps taken to preserve the peace, and the action of the authorities in suppressing the riot, and to report with their recommendations, if any, upon the whole matter of the enquiry."[47] Appointed by the secretary of state for the colonies, the commission was made up of Sir Cecil Clementi Smith, former governor of the Straits Settlements, as chairman, Sir Henry E. M. James, one-time commissioner of Sind, and Stuart Macaskie, recorder of Sheffield. R. V. Vernon, an official at the Colonial Office, was designated by Chamberlain to act as secretary to the commission.

Upon arriving in Port-of-Spain, the commissioners quickly began their inquiry, holding a series of public meetings and conducting on-site inspections. The commission convened twenty such meetings from April 29 to May 22 and took testimony under oath from 146 witnesses, including government officials and others. Many of the witnesses were examined and then cross-examined by the commissioners and by representatives of the colony government and of various unofficial interests. Individually or as a group, the commissioners visited the riot area, the main pumping stations and reservoirs for the Port-of-Spain waterworks, the sources from which the capital drew its water supply, and the sewage pumping station to ascertain the operations of the municipal drainage system. Some private residences were also visited, to appraise the system for distributing water to poor and affluent households.

Its work in the Crown Colony completed, the commission departed Trinidad on May 22. On July 2, it presented its findings and recommendations to the secretary of state in London, along with the testimony of witnesses and various documentary submissions. The official record of the commission was contained in more than a thousand closely printed pages; the document exceeded in length even the massive report prepared in 1898 by the Royal Commission established the year before to investigate the condition of the sugar industry in the West Indies.[48] Remarkably, the commissioners had completed their arduous task in Trinidad in less than four weeks, finding time in the meanwhile to be entertained by high officials in the colony's government. (On the penultimate day of the inquiry, the commission would be formally charged by counsel for the Port-of-Spain Ratepayers' Association with having displayed favoritism toward the official side.)[49]

IV

By the time they arrived in Trinidad on April 28, the three commissioners already had in hand the report that Osbert Chadwick had prepared in 1895 outlining the problem of water supply in Port-of-Spain and the failure of successive administrations in London and the Crown Colony to deal effectively with it.[50] Chadwick's report made clear that there was no dearth of technical imagination equal to the task. Expert investigations had routinely been undertaken over two decades, each one culminating in a meliorative scheme laid before the authorities. But none of these schemes was ever adopted by the colony government as the basis for decisive action. Sir Alfred Moloney was the eighth governor in the Crown Colony in the period 1875–1903; his administration had come closest to enacting a coherent water policy for Port-of-Spain.

Perhaps the earliest contemplation of a long-term solution, Chadwick wrote, could be found in the Unsworth Report; the author, Hugh Unsworth, was a civil engineer who had been dispatched to Trinidad in 1875 (during the administration of Governor Sir Henry Irving) to inspect Maraval, the only source of water for Port-of-Spain. Concluding that the problem was indeed serious, Unsworth proposed that a system of subterranean collecting pipes be set beneath the sandy bed of the Maraval River to obtain water filtered by natural processes. Essentially the same plan had already been implemented successfully under similar conditions elsewhere in Trinidad and in other territories.

Seven years later, in 1882, a special committee, appointed by Governor Sir Sanford Freeling, recommended a strict program of water conservation; one committee member was G. W. Dickson, a specialist on water supply who was serving as assistant director of public works in Freeling's administration. Nearly a decade passed, and in 1890, J. E. Tanner, the director of public works in the administration of Governor Sir William Robinson, proposed that a large storage reservoir be constructed in the Maraval Valley, above the intake of the existing waterworks, for storing water in the wet season for use during the dry season. Three years later, Tanner was still urging that the colony's government attend to his proposal.

Doubtless the most comprehensive and influential investigation to be undertaken was Chadwick's in 1895, during the administration of Governor Sir Napier Broome. Chadwick had been employed for many years by the Colonial Office to report on problems of water supply and drainage in various colonies. In that capacity, he had visited Port-of-Spain several times, usually in connection with water projects being developed elsewhere in the Crown Colony. In 1895, he paid his first visit to the municipality to report on its waterworks. On that occasion, he assailed Tanner's scheme for constructing a reservoir in the Maraval Valley. Stressing economic and technical factors, he criticized Tanner for the costliness of the proposed project, for assuming that there would be a watertight substratum for the new reservoir, and for predicting that the facility would yield Port-of-Spain an adequate supply.

On the last point, Chadwick insisted that even if successfully constructed, the impounding reservoir would add little to the town's annual supply, contending that it would merely equalize supply in the wet and dry seasons. Except during periodic floods, he maintained, the flow of the Maraval River would be insufficient to meet the needs of a growing population in Port-of-Spain.[51]

Chadwick proposed that priority be given instead to conservation and to locating new sources of water for the municipality (in the Diego Martin Valley west of Port-of-Spain, for example, and perhaps in the Santa Cruz Valley to the east). Concluding that the supply would be more abundant and economical at Diego Martin, he recommended that borings and trial pits be made there. He was certain that a water-bearing stratum lay beneath the alluvium of the Diego Martin Valley, fed by streams running down the surrounding hills, disappearing in the sandy plain, and reappearing lower down the valley in the form of springs. But, despite the obvious existence of a major supply, the borings yielded disappointing results.

Chadwick advised in 1898 that a large well be constructed on government land at the head of the valley. This calculation proved correct, the well yielding approximately one million gallons of water per day. Next he turned to the difficult question of how best to draw the new supply. Several alternatives were considered: transporting the water, by gravitation, to a pumping station at Mucurapo Point or, as he preferred, constructing a gallery to tap the water-bearing stratum and conduct the water to the pumping station. Nearly two years passed before a recommendation was finally settled upon.

In the autumn of 1900, Chadwick met in London with Walsh Wrightson, who had succeeded Tanner as director of public works in the Crown Colony. The two engineers agreed that while constructing a gallery (or galleries) to conduct the water to Mucurapo Point was technically feasible and likely to yield the largest supply, it would take a lot of time and probably be unacceptably expensive. Two other considerations caused Chadwick to lose his early enthusiasm for that plan. He feared that it might result in widespread contamination of private farmland under cultivation in the lower Diego Martin Valley (a major political risk unless the colony government could be persuaded to expropriate a large section of the land); and he recognized that the larger supply made available would require prohibitive initial outlay in machinery and an increased annual expenditure for fuel. Weighing all of these factors, Chadwick and Wrightson concluded that the most expedient course would be to construct a pumping station at the site of the well.

The Chadwick Report of 1895 had concluded on a somber note of warning: Because a small island like Trinidad could not hope to have an inexhaustible supply of water, it would have to institute a strict program of conservation. Though the water supply had doubled in recent years, Chadwick stressed that the limits of practical engineering prevented its continuing growth at that rate. If consumption were to continue at current rates, he observed, no amount of water that might become available would be sufficient to maintain a constant supply every year in both wet and dry seasons. In addition to the customary inconveniences associated with an inadequate supply, Chadwick foresaw a serious threat to public health and social order if waste were not soon curbed. He noted that investigators had recently discovered a connection between the mosquito and malarial fever and that insects tended to breed in stagnant water and on irrigated land. Accordingly, he urged strong measures to prevent waste and to ensure that the vast amount of water sent into municipal sewers was swiftly pumped from them into the sea.[52] Chadwick proposed in 1895—and reaffirmed in his endorsement of the consolidated water ordinance framed by Wrightson[53]—that conservation be promoted principally by installing water meters. At their meeting in London, the two engineers agreed that meters would be the best means also to make payment proportionate to use and to prevent the poor from paying for the extravagant practices of the affluent.

The Commission of Enquiry concluded that although the recommendations made by Chadwick in 1895 were regrettably not yet fully implemented, the work completed at the time of its public sitting, in May 1903, "had been entirely successful." By that date, the additional daily yield from all the new sources of supply Chadwick had contemplated was 1.6 million gallons, thus neutralizing the dearth from the previous five years' drought.[54] The commission had, in effect, endorsed the argument propounded eight years earlier by Chadwick that the problem of supply in Port-of-Spain had all along been exacerbated by official irresolution and inaction.

V

Its charge from the secretary of state essentially unbounded, the Commission of Enquiry probed extensively for information pertaining to the Port-of-Spain water riot of March 23. The 146 witnesses were allowed—even encouraged—to fill the official record with facts and opinions on diverse subjects: the historical and technical aspects of the problem of water supply in the capital; the proposed water ordinance and the popular opposition to it; the causes, underlying and proximate, of the water riot; the details of the affray; and the relationship between the population of Port-of-Spain and the Crown Colony government in Trinidad. In the process, attention was drawn to the controversial role of certain government officials, public institutions, and private citizens and organizations: Governor Moloney and his colonial secretary, Knollys; Wrightson, the director of public works; the militia, constabulary, and fire brigade; the Legislative Council and several of its unofficial members; the defunct Borough Council in Port-of-Spain and the "no surrender party"; the Ratepayers' Association and its leaders; Mole and his newspaper, the *Mirror*; and the press generally. Chamberlain also loomed large in the proceedings. Whether or not the secretary of state was mentioned, his "presence"—embodied in the strict paternalism of his imperial policy in Trinidad—could be felt by the participants.

The principal government witness was Knollys. He had been colonial secretary for nearly a decade, in the Broome, Jerningham, and Moloney administrations. His power in the colony's government was surpassed only by that of the governor. Knollys had also served as officer administering the government for varying periods in all but one year.[55] He was regarded as the leading foe, among colony officials, of the Trinidad reform movement. In that role, he had had an important influence upon Chamberlain and the officials at the Colonial Office. For example, it was Knollys who, as officer administering the government in June 1898, advised the Colonial Office that the unofficial members of the Legislative Council had organized as an opposition bloc. That misleading report was the pretext on which Chamberlain had moved to restore the official majority in the legislature.[56]

Knollys, echoing Governor Moloney, alleged that three elements had combined in the campaign against the proposed water ordinance: a segment of the population of Port-of-Spain hostile to the particulars of the legislation; a reformist vanguard zealously pursuing the larger political goal of representative government in the colony; and an irresponsible press bent on inciting local passions.

The colonial secretary told the commission that opposition to the proposed waterworks scheme could be traced back at least to January 1897. At the time, George Gordon, an unofficial member of the Legislative Council, had voiced his strong objection to the government's decision to purchase the River Estate for the project, not the rival Moka Estate. By March 1902, Knollys testified, another unofficial member, George Goodwille, had begun to publicize what he saw as flaws in the scheme. The *Mirror,* published by Richard Mole, joined forces with the other foes of the waterworks; in due course, the *Mirror* emerged as the organ of the Ratepayers' Association, which spearheaded the opposition movement. Knollys revealed that he had made several fruitless attempts to persuade Mole to adopt a more reasonable course in the dispute, all the while continuing the official practice of being accessible to all who wished to address him on the matter. By the spring of 1902, Knollys testified, opposition to the proposed water ordinance had crystallized around these major interests: the leadership of the Ratepayers' Association, which, in his view, was comprised of "adventurous spirits [who], desir[ing] a reform . . . , saw their opportunity of introducing a political question in the Colony";[57] the *Mirror* and its firebrand publisher; and a reform-minded minority among the unofficial members of the Legislative Council. Knollys would not concede even the possibility that the general population in Port-of-Spain might have some legitimate grievance against the colony's government over the water issue.

Knollys contended also that misstatements about the ordinance had helped incite public opinion. He noted, for example, that the government had been charged with having planned all along to maximize revenues from the water rates. Rebutting that allegation, he stressed that the authorities had wished only to raise revenues sufficient to maintain the waterworks and to pay off the interest on the waterworks loan.

Other testimony entered into the official record of the inquiry seemed to bear out Knollys's contention. In this regard, light was cast upon the role of Richard Mole and the *Mirror*. For example, Commissioner Stuart Macaskie referred Mole to the lead article in the March 23 edition, in which the government was accused of scheming to stir up "a row" on that fateful day. Macaskie asked the publisher for his evidence. Mole replied that he had heard something on the Sunday preceding the riot which led him to inquire of Lieutenant-Colonel H. E. Brake, the inspector-general of police in Trinidad, whether a police detachment was being brought into Port-of-Spain from the country districts for special duty on March 23 and whether the authorities were prepared to use water hoses and to barricade Red House. Rebuffed by Brake and unable to confirm the rumor by any other means, Mole simply concluded that the government was indeed bent on precipitating a row just as the legislative session was about to begin.[58]

Macaskie also asked Mole why, on the day of the riot, the *Mirror* had published the allegation that the ticket regulation for admission into the visitors' gallery was illegal and that the acting chief justice had advised against its use. Mole retorted that he had acted on the basis of confidential information. Pressed by Macaskie to divulge his source, the publisher refused on the ground that such a revelation would surely mean his loss of all future sources of information. Macaskie persisted, and Mole finally admitted that the published allegation regarding the behavior of the jurist was hardly more than "an idea" based on false information that had been obtained from a source whose identity Mole could no longer remember. The publisher acknowledged that he often failed to remember the identity of sources to which the *Mirror* turned for information.[59]

Taking his cue from the two dispatches sent by Governor Moloney to the secretary of state on March 24, Knollys had sought in his testimony to demonstrate that the sources of tension surrounding the proposed water ordinance were mainly outside the administration. The government would take responsibility neither for the water riot nor for the events that had led up to it.

VI

In the charged atmosphere of Port-of-Spain in the spring of 1903, there was no dearth of individuals or organizations to rebut the official position on the water riot and its causes. Some appeared as witnesses before the Commission of Enquiry to detail their specific grievances against the government for its handling of the water issue; others came to decry official behavior on that issue as part of their sweeping attack upon the system of Crown Colony government in Trinidad. The comprehensive indictment laid before the commission merits attention. By linking popular ferment over the proposed water ordinance, culminating in violence on March 23, with the fundamental character of government in colony, those critics achieved their principal goal: to make sure that, whatever the findings of the commission, the water issue in Port-of-Spain would have political (and perhaps constitutional) effects beyond the municipal boundaries. In that event, urban nationalism—born of anticolonialism based on issues of municipal public policy that affected both the colony and the capital—would be a boon to the reform movement in Trinidad.

There were two types of criticism leveled against the government. Among the many witnesses who alleged specific abuses and errors of judgment in the water issue was the representative of the United Trinidad Committee, E. A. Robinson. He testified that the government had wrongly insisted on pressing ahead with the second reading of the proposed water ordinance on March 23, even after two unofficial members of the Legislative Council, George Gordon and Henry Alcazar, had withdrawn from the chamber. According to the witness, their departure had been interpreted by the mass of ratepayers in the crowd as a signal to abandon the protest that day, leaving only a small rowdy element for the police to dispatch. Robinson offered the opinion that a disorganized police detachment had instead fired on what was still a peaceful gathering in the vicinity of Red House, adding that bloodshed could have been averted if Governor Moloney had earlier withdrawn the ordinance. Robinson concluded that primary responsibility for the tragedy must be borne by Colonial Secretary Knollys for evincing his characteristic dogmatism, by the governor for acting as an autocrat, and by Colonel Brake for the excesses of the police.[60]

Henry Alcazar appeared before the commission with a broader purpose in mind: to point out how a stunted constitution in Trinidad had affected the stormy history of the water ordinance. Carrying his opposition to the proposed legislation from the Legislative Council to the Commission of Enquiry, he availed himself of the opportunity to deliver a general indictment of the system of Crown Colony government in Trinidad.

Beginning with the particulars of the water issue, the distinguished King's Counsel built gradually toward an assault upon Trinidad's constitution. He began by drawing the attention of the commission to Knollys's allegation that foes of the water ordinance had deliberately misrepresented the position of the government. Alcazar observed that Robert J. Nanco, of the Ratepayers' Association, had properly informed the members of that organization that the government might be tempted to profit from the water rates set by the new Water Authority. He observed that the government had long felt pressed to raise revenue to support a burgeoning civil list in the colony. Referring to Section 28 of the proposed ordinance, Alcazar also rebutted the government's charge that its critics were wrong in their contention that the authority would be empowered to refuse water to any tenement or premises rented at less than £10 annually. Apropos of the ticket regulation, he remarked that the people had a right and a duty to resist what they believed to be illegal and that Edgar Maresse-Smith, of the Ratepayers' Association, had properly urged them to do so. According to Alcazar, it was constitutional and legal for the people to assemble in Brunswick Square on March 23 to protest the water ordinance.

Alcazar went on to denounce the confusion, ineptitude, and secrecy that he ascribed to official efforts over a generation to formulate a coherent water policy for Port-of-Spain. He recounted the many solutions that had been proposed, some workable, others not. In 1875, the Unsworth Report had recommended that the water supply from the Maraval River be increased and purified with a system of subterranean collecting pipes; seven years later, the Dickson Report had recommended instead a strict program of conservation. In 1890 and 1893, Alcazar continued, J. E. Tanner, the director of public works, had urged a filtration scheme to increase and purify the Maraval supply; but this recommendation also was never implemented—despite the report by Osbert Chadwick, in 1895, that Maraval water was impure and dangerous. While endorsing the emphasis on conservation, Tanner had advised that the installation of water meters for that purpose would be too expensive. Alcazar then noted that Tanner's successor, Walsh Wrightson, had vigorously opposed Tanner's filtration scheme, fearing that it would interfere with the Maraval supply and cause the municipality to be without water while the purification process was in operation. Wrightson had also registered strong objection to earlier schemes for increasing the water supply by constructing new reservoirs. When Chadwick dissented from the view held by Tanner that water meters were economically infeasible, Wrightson enthusiastically embraced Chadwick's proposal that they be installed in homes and business establishments as a means of enforcing conservation.

Alcazar also charged that between 1895 and 1900 the government had failed to communicate with the populace about rumors that it was digging wells at Diego Martin and erecting pumps at St. Clair. Moreover, he accused the government of having concealed its decision in 1897 to purchase the River Estate, just about the time when public agitation against the proposed water scheme had forced the authorities to abandon it temporarily. Alcazar testified that if the government felt it necessary to embark upon a costly new scheme, it was obliged to make public all the important details.[61] He observed that a rising public clamor had failed to cause officials to renounce their secret ways: In April 1902, he alleged, Governor Moloney had revealed incomplete details of the waterworks policy to be embodied in the water ordinance—details that, Alcazar insisted, were sufficient to point up "a very unsatisfactory state of things, that the Maraval supply had dwindled in consequence of the neglect of the Government." In that political climate, an inept and secretive government had tried to defend itself by "blacken[ing] the character" of its many foes on the water issue, including George Gordon of the Legislative Council.[62]

Reflecting on the tortuous evolution of the issue over a generation, Alcazar was moved to remark to the Commission of Enquiry that the current opposition of a bewildered public to the proposed water ordinance was hardly surprising—"the more so because there exists such a complete want of confidence in the Government of the Colony," especially among the population in Port-of-Spain. According to the witness, antagonism had grown between the government and the people over water policy because, despite many administration plans over the past thirty years, "we [are] . . . today no better off than then."[63] For Alcazar, mismanagement of the water problem by officials was not merely a hardship too long borne by the entire population but also a symptom of the generally bad state of government in the colony. Having restricted his testimony thus far to the water issue, he proposed to consider the general condition to which it pointed.

Alcazar began his testimony on the system of Crown Colony government in Trinidad by observing that the administration had failed to engender public confidence by promoting the ideal of self-rule as a legitimate aspiration. On the contrary, it had usually behaved in ways that strengthened the perception that the government's interests differed from those of the people. As a case in point, he cited the history of the Stamp Act. Enacted ostensibly to compensate for declining revenues from the Pitch Lake at LaBrea, the act had been retained despite the fact that revenues from the lake, which contained a limitless supply of the highest quality pitch, proved much larger before passage of the legislation than the authorities had claimed. According to Alcazar, official behavior in the matter had lowered public confidence. First, the public resented the government's refusal to abrogate what it regarded as an unwarranted piece of legislation; second, all segments of the population were further alienated when the government failed to allocate revenues obtained from the act, the burden of which fell heaviest upon the affluent classes, to relieve the poorer classes. Alcazar discerned in this case solid evidence of an "absolute lack of sympathy with the people displayed by the Government," of "officials ... not in touch with the public." [64]

Alcazar accused some leading officials of having recently exacerbated the breach between the people and their government by their disdainful attitude toward public opinion. He rebutted the claim of Knollys that, as colonial secretary, he had pursued an "open door" policy in the water issue. Alcazar testified that before March 23, Knollys had studiously avoided encouraging people to come to him for information on the matter and that, following the riot, he had tried to exculpate the administration by charging that some prominent citizens, among them several unofficial members of the Legislative Council, had conspired with the riotous crowd. Alcazar asked, rhetorically, is it "likely that anyone of the ordinary class would go to see the colonial secretary after noting the treatment meted out [by him] to the unofficial members of the Legislative Council?" [65]

The contemptuousness that the witness ascribed to leading officials in the administration was for him but a symptom of the weakness of legislative institutions in the system of Crown Colony government. According to Alcazar, the inhabitants of Trinidad, and of Port-of-Spain particularly, were without representative institutions. Pursuant to the abolition of the elective Borough Council in January 1899, control over municipal affairs in the capital passed into the hands of the colony's government. And at the center, he observed, the executive retained control over the Legislative Council: The legislature was still a purely appointive body, with the majority on the official side.

The official members, ordinarily high officials of the colony serving also on the governor's Executive Council, were expected to back the government in the formulation of public policy. The bias of the majority official bloc in the legislature, Alcazar testified, was reinforced by the origins of its members. Not natives of Trinidad— people from the colony were only occasionally appointed to the Executive Council and then usually in an acting capacity—those officials often behaved without proper regard for local interests and sensibilities. According to Alcazar, this had not always been the case. When in past years the unofficials formed a majority in the Legislative Council and, in turn, controlled its Finance Committee, they were accorded some courtesy by the official side; but the situation changed when the official side once again became the majority and, as a consequence, the Finance Committee fell into desuetude. In the present circumstance, he observed, the administration preferred to decide in the Executive Council which measures to introduce in the legislature; these were then passed into law, whether or not they were acceptable to the unofficial side or to the Finance Committee.[66] On rare occasions, the Executive Council was unwilling or unable to monopolize a particular matter—for example, when policy had to be established for the sugar interests or for other industries in the colony; only then would the Executive Council seek the assistance of the unofficial side and, in the process, accept its recommended amendments. Alcazar thus regarded the unofficial members (including himself) as having no real power and as only occasionally influencing the administration with their advice and recommendations. In his view, those members were not merely unrepresentative of the general population—most of the unofficials had strong ties with the rural planters, especially those in sugar— but they were also "absolutely useless" in their powerlessness.[67]

The witness next sought to demonstrate to the Commission of Enquiry that a pattern of precipitate action by the administration had further contributed to alienating public opinion. As cases in point, he cited the Borough Council crisis and the water issue. From those records Alcazar hoped to draw the lesson that government policy, usually formulated in haste, had often been dangerously shortsighted.

Alcazar recounted for the commission how, in his view, the Borough Council had unwisely refused four years earlier to accede to a greater role for the government in the financial affairs of Port-of-Spain. He conceded that the municipal council had not been an ideal body. It had not always attracted the most able men to its ranks;

and, unfortunately with government authorization, it had long relied on raising loans, not taxes, for the ordinary work of the municipality. Nevertheless, Alcazar decried the decision to abolish the leading representative institution in the Crown Colony. The administration had not given sufficient weight to certain developments in the crisis: to improved prospects for more reasonable conduct of municipal affairs when the best men did contest for council seats in the last election in November 1898, and to antiabolition sentiment spreading throughout the colony, even in official circles. (Alcazar observed that the acting chief justice and the acting attorney-general had both tried to prevent the abolition of the Borough Council, urging instead that various measures be adopted to effect reform, including a government audit of the municipality.) Alcazar testified that the government should not have moved, with unseemly haste and against the drift of public opinion, to abolish the council; rather, it should have passed an ordinance in the Legislative Council compelling acceptance by the municipality of the terms imposed by Joseph Chamberlain. (It should be noted here that Chamberlain's ultimatum probably foreclosed Alcazar's option; the secretary of state had stipulated that the Borough Council itself had either to accept his four conditions or face abolition.)[68]

Alcazar had now arrived at a curious juncture in his testimony. The liberal reformer had put the case forcefully that the Borough Council crisis and the water issue were exacerbated by a colony government given to ill-considered, precipitate action. But was not his own prescription in the former case an invitation to the government to rush ahead highhandedly? In his testimony, Alcazar reaffirmed the pragmatic line he had adopted in late 1898: that whatever the provocation by the secretary of state, or the disability imposed by him upon the Borough Council, the survival of the municipal body was a matter of surpassing importance; and that to save the representative institution in Port-of-Spain, it was, paradoxically, necessary for a powerful government, exercising its legislative privilege, to gather even greater authority over the affairs of the municipality. That that development might leave the Borough Council with hardly more than the patina of representative legitimacy did not appear to disturb Alcazar, either during the crisis over the municipal question, in 1898–99, or, four years later, when he appeared before the Commission of Enquiry to testify against the system of Crown Colony government over the water issue. Or was his apparent equanimity over the accretion of political power at the center in Trinidad a mask to cover some deep anxiety, perhaps that the abolition of the Borough Council might set the dispirited reform movement on a perilous course? Alcazar had, after all, lashed out against the "no surrender party" in January 1899 for its having "strain[ed] every muscle to destroy," sacrificing the municipal council in Port-of-Spain in the cause of an emergent radical politics of confrontation.[69]

VII

The official inquiry into the Port-of-Spain water riot proved disastrous for the Crown Colony government in Trinidad; the commission found, among other things,[70]

1. "that the agitation for any change in the system of the Government formed an insignificant element in creating the riot" (this finding discredited the claim of Governor Moloney and his administration that the public excitement that precipitated the riot "had been increased by several public meetings called together by those who demand representative Government, [turning] ... the whole excitement ... in that direction");[71]

2. that in fact the riot was caused by public opposition to the proposed water ordinance and to the ticket regulation for admission into the visitors' gallery in the legislative chamber;

3. that the Ratepayers' Association and the press had stimulated public opposition by disseminating falsehoods regarding the proposed ordinance and the ticket regulation and by inciting violence;

4. that the executive authority had failed to allay public excitement by taking adequate measures to correct misrepresentations made by the association and the press (particularly by the *Mirror*);

5. that the ordinance was "defective in many respects";[72]

6. that the ticket regulation was proper but poorly administered;

7. that the executive authority had failed to anticipate and prevent the riot;

8. that the executive authority had displayed poor judgment in the timing of the water issue (by instituting cutoffs as the ordinance was being introduced into the Legislative Council

for the first reading, by commencing to sweep dry streets as an epidemic of smallpox was raging through the colony, etc.);

9. that while most policemen and various civilians properly fired their weapons, other policemen were responsible for several deaths caused by the improper use of bayonets;

10. that the police force was "inefficient and wholly untrustworthy";[73]

11. that the failure of the fire brigade to provide timely assistance raised grave questions as to its loyalty and efficiency;

12. that a "most deplorable delay ... in prosecuting the rioters" and their leaders (especially Edgar Maresse-Smith) brought the law under contempt;[74]

13. that the executive authority had traditionally been too secretive in the conduct of public affairs, vis-à-vis the unofficial members of the colony legislature and the general population; and

14. that there existed "a regrettable and serious division between a large and influential portion of the Community in Port-of-Spain and the Executive Government regarding public affairs"—a division which, the commission concluded, would likely take many years to overcome.[75]

The Commission of Enquiry made these recommendations: that the rioters and their leaders be swiftly prosecuted; that the police force be thoroughly reorganized and its inspector-general granted authority over the Fire Brigade; that a Select Committee be established to consider the proposed water ordinance before a new Water Authority was created by the Legislative Council; and that legislation be passed to deal with offenses committed by the press, to restrict the right of public assembly in the vicinity of the legislature during its meetings, and to regulate the sale, carrying, and use of firearms. In due course, most of the recommendations were adopted, the single major exception being the proposal that a curb on the press be enacted.

VIII

Labor as it did to clarify the circumstances of the water riot, the Commission of Enquiry left unanswered many questions. Some touched upon interests directly connected with the riot on March 23, others upon the interest of the commission itself.

1. On March 28, the secretary of state had cabled Governor Moloney, "What steps are being taken to bring to justice leaders of riot?" The governor cabled in reply to an impatient Chamberlain that "No leader has yet been arrested. Matter is in hands of Inspector-General of Police," implying that justice was taking its course. But the commission report revealed that the inspector-general had concluded early that "it would be better to wait till this commission had assembled before taking any steps which would be likely to precipitate a riot or other disturbances, as if we were taking action whilst the matter was *sub judice*."[76]

Having secured the tacit approval of the acting attorney-general, the inspector-general decided "that pending the sitting of the commission no action should be taken" against the malefactors.[77] Had Governor Moloney known of this decision when he replied to Chamberlain's inquiry? If so, why did he not transmit that information to explain the delay in making arrests and prosecutions? Could he have been trying to mislead his superior in London and, if so, for what reason(s)? Had the acting attorney-general ever consulted with the governor to clarify official policy in the matter? The commission report reveals a curious (and, in the view of the commissioners, disturbing) indisposition on the part of the executive authority in Trinidad to assume its legal obligation here—preferring to allow the inspector-general to decide on his own responsibility whether to proceed. Had any of these high officials in the colony's government eventually determined to take a cue from Chamberlain himself, who had written to Moloney on March 31 that "pending report [of] the commission, I will withhold judgment entirely on what has taken place"?[78] Had the executive authority in the colony, confused perhaps by the incongruous dispatches sent by Chamberlain on March 28 and 31, decided to act in its own interest in the more prudent spirit of the latter communication? In that event, should not the commission have muted its criticism of the Trinidad government in the matter of arrests and prosecutions—or assigned some responsibility also to the secretary of state for what it concluded was a "most deplorable delay in prosecuting the rioters" and their leaders?

2. The commission report had dropped a bombshell with its statement that while "the abolition of the Borough Council at the close of 1898, and the fact that representatives of the people are not elected

to take part in the local Government, were unquestionably prominently brought forward by speakers at the public meetings in order to promote the agitation ... no evidence was submitted to us that 'the whole excitement was turned in that direction.'" [79] The commission had concluded, therefore, that this factor was unimportant in precipitating the water riot.

Officials in the colony were stunned by the charge that the government had failed to submit evidence to support the view of Governor Moloney and his administration. Thus, the Crown's law officers in Trinidad wrote that "we certainly thought that this was obviously beyond the scope of the enquiry and we therefore made no attempt at producing evidence to justify the governor's telegram [of March 24]." In the law officers' view, those who agitated for representative government "form a considerable portion of the community ... and we fear that the commissioners have gauged neither their numbers nor their strength." [80] Writing in the same vein, Walsh Wrightson, director of public works, observed that "it is quite true that no direct evidence was brought forward to show that the real object of the ... Ratepayers' Association was and is to obtain some form of representative government at least as far as the municipal affairs of Port-of-Spain are concerned nor was any asked for by the commissioners but no doubt exists locally on the subject. . . . the Water Works question was the spark which caused the explosion." Wrightson emphasized his conviction that the issue of representative government was the key factor in the water riot by recommending in the same communication that the elective Borough Council be restored immediately in Port-of-Spain. [81]

How credible is the law officers' defense that, because "it was obviously beyond the scope of the enquiry," the government did not try to present evidence that political agitation for representative government was at the center of the water issue? Governor Moloney had alleged the great importance of political agitation over the issue of representative government in his two dispatches to the secretary of state on March 24, and Colonial Secretary Knollys had followed suit in his testimony before the commission on May 5, 11, and 12. Knollys had obviously proceeded on the assumption that he could properly state that claim within the broad scope of the inquiry, and no commissioner indicated otherwise. On May 18, Moloney had written Chamberlain a letter outlining his evidence "that the whole excitement was turned in the direction of representative Government," and the next day he sent Chamberlain by post a copy of the memorandum on the causes of the riot that he had recently submitted to the commission.[82] (It appears from the contents of the two communications, and from their timing, that the governor had calculated that he should make his strongest case to Chamberlain. The letter that he had sent to Chamberlain on May 18 was longer and contained more details than the memorandum that he had prepared for the commission. Moloney's dispatches of May 18 and 19 arrived at the Colonial Office on June 4, nearly two weeks after the inquiry had ended; by then, Chamberlain and his officials could be expected to give serious thought to the water riot and the official inquiry in Port-of-Spain and to their possible implications.) In light of the record, the law officers' defense is singularly unpersuasive.

But how to explain the curious role of the commission in this matter? Why hadn't it pressed Knollys to justify the claim that public excitement over the water issue was rooted in political agitation for representative government? And why hadn't it recalled the colonial secretary after receiving a brief, insubstantial memorandum from the governor himself? The commissioners had displayed no similar reticence when questioning Richard Mole, publisher of the *Mirror,* and other witnesses on important matters pertaining to the water riot.

Conceivably, some weighty consideration led the commissioners to refrain from pressing Knollys to justify the administration's claim regarding the role in the water issue of political agitation for representative government. They may have felt that the government could not adduce persuasive evidence, or that it would be unseemly for them to subject a high official of the colony government to close questioning, or, perhaps, that by pressing Knollys in this matter they might appear to be encouraging the official side to strengthen its hand in the proceedings. Because it is not possible to credit any of these explanations, I have concluded that the commissioners' handling of the principal government witness bore the hallmark of ineptitude, not of design.

3. Yet another bombshell was dropped soon after the Commission of Enquiry submitted its report to the secretary of state. Writing privately on July 7 to Charles Lucas at the Colonial Office, Commissioner Henry E. M. James revealed that the three-man commission had actually been deeply divided over what weight to give the issue of representative government. James noted that his colleagues had

rejected two arguments made by him: that the agitation for representative government had indeed been a significant factor in the water riot and that the Borough Council should be restored in Port-of-Spain. "[R]ather than weaken the report by a dissent," he wrote Lucas, "I accepted the decision." In James's view, because his proposal regarding the council would have been the "most important" of the recommendations made by the commission, its omission was "a defect in the report."[83]

Two considerations had moved James to propose the restoration of the Borough Council: his conviction that the process of political reconciliation must be encouraged in Trinidad and his belief that his own experience in India could point the way.

Ironically, the commission report lent weight to James's two arguments, despite its conclusion that political agitation over the issue of representative government had not been a significant factor in creating the riot.

For some years a group of persons had existed in Port-of-Spain whose main conception of public spirit or independence is to vilify the Government and indulge in personalities regarding the individuals who compose it. Conspicuous among this group are certain coloured lawyers, some of whom have studied law in England, coloured tradesmen doing a substantial business, and some less reputable persons, while a few persons of English birth, including the editors of two newspapers, have thrown their lot in with them. That some of the individuals are actuated by a natural desire to take part in public affairs we have no reason to doubt, but others are inspired by a vague aspiration for representative Government. They feel aggrieved at the abolition of the elective Borough Council. . . . They have formed themselves into a Ratepayers' Association . . . [that] at present . . . affects to act on behalf of the whole body of ratepayers in Port-of-Spain. . . . The influence of such a party is usually neutralised by the much larger body of quiet self-respecting persons, when satisfied that the Government is just and sympathetic. But in Trinidad it appears to us unfortunately true that the Government of the colony have not in the past, by continuously endeavoring to keep in touch with the more respectable and intelligent members of the public, by invariably consulting them as to legislative measures beforehand, and by showing every possible consideration for the

views of the nonofficial members of the Legislative Council, secured for the Government as such, and for their measures, the
strong unswerving confidence and support of the community of
Port-of-Spain, which would make a few agitators a negligible
quantity. We must acknowledge that any Government would
have a difficult task in a society where it seems a tradition even
for its leading and most respected members to be usually in opposition to the Government. The Government seem in consequence rather to have taken refuge in a policy of stolid, if not
unsympathetic, isolation, which has ended in a kind of cleavage existing between rulers and ruled which we think many
years will be needed to correct. The Government must have
been aware of the feelings of the public toward them, and
should therefore have been doubly careful to move warily in
grappling with a thorny subject.[84]

James observed to Lucas that India and Port-of-Spain had "the
same kind of educated and semi-educated malcontents. . . . to my
knowledge the establishment of Municipalities and Local Boards in
India has been of greater value, if only by diverting restless spirits
from politics, and giving them opportunities of 'blowing off their
steam.' . . . The very touchiness and violent temper . . . of the coloured creole are reasons for taking away any legitimate grievance
and I am quite sure that there are materials in Port-of-Spain out of
which to make an efficient Municipality." Accordingly, he proposed
that the Borough Council be restored in Port-of-Spain with half its
members elected on the basis of a high franchise and the other half
nominated partly by the government and partly by the Trinidad
Chamber of Commerce. The chairman of the council would be a government nominee, and there would be "what the Indian Native
Press used to call 'bludgeon clauses,' enabling the Government to
control taxation, call for returns and order certain things to be taken
into consideration, or to be done or omitted."[85]

Why did the other commissioners refuse to adopt James's modest
proposal as a concession to reform opinion in the colony? Had they
taken a hard line on the matter of the Borough Council in Port-of-
Spain (and on the importance of political agitation over representative government in the water riot) out of personal conviction? Or,
perhaps, had they done so because of a reluctance to take a stand
against Chamberlain's stern position on the municipal question in

1898–99 (and against his retrogressive policy on constitutional advance in the colony)?[86] One can only speculate. In any event, as we shall see, James's cautious proposal for a partially elective Borough Council in Port-of-Spain was destined to strike a more responsive chord at the Colonial Office than it had among his fellow commissioners.

8

Urban Nationalism IV: A New Normalcy

I

THREE DAYS AFTER the Commission of Enquiry departed Trinidad, the Port-of-Spain *Mirror* proclaimed that "the Ratepayers' Association and the United Trinidad Committee had won 'hands down' easily,"[1] a conclusion that seemed to prophesy the principal findings of the commission's report, soon to be released. But viewed from a longer-term perspective, the reality would prove less clear-cut than that radical reformist newspaper had imagined it to be. For sure, the retrogressive policy that Joseph Chamberlain had fastened on the colony since 1895 was a shambles: The commission report would stimulate a major shake-up of the discredited administration in Trinidad and changes in public policy affecting the colony and Port-of-Spain. These political developments would have a dual significance: They would point out that the imperial power had been obliged to defend its own interests by responding affirmatively to urban nationalism, that is, to a rising tide of anticolonial sentiment in

Trinidad based on issues of municipal public policy that affected both the colony and its capital; framed as concessions to reform opinion in the colony, they would be part of an emergent "new normalcy."

The political concessions would be piecemeal and slow to come—consistent with the Colonial Office practice of advancing any particular Crown Colony by small, hesitant steps, usually under the pressure of a troublesome anticolonial militancy.[2] Accordingly, it would take more than a decade to arrive at the new normalcy, virtually until the outbreak of the First World War. Its evolution would reflect also demographic changes in Trinidad and their effect on politics; against this backdrop would have to be managed conflicting pressures within and among the Colonial Office, the Crown Colony government, and the Trinidad reform movement. Trinidad would experience limited political change in the period 1903–14, within its basically conservative constitutional framework. During that decade Chamberlain and his successors at the Colonial Office would adopt a more conciliatory attitude toward the island colony, principally to prevent any serious weakening of the key premise on which imperial policy in the British West Indies had long been based: that the only alternative to Crown Colony government, with its idea of paternalistic trusteeship, was misrule either by a white oligarchy or by the majority of color.

II

Barely a week after the Commission of Enquiry delivered its report to Chamberlain, he began to make known to the Trinidad government both the contents of the document and his own pained reaction. He cabled Governor Moloney on July 13 that the report "contains the strongest condemnation of the apathy which the Colonial Authorities have shown in failing to bring persons who were employed in, or who instigated, the riot to trial. Full information as to what persons have been charged as taking part in, or instigating, the riot, and on what charges, should be sent at once. The Commissioners report strongly on [J. C.] Newbold's and [Robert J.] Nanco's inflammatory speeches, and state that [Edgar] Maresse-Smith incited people to violence, and intended so to incite them. They state, further, that they do not believe his evidence, which was given on oath. They find that [Richard] Mole either invented false statements or published rumours, not knowing or not caring whether they were true or false, and they sum up that the riots are to be attributed to the proposed Water Works ordinance, stimulated by the falsehoods and incitement to violence to which previous reference has been made in the report." Moloney was instructed to "report what action you are advised to take as regards the prosecution of these four persons."

Chamberlain noted also the commissioners' view "that there was, in several instances, uncalled-for and excessive shooting, . . . that there was no justification for the use of the bayonet . . . that the perpetrators of these atrocities have not been discovered, and . . . that even now no effort . . . [should] be spared by the authorities to obtain further evidence with a view to the conviction of the guilty." Moloney was further instructed "to appoint a formal commission of enquiry into the conduct of the police on these points . . . [the] enquiry . . . [to] be conducted by the acting Chief Justice . . . [with] evidence . . . taken on oath . . . and counsel . . . allowed."

The secretary of state approved the recommendation that a select committee be established to consider the proposed water ordinance and informed the governor that he would address him "on the remaining recommendations, and on many other points which are raised in the report, when I have received your comments on the report, which you should send at the earliest possible date after its receipt."

Finally, Chamberlain revealed that a purge of the administration in Trinidad was already under way. The governor was instructed to demand the immediate resignation of the deputy inspector-general of police and to dismiss from government service two officers in the Trinidad Light Infantry and the Fire Brigade. The likelihood that punitive action would be taken also against the highest officials in the government was signaled by these concluding remarks in Chamberlain's cable: "I understand that [Colonial Secretary] Knollys has postponed his leave on public grounds. I see no reason why it should be further postponed, and I shall have the opportunity of further communication with him on his arrival . . . [in London]. I will take steps to appoint a special *locum tenens,* on learning that he has arranged to leave, and you will hereafter ask the Legislative Council to make special provision for this temporary appointment."[3]

The fate of Governor Moloney and Colonial Secretary Knollys was soon decided. On July 21, Chamberlain sent the governor his stern judgment: "I cannot acquit you, as Head of the Executive Government, of blame in the respects in which the commissioners have found that the Government was to blame and I cannot bring myself to think that the riot, which had such deplorable results, would have attained the dimensions which it did if the heads of the Executive had been more fully advised as to the temper of the people and better prepared to meet a serious crisis."[4]

Chamberlain observed, in the same vein, that "The success of Crown Colony government—*and no other form of government is suited to the conditions of Trinidad*—depends upon the mutual co-operation of the official and the unofficial sections. The fact that the ultimate power as well as the ultimate responsibility rest, subject to the secretary of state, with the governor and the heads of the principal departments of the Executive Government, makes it absolutely imperative to defer, whenever it is reasonable to do so, to the wishes of the Unofficial Members of the Legislative Council, to consult them on matters of legislation and expenditure, to treat them with the consideration and confidence which is due to representative members of the community."[5] A sharp rebuke was also delivered to Knollys for having failed to conciliate the reformist opposition when it was still possible for him to do so.[6]

On these judgments, the secretary of state decided that Knollys should be transferred to another, less important colony in the West Indies; within a year, he would be governor of the Leeward Islands.[7] Moloney was requested in a secret dispatch to resign as governor at the earliest opportune time. Because he had had a long career in the colonial service—in West Africa, British Honduras, and the West Indies—the Sandhurst graduate was offered a post in other than a first-class colony.[8] Quickly the contents of the dispatch began to circulate in Port-of-Spain and then throughout the colony, undermining what little credibility Moloney still had. When the new secretary of state for the colonies, Alfred Lyttelton, moved to implement his predecessor's decision on Moloney, the embittered governor wrote him in early November 1903 that "the section of the population most inimical to law and order has long been agitating in the direction at which you have now arrived . . . these people will be strengthened at the expense of the Executive at a very critical time."[9]

Knollys took his terminal leave of Trinidad soon after Chamberlain had dispatched his cable to Moloney on July 11. By September 1903, the new *locum tenens,* Hugh Clifford, had arrived in Trinidad to take up his post as acting colonial secretary. (He was confirmed in that office a year later.) Moloney resigned from the colonial service in early 1904. He was succeeded as governor of the Crown Colony by

Sir Henry Moore Jackson, who took up his new post in September of that year.

III

What manner of men were Clifford and Jackson, and what attributes did each one bring to his high office in Trinidad at a time of public distress?

Hugh Charles Clifford was born in 1866 in London, the eldest son of Colonel (later Major-General Sir) Henry Hugh Clifford and a grandson of the seventh Baron Clifford of Chudleigh. He was educated at Woburn Park, a private Roman Catholic school, under Monsignor William Joseph (later the thirteenth Baron) Petre. Intending originally to pursue a military career—he passed the Sandhurst examination—Clifford changed his mind in 1883 and joined the Malay Civil Service as a cadet; at the time, his father's cousin was governor of the Malay States. Thus began a career of administrative service in the overseas empire that would span nearly half a century (1883–1929).

Clifford remained in the Malay Service until 1899, holding various posts as resident, commissioner, and government secretary. He became expert in Malay, translating the penal code into that language and producing (with Sir Frank Swettenham) the first Malay dictionary. His great affection for Malaya and its people is conveyed in more than a dozen novels and collections of short stories he published between 1897 and 1929.[10] Many of these works have autobiographical content, pointing up Clifford's own character, values, and experiences. Thus, his heroes, white men and brown, are generally adventurous and passionate men who evoke two major virtues, compassion and honor. Conversely, his villains, white and brown, too, are usually cruel and vicious oppressors of a gentle and hapless peasantry. Posted to North Borneo and Labuan in 1899, Clifford served there as governor until 1901. He returned to Pahang (in the Malay States) for a short tour as resident, then went to Trinidad as colonial secretary (1903–7).[11]

Henry Moore Jackson was born in 1849, the youngest son of the Right Reverend W. W. Jackson, Anglican bishop of Antigua, British West Indies. Educated at Marlborough and at Clifton, he was a graduate also of the Royal Military Academy. He cut short his military career, retiring from the Royal Artillery in 1885 as a captain.

His service in the colonies began in 1874, when he took up the post of aide-de-camp to Governor Sir Henry Irving in Trinidad. After two years, he moved on to Newfoundland, where he served for three years as aide-de-camp to Governor Sir John Glover. His next tour of duty was in Sierra Leone, West Africa, where, in the period 1880–84, he was successively commandant of police and aide-de-camp and private secretary to Governor Sir Arthur Havelock. When Havelock moved on to Trinidad in 1885 as governor, Jackson accompanied him there as aide-de-camp and private secretary. He remained in the West Indies for some years after that, serving as commissioner for Turks and Caicos Islands (1885–90) and as colonial secretary in the Bahamas (1890–93). Subsequently, he was colonial secretary in Gibraltar (1894–1901) and during that tour he earned a knighthood. He then returned to the West Indies, this time as governor of Leeward Islands (1901–2). Following that short tour, he served simultaneously as governor of Fiji and high commissioner for the Western Pacific (1902–4). His final assignment in the colonial service, soon after which he died, was as governor of Trinidad (1904–7).[12]

Clifford was only thirty-seven years old when he arrived in Trinidad in September 1903 to take up his new post. All of his service in the overseas empire had been in Southeast Asia, in and near the Malay Peninsula. Intelligent and foresighted, and also ambitious for advancement, he would make of his appointment in Trinidad a stepping-stone to higher office in the colonial service. After nearly four years in Trinidad, he returned to Asia as colonial secretary in the Crown Colony of Ceylon (1907–12). From there he went to West Africa as governor of the Gold Coast (1912–19) and of Nigeria (1919–25), succeeding Sir Frederick (later Lord) Lugard in Lagos. In the twilight of his long, distinguished career, he returned to Asia, as governor of Ceylon (1925–27) and (1927–29) as high commissioner for the Malay States and British resident in Borneo. His second wife, a writer, became seriously ill, and Clifford resigned from the colonial service in 1929. He died in 1941.

The historian J. de V. Allen has discerned in the record of Clifford's early years in Asia, and in his voluminous writings, a standard by which that scion of the English Catholic aristocracy seemed always to judge individuals and the imperialist ethos and its accomplishments. According to Allen, by the dawn of the twentieth century Clifford had already become disillusioned with the civilizing mission of British imperialism and self-critical about his own role in it.[13] Perhaps so. But having lived and written intensely on a heroic scale,

Clifford rarely, if ever, betrayed in public forum any misgivings he might have had about imperialism or his own colonial service. Before arriving in Trinidad, he delivered with great eloquence two lectures at the Royal Colonial Institute in London, each extolling the British achievement in Malaya.[14] Early in his tour in Trinidad, he wrote of his enduring love for Malaya above all other colonial societies, evincing at the same time satisfaction with his new appointment and a desire to get on with his life's work.[15] During his seven years in the Gold Coast, Clifford often displayed his deep compassion for exploited native peoples. In 1918, for example, he entered an eloquent plea on their behalf in a short work on Imperial Germany in Africa.[16] In Nigeria, he expressed the same sentiment in addresses to the Nigerian Council and in lengthy dispatches to the Colonial Office.[17] Even as his bouts with cyclical insanity (manic depression) grew in number and severity, especially after the First World War, Clifford continued to work on behalf of humanitarian causes.[18]

Another historian of Malaya, Sir Ralph Winstedt, has identified some of the key attributes of personality that Clifford brought to his new assignment in Trinidad. According to Winstedt, he was a "charming, forceful, but never dictatorial personality . . . [which] won him the respect and confidence of all races, even when the onset of cyclical insanity led to eccentricities of behavior. Neither by education nor by temperament was he tempted to political innovations."[19] Clifford, like Jackson, was a colonial administrator of impressive ability. But unlike his new chief, Clifford was a conservative, if open-minded, imperialist, sometimes given to impulsive decision making in that cause. Jackson arrived in Trinidad a year after Clifford, with a reputation as an intelligent man of measured judgment and as a strong advocate of political and constitutional advance in the British West Indies. Despite differences between them in personal and career background and in political outlook, the two men grew to like each other. Their mutual respect and admiration withstood the test of their disagreements over policy for Trinidad.

Jackson came to Trinidad exhausted by nearly three decades of service in the overseas empire—in the West Indies, North America, West Africa, the Mediterranean, and the Pacific. Chronic illness prevented him from being a vigorous governor in the Crown Colony, either in day-to-day administration or in his many social responsibilities. The self-confident Clifford lent Jackson strong support in both roles. A gregarious ladies' man, the colonial secretary moved to the center of social life in the colony. His wife joined him there, until her death in Trinidad in late 1906. The Cliffords participated also in diverse literary, philanthropic, and religious activities.[20]

On more than one occasion Jackson referred to his younger colleague as the "deputy governor." Given the anomalous condition of Trinidad's government from 1903 to 1907, that appellation would have a more complex meaning in Clifford's case than it would have had for an ordinary man in a more conventional situation. In his cable dispatch of July 11, 1903, to Governor Moloney, Chamberlain had noted that he would soon appoint "a special *locum tenens*" in the Crown Colony. As such, Clifford would be the acting colonial secretary, in place of the departed Knollys. But Moloney himself was a discredited lame duck by early November of that year, destined to depart the colony in March 1904. In that circumstance, Clifford was, in effect, "a special *locum tenens*" also for the outgoing governor.[21] Following Moloney's departure, Clifford administered the Trinidad government for six months, until Jackson arrived. Nearly a quarter century later, Clifford wrote self-effacingly of the important, albeit secondary, role of the colonial secretary vis-à-vis the colonial governor.[22] But an examination of his record in Trinidad reveals otherwise. There he was a resourceful leader in his own right, able to capitalize on a fluid political situation that required strong but flexible administration, on the early departure schedule for Knollys and Moloney, on the late arrival of Jackson, and on Jackson's continuing debility. (Clifford administered the government also when Jackson went on sick leave for seven months in 1906.) Throughout Clifford's tenure in Trinidad, the executive authority would be a virtual duopoly.

IV

Clifford had an auspicious beginning in Trinidad. Even the *Mirror*, which had no rival as the bête noire of government in the Crown Colony, waxed lyrical over the new appointment. Its publisher, Richard Mole, wrote on September 29, 1903: "If one may judge a man by his books, one is inclined to think the new exile to Trinidad brings with him a great amount of ability and tact, the polished bearing of a highly cultured gentleman and student of men and letters, as well as a liberal receptive mind which will take in rapidly accurate conceptions of local conditions to the benefit of the colony and those who live in it."[23] Mole went on to point out the contrast with Knollys, whom he characterized as an astringent man of extremely narrow vision, lacking in tact and executive ability.

Governor Moloney introduced Clifford in the Legislative Council on October 5. The governor apologized for Joseph Chamberlain not having consulted the legislature in the matter of Clifford's appointment and for the extra burden it would impose on the colony treasury. According to Moloney, "it was not possible to secure Mr. Clifford's services upon other terms, and . . . in view of the necessity for selecting an officer of special ability and experience as soon as possible, the secretary of state found himself obliged to sanction the . . . arrangement without previously consulting the Legislative Council as would certainly have been done in ordinary circumstances."[24]

Clifford quickly established himself as an effective "presence" in the administration, earning much praise in public circles.[25] On the eve of Jackson's arrival to take up his post as governor, the acting colonial secretary was lauded in the Legislative Council: "He had arrived here some months ago at a memorable and exciting period when there was a cleavage between the Governed and the Government, and when public affairs were in a state of chaos. In a short time, Mr. Clifford reduced chaos to order and by his sound and steady policy, marked by a spirit of conciliation, had restored confidence in the good intentions of the Government. . . . Mr. Clifford had earned the sincere appreciation of . . . all."[26] Clifford responded to this paean, and to the accompanying loud applause and cheers, by expressing sentiments that would not fail to move his listeners: Doubtless, he said, he had made many mistakes, unwitting and inadvertent, in his short time in Trinidad. But his devotion to the interest and welfare of the colony, he noted reassuringly, had suffered no diminution.

Clifford indeed performed with great political skill in that critical first year. His ability to balance firmness with tact was nowhere better evidenced than in his relations with the bullying radical journalist Richard Mole. Clifford knew of Mole's penchant for rumor-mongering, and he was poised to meet any test or challenge that the publisher of the *Mirror* might raise. The first one came on November 17, 1903, when it was already public knowledge that the discredited Governor Moloney would soon depart the colony. On that date, Mole wrote a private letter to Clifford, who would, on Moloney's departure, become ad interim the officer administering the government of Trinidad. The letter badgered Clifford with interrogatories which, Mole acknowledged, were based only on rumor:

1. Has the Abolition of Trial by Jury been under the consideration of the Government?

2. Is the Abolition of Trial by Jury under the consideration of the Government?

3. Is it intended by the Government to abolish Trial by Jury after the December Sessions [of the Legislative Council], or at any time, either before or after December?

4. Has it been the contemplation of the Government to abolish the Carnival?

5. Is the abolition of the Carnival still contemplated by the Government?

6. Will an Ordinance abolishing the Carnival be introduced into the Legislative Council, either before or after Christmas, 1903?

7. Is it in contemplation to make the regulations governing the Carnival more stringent?

Mole observed that he "should very much like to know if there is any foundation for these reports, as their truth would very materially affect the attitude of ... [his] paper toward the Administration." He concluded by expressing his intention to publish in the *Mirror* both his letter and Clifford's rejoinder. Clifford replied at length by private letter.

Dear Mr. Mole,

Referring to your letter of yesterday, I must decline utterly to treat it as an official document because, were I to do so, I should have no alternative but to point out to you in quite unmistakable terms that I, as Colonial Secretary, cannot recognize your right to catechise me in this fashion concerning, not facts or events, be it remembered, but the *alleged intentions,* or suggested future policy of Government. If your experience of the conduct of a newspaper was somewhat more extended than I conceive it to be, you would have appreciated the fact that such enquiries cannot be made with propriety on the strength of a "rumour" which, as you state, has reached you from certain irresponsible persons, and I venture to hazard the opinion that your letter would never have reached me in the form in which it is written.

You must further excuse me for saying—writing in my purely private capacity I may take the liberty of speaking plainly—that "the attitude" which your paper may or may not adopt toward the Government of this Colony is a matter which leaves me comparatively unmoved. Any "marked change" in that attitude is something, however, which personally I should be disposed to welcome. Change is always refreshing, and in this instance (or so it seems to me) the change could hardly be for the worse.

Turning now to the real subject of your letter, and writing still in my private capacity, I am able to give you the following information, of which you are at liberty to make use without the authority of my name, though I must point out to you that your expressed "intention" to publish your letter to me and my reply to you cannot with propriety be carried out lacking my permission, in view of what I may call the "dagger and bowl" tone of your communication, I absolutely withhold.

The *abolition of Trial by Jury* has not been under the consideration of Government; is not now under the consideration of Government; nor is it intended or contemplated.

The *abolition of the Carnival* has never been so much as spoken of, so far as I am aware, nor have I seen it suggested that the existing regulations are inadequate to govern it.

So much you are at liberty to make known to those who are responsible for the rumours of which you speak. For your private information, and speaking always in my private capacity and for myself alone, I may add that if, in the future circumstances were to arise which demonstrated the necessity of any action either in the direction suggested, or in any other directions, I, for one, should not hesitate to recommend the adoption of such measures as might then appear to be required by the circumstances. It is not normally my practice to make statements as to what I should or should not do in hypothetical situations, but as you have made an attempt to delve into the future, I find myself constrained for once to follow your example. Please God an "impossible" situation may never be created in this Colony and in my time; were such a situation to arise, it might have to be met, not improbably, by "impossible" measures. I am glad to think that that at any rate is not yet.

In future I shall be greatly obliged if you will confine your enquiries to matters of fact and not to speculations based upon irresponsible rumour, as I shall have no alternative but to refuse an answer to questions of the last named character.

Believe me, faithfully yours,
Hugh Clifford

An apologetic Mole wrote his appreciation to Clifford: "Thank you for your last letter and the information it contained. The 'dressing down' you gave me I enjoyed because I think I deserved it—I must confess I behaved rather badly. I apologize. At the same time I must point out to you that my informant was not an 'irresponsible' person though he seems to have been misinformed on this occasion." [27]

No part of this remarkable correspondence was ever published in the *Mirror*. However, in the future Mole would often use his newspaper to goad and hector Clifford, who he had come to regard as a formidable adversary indeed.

V

Soon after receiving the report of the Commission of Enquiry, Chamberlain signaled his willingness at last to return Trinidad to a course of political reform. He would do this by, in effect, disavowing the majority opinion of the commission that the water riot had resulted essentially from the dispute between the Ratepayers' Association and the colony's government over the proposed water ordinance. Chamberlain was clearly impressed by the dissentient view that Commissioner Henry E. M. James had communicated privately to Charles Lucas at the Colonial Office—that political agitation for representative government had indeed been a significant factor in the water issue and that the Borough Council should be restored in Port-of-Spain on the Indian model, with limited powers and with a limited elective principle. James had proposed this measure, it will be recalled, partly to conciliate reform opinion in the colony and partly to divert the energies of political hotheads. [28] Chamberlain knew that important officials in the colony's government had already urged the Colonial Office to restore the municipal council. [29] Accordingly, on July 21, 1903, he wrote to Governor Moloney: "When [the constitution of the water authority] and other matters connected with water and sewerage have been settled for the time being, I should hope that it may be possible to go a step further and consider whether a

Borough Council should not be revived, modified [as James had counseled] on the lines which are followed in India and some of the Eastern Colonies but containing a proportion of Elected Members."[30]

The question of which political formula to use in restoring the Borough Council would prove deeply divisive, however, absorbing the energies of both the Crown Colony government and the Trinidad reform movement for more than a decade. Its resolution would come by stages, the first of which involved the resolution of the water issue in Port-of-Spain.

The executive authority in Trinidad would be spurred into action by the criticisms that Chamberlain had lodged against it in his dispatches of July 11 and 21—and by his apparent willingness to revoke the decision he had taken against the Borough Council nearly five years earlier. Following up on Chamberlain's initiatives, the colony's government proposed a series of reforms. One involved the Executive Council, another the Legislative Council. With an eye also to the incoming secretary of state, who would decide whether to implement Chamberlain's decision regarding Moloney, the governor ascribed the breach between the people of Trinidad and their government to "the official character which the Executive Council has been allowed unfortunately to assume and maintain, a fact which doubtless served, in the eyes of the public at large, as an unattractive and distasteful exclusiveness."[31]

Accordingly, Moloney proposed that the Executive Council should be enlarged to include two unofficial members, one chosen by the unofficials in the Legislative Council, the other nominated by the Trinidad Chamber of Commerce. If implemented, he observed several weeks later, this reform would have the effect of ensuring that the merchant and planter interests were represented in the leading council in the colony.[32] Moloney's proposal was mindful of Chamberlain's stricture that the executive authority in Trinidad must be especially sensitive to the interests of the unofficial members of the legislature; and it was, moreover, consistent with the formula that Commissioner James had proposed for reconstituting the Borough Council in Port-of-Spain: that the conservative Chamber of Commerce should nominate some of the members of the restored municipal council.[33]

Moloney's proposal had a mixed reception at the Colonial Office. Two clerks with prior service in Trinidad recommended its adoption to Alfred Lyttelton, the new secretary of state. R. V. Vernon, who recently had been secretary to the Commission of Enquiry, wrote that

"The Trinidad system of a purely official Executive Council is practically unique in the West Indies. *British Guiana* has three unofficial members on the Executive Council. On the *Jamaica* Privy Council are two unofficials . . . two years ago the governor was authorized to add a third. . . . In Barbados we have reduced friction and facilitated Government by establishing the extra-constitutional Executive Committee on which the elective House of Assembly is represented by four members. Among the smaller islands, Antigua, St. Kitts, Nevis, Dominica, Montserrat (as well as the Federal Executive of the Leewards), Grenada and St. Vincent all have unofficials on the Executive Council. St. Lucia apparently has none." Vernon was seconded by his colleague H. C. Bourne, who had been registrar-general of Trinidad in the administration of Governor Jerningham;[34] Bourne, it will be recalled, had adopted a strong reformist position in the struggle between Chamberlain and the old Borough Council over the municipal question in Port-of-Spain.[35] But the cautious Lyttelton rejected the recommendation of his two subordinates, on the ground that "the status quo must be maintained till a new governor is appointed. The matter . . . [should] then be considered in the light of any opinion which he may express after deliberation."[36] That decision sealed the fate of Governor Moloney. The Executive Council was destined to remain an exclusively official organ until 1915, when (Sir) Henry Alcazar, an unofficial member in the Legislative Council, was nominated to be an unofficial also in the former body.

Because the Colonial Office and the Crown Colony government were both opposed to conceding the elective principle in the Legislative Council, Governor Moloney resolved to introduce political change in that body as it was then constituted. His principal objective was to conciliate the majority of color in Trinidad. Over the past half century, that element in the population had become more alienated and restive—as evidenced, for example, by the social pathology of vagrancy and crime in the towns, where most blacks lived,[37] and by the preponderance of blacks in the Port-of-Spain prison riot in October 1849,[38] the public disorder that had come to be associated with the annual festival of Carnival,[39] and the water riot of March 23, 1903. It was time, Moloney concluded, to try to counter this tendency by constructive political action—and, in the process, to arrest the radicalization of blacks under the influence of such self-appointed, irresponsible spokesmen as Emmanuel Lazare and Edgar Maresse-Smith. Accordingly, in early February 1904 he proposed that the first black be appointed to fill a vacancy among the unofficials in the Legislative Council.[40] Taking note on that occasion of the growing size and restiveness of the Indian community,[41] the governor proposed also that an Indian soon be appointed an unofficial in the legislature.

On the advice of the acting colonial secretary, Clifford,[42] Governor Moloney nominated the creole barrister C. Prudhomme David to fill the "black seat" in the Legislative Council.[43] David had read law at Gray's Inn, London; in Trinidad he had built an admirable reputation in his profession and as a political radical. In the latter role, he wrote a critique of the system of Crown Colony government, and he was an official in the Reform Committee, a group founded several years before to press for elective government in Trinidad.[44] But David was no street agitator in the cause of radical reform. A judicious man, he was regarded by Clifford and Moloney as having great potential to play a constructive role in legislative affairs.

David's nomination was well timed to conciliate black opinion in the colony. Just three months before, Moloney had (on Clifford's advice) recommended David to be the new stipendiary magistrate in Couva, presenting this testimonial on his behalf: "Mr. Prudhomme David is a lawyer of high standing: he has the reputation of being a man of strong character and undoubted probity. He is a coloured man and one of the best representatives of his race, he is not, however, and has never been a member of the Public Service. . . . From the point of view of qualification for the post, Mr. David is undoubtedly the most suitable selection open to our choice."[45]

However, acting upon the recommendation of C. A. Harris, a principal clerk at the Colonial Office, the new secretary of state, Lyttelton, had refused to confirm the appointment. Harris had written, "As a matter of policy I consider it would be the greatest mistake to give another legal appointment at present to a black man. Of course the black A.G. will favor black men: but this is to be resisted except in moderation. I have no doubt that the right thing to do in this case is to transfer a deserving officer from another colony."[46]

Harris's rationale offended many in Trinidad, on racial, political, and "national" grounds. The colored Vincent Brown had recently been elevated to the office of attorney-general, but he was a controversial figure in the public life of the colony. Because of his long service as a Crown law officer in Trinidad, and because he had been scored by many for his advocacy of the proposed water ordinance, Brown's credentials as a reformer were suspect, particularly in radical circles.[47] Of the two men, David was more popular among colored professionals and ordinary blacks, so the veto of the magistrateship was met with bitter resentment among those elements in the population. Moreover, Harris (and then Lyttelton) had failed to take account of the antipathy of most Trinidadians toward the longtime practice of appointing foreign officials in the colony. The nomination of David to the Legislative Council was an opportunity for the Colonial Office to make amends, as it were, for the racial and "national" slurs that many Trinidadians had discerned in the earlier rejection of the black creole as a magistrate. Lyttelton moved swiftly to make this appointment, which, Clifford later advised the secretary of state, was met "with practically universal approval."[48] Desiring now to enhance the prestige of the multiracial legislature, Lyttelton acted on the precedent in the Crown Colony of Ceylon and instituted the practice of allowing all former members of the Trinidad legislature to retain the title "Honourable."[49]

VI

Doubtless unwittingly, the Commission of Enquiry had urged upon the Colonial Office and the Trinidad government a course of action that contained a self-defeating inconsistency: that even as the authorities were seeking to promote political reconciliation with moderate reforms based on the constitutional status quo, they should institute judicial proceedings against the leading instigators of the water riot. A powerful political logic had eluded the commissioners: that reconciliation would probably require, among other things, a show of leniency toward the instigators, all of whom were popular radicals.

Early on, Joseph Chamberlain had appeared to signal the Trinidad government that it should proceed to prosecute the malefactors. On March 24 he had cabled Governor Moloney, "What steps are being taken to bring to justice [the] leaders of [the] riot?" Moloney had quickly replied that "No leader has yet been arrested. Matter is in hands of Inspector-General of Police."[50] Colonel Brake had decided, in consultation with Vincent Brown, acting attorney-general, to delay taking action until the Commission of Enquiry had concluded its work.[51] By early May, the secretary of state and his officials at the Colonial Office had begun to communicate to each other their growing concern about the delay. Charles Lucas had stated his dissatisfaction "that no arrests seem to have been made."[52] Chamberlain had concurred, observing that "It is most unsatisfactory and requires full explanations."[53] But the Colonial Office had not adopted a firm stand until the commission report (submitted to Chamberlain on July 2) was seen to point up the gravity of the delay and the need to accelerate the judicial process.

On July 11, the secretary of state cabled Governor Moloney to "report what action you are advised to take as regards the prosecution of . . . four persons":[54] Richard Mole, publisher of the *Mirror*, and J. C. Newbold, Robert J. Nanco, and Edgar Maresse-Smith of the Ratepayers' Association. No progress had been made by the end of August; the deputy inspector-general of police advised the governor that "The people, high and low, stood together in one impenetrable mass declining emphatically and sometimes rudely to give any information."[55] (The inspector-general of police, who was also commandant of local forces in the colony, had earlier reported that many people refused to give evidence against the accused, citing as reasons their hostility to the government or their fear of reprisal.)[56] Frustration over the delay built rapidly among Colonial Office officials; one, H. C. Bourne, remarked vituperatively, "The Crown Solicitor [in Trinidad, Leon Agostini] is a [French] Creole and a coward of a man of very different stamp in character and intellect."[57]

Chamberlain would brook no further delay; in early September, he demanded that there be prosecutions on "grounds of public policy."[58] Governor Moloney advised him that among the five leading instigators of the riot, there was sufficient evidence to try only three: Henry Hall, publisher of the *Pioneer*, and Edgar Maresse-Smith and Emmanuel Lazare of the Ratepayers' Association. Only weak cases could be made, he observed, against Richard Mole and Robert J. Nanco. (J. C. Newbold was not mentioned in this dispatch from the governor.) Moloney went on to warn the secretary of state that even the three strongest cases would "almost certainly fail, and this not through lack of ample evidence but owing to the determination of local juries not to convict."[59]

As the attitude of the Colonial Office hardened against the riot leaders, public opinion in Trinidad came to regard the impending trial as a test of strength between radical sentiment and an oppressive imperial authority. By the end of November 1903, a substantial defense fund was raised by the Ratepayers' Association in Port-of-Spain. Lending strong encouragement to the fund-raising effort was the *Mirror*, which highlighted the political character of the trial: "[The] Defense Fund [is] devoted to agitating against Government misrule. It is intended to prosecute a vigorous, well-directed and perfectly constitutional campaign, which we hope will . . . strengthen . . . [the] hands [of Hugh Clifford, the new acting colonial secretary] in carrying out that policy of conciliation whereby people and rulers will soon be drawn together in harmony and a complete understanding of each other's intention." [60]

The campaign to rally popular support for the defendants was facilitated also by the action of the Colonial Office on another policy matter, additional taxation in Port-of-Spain to repay expenses caused by the water riot. On June 5, 1903, Moloney wrote to Chamberlain that the value of public property destroyed in the affray amounted to about £40,000. [61] Nearly £13,000 more had been expended to restore peace in the capital and to maintain the Lancashire Fusiliers sent from Barbados; to repair buildings partially destroyed by the Red House fire; and to meet certain legal expenses along with costs incurred by the Commission of Enquiry. [62] Six weeks later, Moloney proposed to Chamberlain that these expenses should be met by levying additional rates upon private property in Port-of-Spain or by drawing from the general revenue of the colony. Taking a cue from the commission report, which stressed that the colony's government must work closely with the unofficials in the Legislative Council, the governor proposed also that the matter be "entrusted to a Select Committee of the [legislature]." [63]

But Chamberlain preferred "on the present occasion to prescribe the course to be adopted": that the riot expenses should be defrayed with a payment of £50,000 by Port-of-Spain over a period of eleven years. The Trinidad government was instructed to raise that amount by levying a special rate of 2 percent on the rental value of property in the capital and by raising a loan. The secretary of state would allow only a small portion of the total repayment to be borne by the colony's treasury. [64]

Chamberlain's decision was met by a volley of criticism representing a wide range of opinion. Strong protests were registered by four unofficials in the Legislative Council, by the Port-of-Spain Ratepayers' Association, and by the Trinidad Chamber of Commerce. [65] Denunciations appeared in the *Mirror,* the *Gazette,* and the *Pioneer.* [66] A. P. Marryat, the town assessor in Port-of-Spain who was also an unofficial member of the legislature, wrote privately to H. C. Bourne at the Colonial Office that the special rate would impose a great hardship upon the poorer classes, and even Governor Moloney voiced outrage over what he characterized as the "penal rate." On

January 28, 1904, he wrote to Lyttelton that the 2 percent rate "does not inflict punishment upon the classes whom I regard as most immediately responsible for the Riot, while it represents a heavy burden laid upon those sections of the community which are most peaceful and law-abiding." [67]

But the Colonial Office refused to yield. The official view in London was put succinctly by Charles Lucas: Chamberlain's decision would "pay off the Scoundrels who have brought it on them. I believe it to be a most wholesome measure." [68] On March 1, 1904, Lyttelton wrote to Moloney that the repayment formula was both "just . . . and expedien[t]." [69]

The popular hostility aroused by the concurrent issues of repayment and prosecution formed the backdrop for the trial of the riot leaders: Henry Hall, Emmanuel Lazare, and Edgar Maresse-Smith were tried in December 1903 and, as predicted by the Trinidad government, acquitted of all charges; the jury took only fifteen minutes to reach a verdict. [70]

VII

Sir Alfred Moloney remained governor of Trinidad for nearly a year after the water riot. During that period, radical sentiment continued to grow in the colony. The radical camp would find vindication for its political cause in the report of the Commission of Enquiry and the decision taken by Chamberlain to replace Moloney and Knollys. Radical reformism capitalized also on the revulsion of most Trinidadians over the repayment and prosecution issues and the refusal of the Colonial Office to appoint C. Prudhomme David as stipendiary magistrate in Couva. David's subsequent appointment as the first black unofficial in the Legislative Council was hailed by the radicals as their triumph.

The gathering strength of radicalism in the first year after the water riot caused Governor Moloney to become increasingly apprehensive about security in the colony. Accordingly, he advised the Colonial Office that white troops should be permanently garrisoned in Trinidad. The proposal precipitated a heated dispute between the Colonial Office and the War Office. In a compromise, the War Office consented to garrison one company of white troops in Trinidad for at least two years, until the barracks in St. Lucia were ready to receive them; as a quid pro quo, Trinidad agreed to reorganize its own local defense force.[71] This security measure had discordant effects among the population of the Crown Colony. The stationing of white troops in Trinidad gave comfort to the tiny white minority, which had long feared violence among the majority of color;[72] the nonwhite majority deeply resented what it regarded as a white military occupation. Unintendedly, the security measure exacerbated racial tension in the colony and strengthened the appeal of radicalism, especially among the nonwhite population.

VIII

Before turning over the reins of government to Sir Henry Moore Jackson in September 1904, Hugh Clifford was able to "close the book" on the controversial Water Works Ordinance, the enactment of which had been prevented by the Port-of-Spain water riot. Under Clifford's skillful direction, in August 1904 the Legislative Council passed an amended version of the original bill. On this occasion, the legislative timetable was unhurried, affording the unofficial members ample opportunity to discuss the measure. The ordinance, as enacted, struck a balance among conflicting interests: Many details were changed but the basic principles on which the Trinidad government had framed its bill were not altered materially.[73]

Despite renewed efforts by the *Mirror* to whip up opposition to the proposed ordinance,[74] no public meetings were convened in August 1904 to denounce the measure. Nor was any public campaign mounted against the colony's government for its continuing refusal to yield in the matter of water meters; under the new legislation, water meters would be the main control on waste in Port-of-Spain. The public quiet was broken only by the protest of a small group of petitioners against one section in the lengthy bill. Among the seven signatories were the familiar names of George Goodwille of the Trinidad Chamber of Commerce, J. C. Newbold of the Port-of-Spain Ratepayers' Association, and J. A. Rapsey of the "no surrender party" in the defunct Borough Council.[75] But their action was overshadowed by the strong support for the revised ordinance by key unofficials in the Legislative Council—Henry Alcazar, the liberal reformer, and the radical C. Prudhomme David. Unable to prevent the ordinance from being passed, the *Mirror* warned that the new governor would encounter great difficulty with its implementation.[76] But reality proved otherwise. Within weeks of the enactment of the Water

Works Ordinance, the legislature paid tribute to Hugh Clifford for his success in the preceding year in the difficult role of political conciliator.[77]

IX

Even before taking up his office, Governor Jackson had received from Hugh Clifford a list of questions that Clifford thought required immediate consideration. Principal among them was the organization and composition of municipal administration in Port-of-Spain, which had been rendered more complicated—and therefore politically more dangerous—by the resolution in August 1904 of the water issue.

By now the administration of the capital was divided among three independent authorities: the Board of Town Commissioners, which had replaced the elective Borough Council in January 1899; the Water Authority, established by the Water Works Ordinance; and the Board of Sewerage.[78] Ostensibly the Water Authority and the Board of Sewerage had both been created to aid the Board of Town Commissioners in administration;[79] in fact, the three bodies achieved little coordination. Each was empowered to raise its own rates, and each could, for example, break up streets in the capital on its own initiative. Their operations involved the keeping of three separate sets of accounts and the payment of municipal officials from three separate funds. Because each body "calculate[d] its rates so as to have a safe balance, instead of trusting to a general balance,"[80] there was no incentive to economize in the rates.

The composition of the three boards revealed the great power of the colony's government in the municipal affairs of Port-of-Spain. It nominated all the members of the Board of Town Commissioners from among those government officials who were ratepayers in the capital. The Water Authority and the Board of Sewerage each had as members the high government official who served also as chief commissioner of Port-of-Spain; three other high government officials, the director of public works, the surgeon-general, and the receiver-general; and up to five ratepayers nominated by the governor.[81] In fact, the Water Authority and the Board of Sewerage were "identical as to personnel but vested with distinct duties."[82]

Under this arrangement, municipal administration in Port-of-Spain was inefficient and uneconomic—conditions which, Jackson and Clifford appreciated, might someday be the object of renewed political agitation.[83] Governor Jackson resolved to check that development by effecting a rational municipal reform in the capital that would have the approval even of the radical element, but he would not be rushed in the matter. He pondered it for more than a year, often consulting with his colonial secretary. Finally, in December 1905 the governor took his first public step.

On December 4, Governor Jackson informed the Legislative Council "that he proposed to appoint a Special Committee to enquire into and report to the Council upon the question of Municipal Government in Port-of-Spain and of the reform, and possibly the extension, of Local Government in the Country Districts of this Colony."[84] He had already discussed the matter at length with Clifford, and together they had decided upon a strategy: A seventeen-man committee would be established, nearly evenly divided between those who were strong advocates of elective institutions and those who were known to oppose such institutions in the present state of political development in the colony. Before meeting with the committee, its chairman, Clifford, would tour British Guiana, which had the most advanced system of local government in the British West Indies (its capital, Georgetown, had had an elective municipal council since 1837, and after 1845 rural administration in the colony had been organized on village councils).

Clifford was buoyed in his new assignment by the reputation he had earned in Trinidad as an effective administrator and conciliator. He expressed confidence that as chairman he would have no difficulty getting the committee to agree to a compromise formula for Port-of-Spain, based on a revived Borough Council with elected and appointed members. On receiving that assurance, Governor Jackson agreed "to assist him as far as possible . . . [by giving] him an absolutely free hand in selecting his Committee."[85] Clifford named as members government officials and spokesmen for a wide range of reform opinion, among the latter Henry Alcazar, a liberal, and the radicals C. Prudhomme David, Emmanuel Lazare, J. A. Rapsey, and Randolph Rust.

But Clifford had seriously miscalculated and had set in motion a chain of events the effect of which he would later characterize in a secret dispatch as "one of considerable embarrassment and difficulty" and which Governor Jackson would describe as "something unique, . . . somewhat disastrous."[86] What led the two officials to these conclusions?

X

The Special Committee met five times during January 1906 and made its report to Governor Jackson and the Legislative Council on February 1. Two questions were formulated as the basis for discussions on municipal administration in Port-of-Spain: Should there be an amalgamation of the existing authorities—the Board of Town Commissioners, the Water Authority, and the Board of Sewerage—exercising municipal functions? And, if amalgamation were recommended, should the superseding authority be based on the elective or the appointive principle or on some compromise between the two? The first question was quickly disposed of when committee members recommended unanimously that municipal functions in Port-of-Spain be amalgamated. The second question proved less tractable. At the outset, Clifford tried to build wide support in the committee for restoring the Port-of-Spain Borough Council as a mixed institution. Several considerations led him to pursue that alternative: he drew from the historical record of elective municipal government in British Guiana and in Port-of-Spain the lesson that it would be politically dangerous to restore the Borough Council as a wholly elective body. On returning to Trinidad from his study tour of British Guiana in November 1905, Clifford wrote a confidential memorandum to Governor Jackson:

> I anticipate that a Town Council, constituted as are those of British Guiana, would, in Port-of-Spain ... be seized upon eagerly as an instrument for political agitation; the temptation to win a worthless popularity, which is one of the curses of our public life in this Colony, would operate as a strong inducement to reduce rates to an impossible figure; financial embarrassment would ensue, as it before ensued, and the spirit of the place, unfortunately, favouring the notion that Government should pay for everything on every conceivable occasion, the General Revenue would be looked to as a means of extricating the Council from a difficulty of its own contrivance. The inevitable refusal would, in its turn, lead to a popular outcry against the Government and to political agitation in a Colony in which, in my opinion, political agitations are highly dangerous owing to the inflammable character of our people whose chief lacks are ballast, sound judgment and common sense.

(This anticipation, I may parenthetically remark, amount[s] merely to a statement that history . . . [is] likely to repeat itself, as an examination of the records dealing with the Borough Council, which was abolished in 1898, very clearly shows.)

I am therefore very strongly of opinion . . . that the absolute quiet and absence of excitement and contention which have now, for many years, characterised the working of the Town Council system of British Guiana, must not be allowed to delude us into the expectation that the creation of a similar [elective] institution in our midst would be attended by the like results. On the contrary, the converse would, I believe, be the case, and the presence on any Municipal Authority that may hereafter be created for Port-of-Spain of a certain portion of nominated members—not necessarily a majority—is, in my opinion, an essential condition of the success of such an Authority. . . . In British Guiana, partly owing to the character of the people, partly also, no doubt, to the knowledge they possess that their system of government places the power of taxation in their own hands, the municipal system works with a quite lethargic quiet; in Trinidad, I do not think that it would have even this advantage.[87]

When Governor Jackson wrote that he "entirely" shared his conclusions in the report on British Guiana,[88] Clifford interpreted it to mean that the governor would not countenance restoring the Borough Council in Port-of-Spain as a wholly elective or appointive body and that Jackson would not concede more than a mixed institution, possibly with an elected majority.

Clifford found further strong support for the alternative of a mixed institution in three official documents: the address of Governor Jackson to the Legislative Council on December 4, 1905, in which he revealed his intention to appoint a committee to inquire into the system of local government in Port-of-Spain and the country districts;[89] the report of the Riot Commission, which expressed the hope that "gradually, and at no very distant date, there will be not only nominated, but elected members on the Board or Boards appointed to deal with such questions [in Port-of-Spain] as water, sewerage, and other Municipal matters";[90] and Chamberlain's dispatch to Moloney on July 21, 1903, revealing that he might be willing to revive the Borough Council "modified on the lines which are followed in India and in some of the Eastern Colonies, but containing a proportion of elected members."[91] Finally, Clifford was sure that the Special Committee, finding itself polarized on interests favoring either the elective or the appointive principle, would follow his lead and recommend a mixed institution.

But the Special Committee rejected Clifford's counsel. Finding the alternative of a mixed Borough Council "plainly distasteful to the community,"[92] the committee recommended unanimously against its adoption. Unable to reach a consensus on either the elective or the appointive principle, it refrained from advising the governor and the Legislative Council on those alternatives.

During the course of its deliberations, the Special Committee tried to stimulate public discussion of the issues before it. But because every individual and organization whose views it solicited declined, the committee had to prepare for the coming legislative debate merely by discussing at length the various alternatives and by tendering its own recommendation against a mixed body.

On February 19, 1906, Clifford moved that the Legislative Council adopt the report of the Special Committee, whereupon Governor Jackson read a statement that included his "personal suggestion"[93] that a municipal council be promptly established in Port-of-Spain, with the same number of members as that contemplated by the committee. All the members of the new body would be nominated by the governor. At the end of five years, the council would be transformed into a wholly elective body; one-third of the appointive members would be replaced by elected members after the third year, another third after the fourth year, and the remaining third after the fifth year. Upon becoming a wholly elective institution, the municipal council would elect from its own members a mayor for Port-of-Spain. Jackson concluded his statement by inviting the ratepayers and the general population to address the Legislative Council by petition on his "personal suggestion"; moreover, he gave strong encouragement to the official members to speak and vote freely in the matter. The Legislative Council held three lengthy meetings from February 19 to March 14, but by the end of that period no action had been taken by ratepayers or others to petition the legislature.[94]

As had the Special Committee, the Legislative Council quickly voted its unanimous endorsement of the recommendation that the three existing authorities in Port-of-Spain be amalgamated. On the second recommendation, to which Governor Jackson had responded with his "personal suggestion," the "evident good temper" of the Special Committee was replaced in the legislature by "a considerable amount of vituperative and heated argument."[95] The acrimony that marked the debate is evidenced in the respective comments of Walsh Wrightson, director of public works, and C. Prudhomme David, the radical unofficial:

> The people of Port-of-Spain and of the colony generally are not yet fitted by their personal qualities, character and education to exercise such an important privilege as self-government on English lines. . . . It would appear to be that in the Tropics the great mass of the people have not that energy, self-reliance and determination to be masters of their own destiny which characterise the people of Great Britain.
>
> [Port-of-Spain and the colony will both progress] only . . . [by] maintain[ing] . . . constant importations—not of ideas only—but of men from the more advanced and civilised races of the world.[96]

In that circumstance, Wrightson observed, a mixed council would be more appropriate in Port-of-Spain than a wholly elective body introduced either immediately or by stages.[97] David replied by bitterly denouncing "the mockery of a representative body so pertinaciously insisted upon by the director of public works . . . [adding that] Anglo-Saxon domination may deny us of our wants but Sir, it is powerless to deprive us of our ideals."[98]

Eventually, various unofficial members of the Legislative Council moved two amendments pertaining to the governor's initiative. The first one, offered by the liberal reformer George Goodwille and seconded by C. Prudhomme David, proposed that the timetable for arriving at a wholly elective municipal council in Port-of-Spain be shortened from five years to three; in that event, the process of annually replacing one-third of the appointed members would begin a year after the creation of the new body. The second amendment, offered and seconded, respectively, by S. Henderson and George Fenwick, the leading progovernment unofficials in the legislature, proposed that the newly established municipal council continue to be wholly nominated by the governor. A protracted debate ensued, whereupon the second amendment was adopted by a vote of fourteen to six. In the division, the majority bloc included nine official members and five unofficials, the minority one official and five unofficials. The outcome was a humiliating political defeat for Governor Jackson, who had proposed the creation by stages of an elective municipal authority in Port-of-Spain. It appeared from the vote that the governor had been repudiated even by his own officials.

Recognizing that he himself had played a major role in the debacle, Hugh Clifford resolved to explain his opinions and actions to Lord Elgin, who had succeeded Alfred Lyttelton as secretary of state for the colonies.

On March 31, 1906, Governor Jackson left for a long leave of absence in England. As colonial secretary, it fell to Clifford to administer the government. On April 24, he sent Elgin two long dispatches—one open, the other confidential.[99] Clifford's open dispatch was essentially a catalogue of the events that had culminated in the legislative vote against the governor. His confidential dispatch contained a briefer summary of those events and, of special interest here, other detailed remarks that threw light upon the connection between Clifford's personal opinions and his political actions; the confidential dispatch is of interest also for the attention it drew to the artfulness of the colonial secretary as a political actor.

When it became evident to Clifford that the Special Committee would refuse to recommend the restoration of the Borough Council as a mixed institution, he gave up advocating that alternative. Believing that the government shared his own strong objection to an elective institution, he decided to press for a wholly appointive municipal council.

Clifford claimed that had he known then that Governor Jackson preferred an elective council, established by stages, over an appointive council, he might have been able to influence the committee to advocate that view. But because he had already persuaded various committee members to embrace a wholly appointive institution, causing them to suffer censure in the press, he resolved to abandon neither his supporters nor their position. In any event, Clifford claimed, he had spoken as an individual in the committee and, as such, had not committed the governor to any course of action.

Clifford emphasized to Lord Elgin his regret that Governor Jackson had communicated his preference to the Legislative Council as a "personal suggestion." Had the governor put forward his scheme to establish gradually an elective council as "his considered policy,"[100] Clifford assured Elgin that all the officials would have supported him as their duty.

Only after the vote against Governor Jackson in the Legislative Council did an organized public opinion begin to be heard on the question of the municipal authority in Port-of-Spain—in a voice that was hostile to a wholly appointive municipal institution. The first group to be heard was the Trinidad Workingmen's Association, which seemed to spring back to life on this issue. Led now by Alfred Richards,[101] the association decried the decision of the legislature favoring a wholly appointive municipal council, and it petitioned Lord Elgin for "a purely elective [municipality] . . . and some measure of reform of the Legislative Council on a representative principle."[102] Elgin was unmoved by this protest and petition, coming as they did from an organization which, from its inception in 1897, had generally been ignored or scorned in Trinidad. He took his cue from Governor Jackson, who advised him to disregard the "irresponsible self-selected body and its Committee [who] are neither ratepayers nor artisans."[103]

Of greater weight was the protest lodged by "nearly 700 firms or individuals comprising with a few exceptions, the leading business establishments, professional men and property owners in Port-of-Spain." Their preference was an elective municipal council along the lines of Governor Jackson's "personal suggestion" to the Legislative Council.[104] Having consistently opposed that alternative, Clifford tried now to persuade Lord Elgin that he should not be unduly influenced by the petition: Many among the signatories, he observed in his confidential dispatch to the secretary of state, had recently appealed privately to him and to the attorney-general and the solicitor-general in Trinidad to resist on racial grounds any temptation to restore the Borough Council as a wholly elective institution. Clifford stressed the great weight he attached to these private sentiments by quoting from a confidential memorandum on "The Existing Condition of Race Feeling in the Island of Trinidad" which he had submitted to Elgin's predecessor, Alfred Lyttelton, in May 1905, and he offered some advice:

The vast majority—I might almost say the whole—of the white population . . . is convinced that popular representation would be the ruin of the Colony and would destroy such security for life and property as now exists. This opinion has been expressed to me with absolute unanimity by numbers of the leading white men of all shades of view and of all the different nationalities; yet no one of them is prepared to express that opinion publicly for fear of the unpopularity which he would thereby incur. It is even probable that if the question were to come prominently to the front, many of them who disapprove of it most completely would pose as its advocates for the purpose of enjoying the admiration of the blacks, trusting to the Secretary of State to veto the proposal. I am aware that to one not personally acquainted with Trinidad this statement may well seem to be incredible, but I make it with a full sense of my responsibility in so doing, and I am convinced that the event, should occasion arise, will prove that my forecast is correct.

It is the duty of the Government of a Colony such as this to decide matters without too great a regard either to the overt support which it may obtain, or to the apparent opposition which it may excite. The newspapers, if they are to secure a sufficient sale, must cater for the bulk of the reading population, whose numbers our schools are annually increasing, by the enunciation of opinions which will prove attractive to the more ignorant and short-sighted masses. The man who in this community speaks publicly of local matters must adopt a like course if he is to avoid very offensively expressed unpopularity. The dry-goodsman cannot afford to offend those who form the bulk of his customers; the businessman, the lawyer, and the doctor are loath to have recourse to any action that may prejudice them with their clients; and accordingly it is, in my opinion, to the personal expression given privately to their views by responsible individuals, who are well acquainted with the Colony, its inhabitants and needs, that the Government must look for advice and guidance, rather than to public actions or to the popular pronouncements which come to us from the Press and from the *quasi* political platform.

Clifford warned against attaching too much importance particularly to the views of prominent colored professionals in the Crown Colony:

Any petition . . . that is submitted for signature by Mr. [C. Prudhomme] David, the Negro Member of [the Legislative] Council, by Mr. [Emmanuel] Lazare, the Negro lawyer and agitator, who was tried for his share in the 1903 Riot, by Dr. [George] Masson, a coloured Doctor, late agitator and present philanthropist, seconded by Mr. [George] Goodwille, one of the leading dry-goods merchants in the place and necessarily the rival of other dry-goods firms, would always be secure of obtaining a large number of supporters even among those who disliked the policy which the petition was designed to advocate. Such a petition, in my opinion, would be signed all the more readily if those signatories who did not at heart approve of it were aware that the policy advocated had already been disallowed by a vote of Legislative Council, since they would count to some extent upon the very natural reluctance of your Lordship to disregard such a vote.[105]

Even as he was emphasizing to Lord Elgin that it was for Governor Jackson alone to recommend a course of action in this delicate situation, the artful Clifford continued to press his own contrary views on the secretary of state. Thus, he highlighted for Elgin the risks that would purportedly attend a rejection of the legislative recommendation that the Borough Council be restored in Port-of-Spain as a wholly appointive institution:

It will prove to be somewhat difficult to give effect to a policy, no matter how publicly, loudly or influentially advocated, which is directly opposed to a vote of the Legislative Council in which the official voting was free, if that Council is still to be retained as at present constituted, and if its unofficial members are to continue to owe their appointment to nomination and not to election. I would submit that either the nominated unofficial members must be recognized as representing some of the sanest and soundest opinion of the community at large, in which case their existence is justified; or they must be held to be unrepresentative of the people whose interests they are appointed to watch. If the latter be admitted, it appears to me to follow that the presence of nominated members on the Legislative Council is of no great utility to the people or the Colony, and may quite conceivably, be highly mischievous to the interests of the community as a whole. . . .

The existence of an elected Body [in Port-of-Spain] would in the future, as was the case in the past, add considerably to the difficulties by which from time to time the local [i.e., Trinidad] Administration must expect to be beset. Apart from complications arising out of disagreements between the Government and the Council upon matters affecting the finances and welfare of the Town, from which, I think, it would be vain to expect complete freedom, there is every reason to anticipate, having regard to the character of our population and their love of public speaking, that the Borough Council would speedily become a platform for the discussion of local [i.e., Trinidad] political questions, and that these would prove to be far more interesting to the members than wearisome details of municipal administration. Whenever this should occur—and again it would invariably be the popular and not necessarily the wise view which speakers would be found to advocate—the fact that the Borough Council was composed of members chosen by election would be used to discredit, as local agitators seek very persistently to discredit, the decisions of a Legislative Council whose unofficial element is wholly nominated. This, I submit, could not but add considerably to the embarrassment of the Government and weaken the authority of its Councils. As a purely personal opinion I would suggest that a complete change in the method of selection of Unofficial Members of Council— viz. by election, not by nomination—would alone suffice to rob a purely elected Borough Council of its power for most inconvenient political mischief.[106]

Clifford wrote shrewdly here in the interest of a wholly appointive institution. He proposed what was, at the time, an impossible resolution of the question of the municipal authority: that restoration of the Borough Council on an elective basis be accompanied by a reform of the legislature to include elected unofficials. Knowing that Elgin would not countenance such an immoderate reform, and daring the secretary of state to risk weakening the Legislative Council by pitting an elective municipal authority against it, Clifford had gone far toward assuring that the Borough Council would be restored as a wholly appointive institution.

Clifford ended his confidential dispatch to Lord Elgin by noting that the appointive Board of Town Commissioners had acted more responsibly in the public interest than the elective Borough Council that it replaced and that the record of the latter and of the municipalities of Georgetown and New Amsterdam, in British Guiana, highlighted the danger of machine politics where few eligible voters exercised their franchise. Clifford warned Elgin that this pattern would likely recur should the Borough Council be restored on an elective basis and recommended as an antidote "that any grant of the right to elect representatives should be coupled with the provision that, in the event of that right not being exercised by a sufficient proportion of the electors of a ward casting votes for or against the candidates who offer themselves, the Government should be required to select the member to fill the vacancy upon the Council. This would not be a limitation of the privilege of election, but it would place the power of nomination in responsible hands in the event of the electors themselves neglecting to exercise their right." [107]

XI

Governor Jackson was on leave in England when Clifford's two dispatches on municipal government in Port-of-Spain, sent on April 24, arrived at the Colonial Office. Soon after, the governor was solicited for his comments.

Jackson was clearly pained by the contents of the two dispatches, which showed clearly that during his absence a "very embarrassing situation" had developed over the question of the municipal authority in Port-of-Spain. His distress was registered in a minute sent to Elgin on May 29. After highlighting the events that had led the Legislative Council to reject his proposal that the Borough Council be restored gradually as an elective body, Jackson pointed out that while he would have preferred appointment to the Special Committee of a large majority favorable to his own position, he had given free rein to Clifford to select the committee. He said that he agreed with Clifford's conclusions in the report on British Guiana but did not endorse "the whole of the personal views which led him to those conclusions, . . . [as] I do not share his strong objections to the elective principle." In Jackson's view, his colonial secretary had erred in issuing a general invitation to all interested persons to give testimony before the committee, especially as Clifford knew that leading citizens in the colony would be reluctant to do so. "Such an invitation," the governor thought, was "foredoomed to failure." [108]

Jackson revealed to Lord Elgin that before presenting his "personal suggestion" to the Legislative Council, he had consulted with Clifford and other principal officials of the Trinidad government and with key unofficials in the legislature and had received their encouragement. Because Clifford had advised against muzzling officials who had spoken freely in the Special Committee, the governor agreed to put forward his proposal in the legislature as a "personal suggestion," not as "his considered policy." Jackson emphasized that his proposal was not intended as a compromise but as a means to ensure that "inexperienced hands" [109] in the restored Borough Council would have time to learn their duties.

According to the governor, a wholly appointive municipal authority would exercise "control without responsibility." In that circumstance, he observed, "the Government which nominates . . . [it] will be held responsible for . . . [its] actions by the public, and rightly so, since the latter are deprived of the only means of bringing the responsibility home to the members of the Board by withdrawing their support."[110]

Jackson was especially apprehensive lest public opinion be aroused by an appointive body that might in the future levy higher rates for a new sewerage system in Port-of-Spain. He feared that such a municipal authority would lead the citizenry to expect the Trinidad government to shoulder the burden of municipal finance and, in consequence, would stimulate public opposition to all future efforts to raise the rates. It was Jackson's view that Port-of-Spain, the largest and wealthiest city in the West Indies, could be educated to act responsibly as an elective municipality with a liberal franchise.

While pleased with Clifford's assurance that all his officials would now render him support, Governor Jackson nevertheless took pains to point out to Lord Elgin that the present situation was "something unique . . . somewhat disastrous":

It has been referred to in the press as a vote by the officials of want of confidence in the Governor, and has been widely accepted as showing differences in the Councils of the Government, which my officials would be the first to repudiate. The fact that the restoration of an elective municipality in Port-of-Spain has been rejected by the vote of the officials has also been quoted in the press as showing that the hostility of the officials to the public, formerly (and very wrongly) attributed to them at the time of the Water Supply disturbances, has been kept under only by the personal control of the Governor, and that directly that is relaxed it makes itself apparent. I mention these matters, not that I attach any great importance to them, but merely because for the moment they add to the difficulties of the situation.[111]

In addition, Jackson was disquieted by Clifford's proposal to Lord Elgin "that it is to the personal expression of their views given privately by responsible individuals that the Government of Trinidad must look for advice and guidance." "Such a principle," Jackson observed, "would be fatal to good Government in Trinidad, or any other Colony, and would inevitably lead to Government by Clique. Such opinions could not fail to be largely inspired by self-interest, and the bare suspicion that the Government was guided by advice so obtained, would result in the deep distrust of the general public. The Governor of a Crown Colony must be accessible to all sorts of conditions of men, 'give every man his ear and few his voice,' but he should receive with the utmost caution opinions, which the holders are afraid of submitting to the judgment of others." [112]

Further emphasis was given to the contrasting outlooks of the two men when the governor remarked: "Mr. Clifford adds [in his confidential dispatch to Lord Elgin] that it is the duty of the Government of a Colony such as Trinidad to decide matters without too great a regard either to the overt support which it may obtain, or to the apparent opposition it may excite. That is true, but with limitations. The 'benevolent despot' is probably the best of all Governments, if the people will accept him, but no reform, however carefully thought out, and however beneficent in intention, will be successful, unless the people can be brought to accept it, or can be educated up to it." [113]

Remarkably, the portrait of Clifford that emerges in Jackson's minute is of a man who, despite his flawed role in the circumstances, still deserved admiration and support. The governor wrote:

> I hope it will be clearly understood that I do not attribute any blame whatever to Mr. Clifford, who is a valuable officer of marked ability, to whose opinions I attach great weight, and for whom I entertain a strong personal regard. His only fault, if I may say so, is a tendency to form his conclusions too rapidly without going carefully enough into all sides of the question. My mistake, if mistake it was, was in placing too great confidence in his sanguine forecast of the action of the [Special] Committee, and in giving him too free a hand. I did not anticipate that he, or the other principal officials, would not foresee the effect on the public of the almost unanimous opposition of the chief civil officials in a Crown Colony to a proposal by the Governor, and I saw no reason to doubt that they would realize that, however much they might object to it, the restoration of some form of elective municipality to Port-of-Spain is inevitable in the near future, as is admitted even by Mr. [S.] Henderson, its strongest opponent [among the unofficials in the Legis-

lative Council]. . . . I ought perhaps to have remembered that, like the majority of people who form strong and uncompromising opinions, it is sometimes difficult for Mr. Clifford to see both sides of a question, or even to admit that there can be any other point of view than that which seems so plain to him. I can only say that although, as he himself admits in the final Paragraph of his confidential despatch [to Lord Elgin], his action has contributed to the creation of a situation of considerable embarrassment and difficulty, my confidence in him is in no way shaken.[114]

Governor Jackson concluded that a compromise formula was needed to resolve the difficulty. Accordingly, he proposed to Elgin that a new Town Board be established in Port-of-Spain, its members nominated by the governor for a period of two years. The board would take over the functions of the three existing authorities in the capital, the Board of Town Commissioners, the Water Authority, and the Board of Sewerage. Jackson proposed also "that at the end of the two years, when the municipal work has been thoroughly reorganized, the question as to whether the nominated Board should be continued, or should be replaced by an elected Board, should be submitted to the vote of the Legislature. This neither sets aside the resolution [of the legislature favoring an appointive municipal institution], nor rejects the prayer of the [nearly 700] Petitioners, as the original proposal [by Jackson], which it asks may be given effect to, provides for a nominated Board for three years. It will be a matter for consideration when the matter comes forward again whether the official members [of the legislature] should record their votes or not. The new Board should not be presided over by the Auditor-Gen[eral of Trinidad] as it seems very undesirable that the chairman, who is directly responsible for the municipal accounts, should also be charged with their audit. The audit should be paid for from the rates, and not merely be added to the duties of the Auditor-Gen[eral]."[115]

Elgin's decision was quickly forthcoming. On June 21, 1906, he wrote to Clifford, who was administering the government of Trinidad, that a new municipal authority should be established in Port-of-Spain along the lines proposed by Jackson. According to Elgin, "the final solution will be all the more satisfactory for being thus gradually worked out."[116] Created by Ordinance 19 of 1907, the new Town Board superseded the three existing authorities in the capital.[117] The ordinance stipulated, among other things, that the board members would all be appointed by the governor from among the ratepayers and that one member would be designated by him to be the chief commissioner of the municipality. The Town Board, as constituted, would serve until May 1909, at which time consideration would be given again to the question of the municipal authority in Port-of-Spain.

9

Urban Nationalism V: The Municipal Question Resolved

I

LORD ELGIN HAVING DECIDED to set an early timetable for reconsidering the municipal question in Port-of-Spain, there was no significant public agitation over the matter during the two years following the enactment of Ordinance 19 of 1907. A wait-and-see attitude was adopted by all parties, even by the radical element in the capital. In its lead editorial of November 29, 1906, the Port-of-Spain *Mirror* stressed the pointlessness of holding any public discussion regarding an elective municipality so long before the question was scheduled to be reopened officially. The *Mirror* was content on that occasion merely to endorse Governor Jackson's view that no official of the Crown Colony government should serve either as chairman of the municipal authority in Port-of-Spain or as mayor of the town.[1]

When the time came to reopen the municipal question in Port-of-Spain, new leaders were in place in the Crown Colony: Sir George LeHunte was governor and Samuel W. Knaggs, an "old Trinidad hand," his colonial secretary.[2] In December 1909, LeHunte asked the Legislative Council to weigh three alternatives: that the appointive Town Board be retained in the capital, that a mixed council be established in its place, or that the municipality be governed by a wholly elective institution.[3]

The strong influence of LeHunte's predecessor, Sir Henry Moore Jackson, could be seen in the ground rules that were established for legislative action. It will be recalled that in his dispatch to Elgin of May 29, 1906, Jackson had rued the conservative bias of his officials regarding municipal administration in Port-of-Spain. He had strongly hinted then that, when the municipal question was brought forward again in the Legislative Council, the official members should not be allowed to record their votes.[4] Governor LeHunte advised the legislature that Lord Crewe, Elgin's successor at the Colonial Office, had expressed his wish that the alternatives "should be decided by the Unofficials."[5] Crewe had determined that the Trinidad government would take no initiative in the matter; only the unofficial members of the legislature would be allowed to move any resolution.

Despite this strong signal from the Colonial Office, in the ensuing months the Legislative Council took no action on the municipal question in Port-of-Spain. An impatient Town Board decided to debate the matter at its meeting in early March 1910. One member, L. A. Wharton, moved that the board petition the Trinidad government to establish gradually an elective municipal institution in the capital, along the lines proposed by the former governor. Wharton argued that the municipality had been punished enough and that "dissatisfaction, unrest and discontent have been allayed and if we remain here any longer we shall be stagnating and incapable of doing anything more in the nature of perfecting the object lesson which we were appointed to give."[6] While there was great sympathy on the board for the grounding principle of the motion—an elective municipality—it was narrowly defeated by the vote of the chairman. Among those voting in the negative were some who protested that the municipal council had no authority to entertain such a motion.[7]

Governor LeHunte now felt himself pressed to report to Lord Crewe on the attitude of the Legislative Council toward the municipal question in Port-of-Spain. Accordingly, near the end of March, the governor formally conveyed to the legislature the substance of the debate recently conducted on the matter by the Town Board, along with a request that the unofficials inform him of what action, if any, they proposed to take.[8] Responding to LeHunte, George Fenwick, a conservative unofficial, observed that those unofficials who were "perfectly content with the present administration" of Port-of-Spain by an appointive Town Board would seek no further reform, and he invited any other unofficials who wished to do so to move a resolution to alter the status quo. The two leading reformers in the legislature, the radical C. Prudhomme David and the liberal Henry Alcazar, both formally dissociated themselves from Fenwick's response to Governor LeHunte,[9] but neither reformer chose on that occasion to move an affirmative resolution on the municipal question.

How to explain this apparent lethargy among the unofficials in the Legislative Council? The answer had a political implication, as revealed near the end of April 1910 by LeHunte himself. Shortly before, he had learned from the unofficials of their decision that they alone should not be called upon by the Colonial Office or the Trinidad government to move a change in the administration of Port-of-Spain. He communicated that decision to the full legislature; and he informed the legislature that, upon receiving the decision, Lord Crewe promised that if the unofficials moved a resolution on the municipal question, he would allow the official members to speak and vote freely.[10] But the unofficials refused again to take the initiative. Whereupon LeHunte communicated his puzzlement to Crewe, registering his surprise especially over the reluctance of David and Alcazar to strike boldly for reform in the municipality of Port-of-Spain.[11]

The Colonial Office proved more discerning. R. V. Vernon, a clerk who had served in 1903 as secretary to the Riot Commission, wrote that the unofficials were refraining from taking the initiative for fear of "being snubbed as they have been on other occasions."[12] There was warrant for Vernon's thesis. Only a few years before, all but one official in the Legislative Council had voted freely for an appointive municipal institution in Port-of-Spain—despite the preference that Governor Jackson had registered for the gradual establishment of an elective municipality. On that occasion, the colonial secretary, Hugh Clifford, and Jackson had both affirmed that leading citizens in the Crown Colony were loath to act boldly in public affairs for fear of incurring unpopularity.[13] And as recently as 1908, the unofficials in the legislature had once again been rebuffed as they tried to assert a more powerful role. In July of that year, the unofficials, who were members of the Finance Committee, protested strongly against the decision of the Trinidad government to allocate a salary for the inspector of docks without addressing the committee on the matter. Following that incident, the unofficials refused to attend meetings of the Finance Committee, and even George Fenwick, a conservative senior unofficial, expressed his disapproval of the government for its unilateral action. But Crewe's reply was dismissive: He reminded the unofficials that since 1895, when Joseph Chamberlain took charge at the Colonial Office, the Finance Committee had never had other than an advisory role in the legislative process.[14]

By 1909, the situation involving the municipal question in Port-of-Spain was an anomalous one. The Colonial Office appeared bent on reestablishing an elective institution. Thus, addressing the House of Commons in July of that year, an undersecretary of state at the Colonial Office remarked that it was not desirable that "this [elective] municipality should permanently remain abolished."[15] But faced with unofficials in the Trinidad legislature who were reluctant to initiate the process of change, the Colonial Office was resigned for the time being to let matters stand in Port-of-Spain: In November 1910, the new secretary of state for the colonies, Lewis Harcourt, instructed Governor LeHunte to inform the Legislative Council that the Trinidad government would not reopen the municipal question until the legislature was ready to assert itself in the matter.[16] This stalemate would last for nearly three more years.

II

In the thirty months following, pressure continued to build in the Crown Colony for political reform. New radical groups emerged in Port-of-Spain, San Fernando, and other smaller towns, directing their appeals especially to blacks, mulattoes, and women. The Indian community, growing in the countryside and restive in its low social status, began to evince political consciousness and an organized political interest.[17]

The radical spirit could be felt also in this period among unofficials in the Legislative Council. The black radical C. Prudhomme David had to resign from the legislature in 1911 when he was appointed the first commissioner of Port-of-Spain. His seat was quickly filled with the appointment of Dr. Stephen Laurence, a colored radical.[18] Nearly a decade before, Governor Moloney had proposed that Indian interests should be represented in public affairs by appointing a member of that community as an unofficial in the legislature.[19] But following the Colonial Office practice of granting only slowly and under pressure what could be seen as inevitable, the first Indian was not seated until September 1912. With the appointment of George Fitzpatrick, an Indian creole barrister from San Fernando, there were four radicals and a liberal reformer among the eleven unofficials: Fitzpatrick; Laurence; C. deVerteuil, a French creole cocoa planter; Dr. E. Prada, a Portuguese creole physician; and Henry Alcazar. The infusion of "fresh radical blood" [20] in the legislature reflected growing radical sentiment in the colony.

Along with the appointment of Fitzpatrick, a minor concession in the conduct of legislative affairs was made to reform opinion in 1912. In July of that year, unofficials in the Legislative Council tried once again to strengthen their hand in the Finance Committee. For some years, the three officials on the committee had refrained from voting on matters before it. Fearing that the official side might someday assert its right to vote, the unofficials pressed for—and were granted—a change in the standing rules that foreclosed that possibility. [21]

Buoyed by these developments, radical unofficials in the Legislative Council began to agitate for an elective municipality in Port-of-Spain. The first step was taken in June 1913 by Dr. Prada, who moved a resolution that was modeled on the gradualist approach of Governor Jackson. He proposed that a new municipal authority be established in the capital on March 31, 1914, and that it evolve by stages over the next three years toward a wholly elective institution. According to his plan, in the first year of its existence the municipal authority would include the eleven members on the outgoing appointive Town Board along with four other members elected by the ratepayers in Port-of-Spain. Four of the appointive members, to be chosen by lot, would be replaced by four newly elected members after the first year. The procedure would be repeated after the second and third years to complete the process. Prada calculated that his motion would more likely win approval in the legislature if it did not include any particular formula for qualifications for voting and officeholding, and he proposed that a Franchise Committee be established to make such recommendations. Tightly drawn to minimize conflict among the unofficials, Prada's motion was carried in the legislature. [22]

The strongest dissent was registered outside the Legislative Council—by the Trinidad Workingmen's Association, which proposed as an alternative that elective government be established "at one and the same time over the entire Colony, Port-of-Spain included."[23] With that proposal, the association underlined the essential character of urban nationalism, with its anticolonialism based on issues of public policy that affected both the colony and the municipality. But Harcourt chose to embrace the more moderate legislative view, which was consistent with his own position "that the time has arrived for the restoration of an elected Municipality."[24]

Passage of Dr. Prada's resolution in the Legislative Council set the stage for a political conflict that would evoke the divisiveness in the Special Committee established in late 1906 by former Colonial Secretary Hugh Clifford. A fifteen-man Franchise Committee was named to weigh possible formulae for qualifying voters and candidates in municipal elections in Port-of-Spain. A rift quickly developed in the group: The six radical members bid strongly for a liberal franchise so that more burgesses could be added to the list of voters; the majority, formed of conservative and moderate members, stood firm for a restrictive franchise. The Franchise Committee submitted its report to the legislature in December 1913.

Even before receiving the report, the Legislative Council was poised for the coming political storm. As early as September 1912, the Trinidad Workingmen's Association had begun to agitate for a liberal franchise in Port-of-Spain, assisted in its efforts by Joseph Pointer, a junior Labor whip in the House of Commons who had visited Trinidad in October of that year as a guest of the association.[25] At its peak under the old Borough Council system, no more than 5 percent of the inhabitants of the capital were listed as burgesses eligible to vote.[26] Pointer lobbied for a break with that tradition, proposing to the Colonial Office in September 1913 a formula that would enfranchise approximately 10,000 (17 percent) among the population of 60,000 in Port-of-Spain.[27] Having learned early that the Franchise Committee would recommend a more restrictive franchise than that which Pointer had urged upon Secretary of State Lewis Harcourt, the association did not wait for the legislature to begin to deliberate the issue. In October 1913, it lambasted the committee for proposing to disenfranchise "large numbers of intelligent artisans quite as capable of having a voice in public affairs as those admitted."[28]

Three criteria were proposed by the Franchise Committee for qualifying voters in Port-of-Spain elections: tenancy in rated property, ownership of ratable property, and personal income. The elector must be a tenant in a house rated at no less than £12/10s. per annum; or own property assessed at an annual ratable value of at least £10/−; or have an annual income of at least £62/10s.[29] A simpler, more liberal formula proposed by Joseph Pointer would base the qualifications for voting on tenancy or ownership, pegged to £10/− in either case.[30]

The Franchise Committee proposed that the qualifications for officeholding in Port-of-Spain be based on the same three criteria. But the committee stipulated more stringent qualifications for officeholding than it had for voting. A candidate must be a tenant in a house rated at no less than £62/10s. per annum; or own a freehold in property with an annual ratable value of at least £50/−; or have an annual income of at least £312/10s., as required for candidates seeking election to the municipal council in Georgetown, the capital of British Guiana.

Another proposal put forward by the Franchise Committee dealt with the role of women in municipal affairs. By 1913, woman had begun to assert themselves politically in the capital, sometimes at great personal sacrifice. For example, among the thousands of rioters on March 23, 1903, many were women, drawn mostly from the black laboring class. Five of the sixteen people killed that day and ten of the forty-four wounded and admitted to hospital were women.[31] In the ensuing years, many women could be seen at political gatherings and protest rallies.[32] Influenced partly by these local developments and partly by the suffragette movement in Great Britain[33] and in the United States, sympathy began to build in Port-of-Spain (and throughout the colony) for granting women a formal, albeit limited, role in public affairs. Accordingly, the Franchise Committee proposed that women be allowed to vote in municipal elections in Port-of-Spain on the same basis as men. But finding itself deeply divided on the role of women as public officeholders, the committee made no recommendation on whether they should be allowed to seek election to the new municipal council.

Finally, the Franchise Committee proposed that the privilege of voting in Port-of-Spain's elections be extended to foreign nationals who had been residents in the Crown Colony for five years preceding their registration to vote. This proposal had been sharply debated in the committee. Among its foes was Henry Alcazar, who contended that because British subjects had no political rights in France, Germany, and other countries in Europe, aliens should not be allowed to vote in British Trinidad. According to Alcazar, any resident foreign national who wished to vote in the colony should become a British subject.[34] The leading proponent in the committee of a liberal franchise for non-British subjects was Adam Smith, an English unofficial in the Legislative Council who served also as chairman of the Port-of-Spain Town Board. Because Smith regarded the proposed municipal authority as essentially nonpolitical, he saw no justification for denying the franchise to resident foreign nationals.[35]

The report of the Franchise Committee precipitated much discussion and disagreement in London and in Port-of-Spain. At the Colonial Office, Harcourt took the position that the proposed qualifications for officeholding were excessive,[36] and he suggested that the Legislative Council lower the property and income requirements for candidates.[37] The colony's legislature refused to do so, contending that the Franchise Committee had gone far enough when it recommended reducing the candidates' tenancy requirement for rated property from £75/– under the old Borough Council system to £62/10s. for the proposed municipal authority.[38] The press in Port-of-Spain rallied behind the legislature; the *Mirror* and the *Gazette* both endorsed a high qualification for candidates, and the latter proposed an even higher qualification for voters.[39]

The Trinidad Workingmen's Association, in turn, proposed to Harcourt that he force the Legislative Council to lower the qualifications for candidates, because, the association held, in England there was "no special qualification for Councillors."[40] Reluctant to offend the unofficials in the legislature, the secretary of state rejected the suggestion of two clerks in the Colonial Office that Governor LeHunte be directed to lower the tenancy requirements for voters and candidates.[41] In due course, Harcourt accepted all the recommendations of the Franchise Committee, and they formed the basis for the new municipal authority that the Legislative Council created in May 1914 with the passage of Ordinance 24.[42]

III

Ordinance 24 established an elective City Council in Port-of-Spain. Under the new system, women could vote but not seek election, and the franchise was granted to all foreign nationals resident in the Crown Colony for five years preceding their registration to vote. Literacy in English was required for members of the municipal council but not for voters.

The municipality was organized around five wards, each represented on the council by three councillors elected to a three-year term of office. Staggered terms were provided in the ordinance, one councillor retiring each year in each ward. A candidate could seek election to the municipal council in more than one ward but could represent only one. Any duly elected person who refused to take his seat was subject to a fine of £100/—.

Joining the fifteen councillors on the Port-of-Spain City Council were five aldermen. According to the ordinance, the full body of councillors would convene to elect their alderman colleagues to a three-year term of office. The principle for this arrangement was that the municipal interest should be served also by qualified people who were themselves indisposed to seek election to public office. Provision was made for a mayor to be elected to a one-year term by the council from its own members; no person could serve in that office for more than three years.

The new municipal authority was granted wide responsibility in "the administration of the Waterworks and the Sewerage Works, the markets, the streets, the buildings, and the things upon which the comfort of the community largely depends." [43] Recalling that intergovernmental relations between the colony and the capital had long been exacerbated by the ambiguity surrounding their overlapping functions, [44] the attorney-general of Trinidad emphasized that the aforementioned "are all powers falling within the corporation unhampered by the governor in Executive Council." [45]

Notwithstanding, the municipal authority in Port-of-Spain remained a weak institution vis-à-vis the Crown Colony government. The City Council was empowered to raise the municipal house rate up to 10 percent, but it had little scope for independent action especially with regard to the passage of original legislation. Both the governor and the Legislative Council had to authorize the enactment of all financial legislation by the municipal council. The annual estimates for Port-of-Spain had to be approved by the legislature, and the governor-in-council had to authorize the supplemental budget. The governor-in-council had also to authorize the municipality to raise loans, acquire property, and establish new markets. New streets could be opened in the town only with the approval of the city engineer, who was appointed by the Trinidad government.

The government had levying powers over rates and charges proposed by the City Council. A large municipal debt pointed up the continuing subordination of Port-of-Spain to the powerful center in Trinidad: The municipality had to repay £57,000 at 3.5 percent interest on money borrowed from the government, along with

£100,000 at 4 percent interest on various loans raised for the municipal sewerage works. Finally, Ordinance 24 stipulated that there should be tight control over the relationship between the mayoralty and the municipal council in financial affairs: The mayor had personal responsibility for any money that was misspent by the council, whether or not he authorized the expenditure. If, however, he had previously recorded his disavowal, responsibility would lie with those members of the City Council who had authorized the improper expenditure.

Not surprisingly, the radical unofficials in the Legislative Council protested the financial powers of the Crown Colony government under the ordinance.[46] But their protest was in vain, failing to arouse popular indignation or official sympathy. The Colonial Office hailed as "a great experiment" the restoration in Port-of-Spain of a municipality whose powers and electoral base exceeded those encountered elsewhere in the British West Indies.[47] Thus ended the long struggle over the municipal question in Port-of-Spain, bringing to a close the period of urban nationalism.

10

Urban Nationalism in Trinidad: Concluding Observations, Pointing Ahead

I

PERHAPS THE MOST SWEEPING indictment of the system of Crown Colony government in Trinidad can be found in Eric Williams's *History of the People of Trinidad and Tobago*, published two years after the island colony gained its independence in 1962. The author, a noted black historian of imperialism and a nationalist politician, was serving at the time as prime minister in the black-dominated People's National Movement government.[1] He could discern little of value in eight-score years of British rule in Trinidad. "Conceived," as Gordon K. Lewis put it, "more in a spirit of hatred rather than of anger," *History of the People of Trinidad and Tobago* decried the hypocrisy and cant that its author saw in the "colonial myth."[2] His words fell like acid particularly upon the record of what I have termed urban nationalism, scoring the imperial power, in effect, for having failed to learn in the "schoolhouse" of colonial Trinidad, from 1895 to 1914, the lesson that quicker steps must be taken to advance the colony toward responsible government.[3]

Exemplifying the opposite view of Crown Colony government in Trinidad and of the period of urban nationalism was the Liberal imperialist Joseph Chamberlain. Writing to Governor Moloney soon after he received the report of the commission that inquired into the March 1903 water riot in Port-of-Spain, Chamberlain observed: "No other form of government is suited to the conditions of Trinidad. . . . I must confess . . . that I see reason for thinking that what the commissioners call the cleavage between the rulers and the ruled may not have been in fact so complete as might appear at the present moment to be the case. I cannot bring myself to believe that Trinidad would have been so conspicuously prosperous, had not officials and unofficials . . . [in the Legislative Council] been as a rule working hand in hand for the good of the Colony."[4]

Each of these two portraits of Trinidad in the period under review is striking: Crown Colony government and the period of urban nationalism painted darkly by the onetime colonial but seen in a brighter light by the archetypal imperialist. Wherein lay the truth?

II

Trinidad was in a severe economic depression from 1870 to 1901, despite occasional signs of a better future. The economy had recovered by 1870 from dislocations caused by manumission and by free trade,[5] and there was hope of prosperity tied to expanding international commerce. Optimists would later point, for example, to buoyant trade in 1883, when Trinidad's exports exceeded by nearly £200,000 the level in any previous year.[6]

But the island's economy was still closely tied to the vicissitudes of cane sugar, which suffered in the period 1870–1901 from the twin blows of a worldwide depression in cane sugar and competition from European bounty-fed beet sugar.[7] (A similar fate befell molasses and rum, and prices for those two by-products of cane sugar declined sharply during the last quarter of the nineteenth century.)[8] The plight of cane sugar in Trinidad caused pressure for changes to ensure a more diversified and stable economy. This stability was to be achieved after the turn of the century by introducing new crops, new methods of production, and new agricultural technologies based on scientific knowledge.[9]

The worst year of the sugar crisis in Trinidad was 1884,[10] and a scramble for remedies ensued. One proposal, based on the culpability of the industry for its noncompetitiveness, was that the last barriers to free trade should be eliminated throughout the British West Indies. But this measure failed to win significant political support in the region. Colonial governments were accustomed to raising revenues partly by imposing small duties on exports and imports; they preferred to increase the levies, not to lower or abolish them,[11] and the sugar plantocracies joined forces with them.

Urged on by the West India Committee, which spoke for the sugar plantocracies in the British West Indies, colonial governments in the region petitioned Lord Rosebery's Liberal government in London to take strong action against bounty-fed sugar, cane and beet. Speaking for the West Indies at the Colonial Conference of 1887, the chairman of the committee, Nevile Lubbock, called for the imposition of countervailing duties as the most practical way to defeat the bounty system. However, committed to a free trade policy, the British government made clear its unwillingness to adopt such a drastic measure except as a last resort.[12]

Faced with official intransigence in London, Trinidad placed its hopes on the McKinley tariff established by the United States in 1890. Consistent with that tariff, in January 1892 the Legislative Council passed an ordinance that repealed the duties on most items and lowered them on others. But the McKinley tariff failed to benefit Trinidad cane sugar. Five years after the enactment of the tariff, the colony reimposed duties on imports.[13]

The controversial question of countervailing duties was raised again in 1897, when a Royal Commission was appointed to investigate conditions in the sugar industry in the British West Indies. The strong case that its chairman, Sir Henry Norman, made for imposing such duties failed to persuade the other two commissioners, Sir Edward Grey and Sir David Barbour. Siding with Norman, Secretary of State Chamberlain lobbied strenuously, albeit futilely, in the Conservative-Unionist Salisbury cabinet for the imposition of a duty on bounty-fed beet sugar.[14]

Hard-pressed now to protect the sugar industry in Trinidad, in 1899 the Legislative Council passed a resolution urging a surtax of 10 percent on all goods imported from countries granting bounties on sugar. But Chamberlain refused to back the proposal.[15] When later that year he empowered Trinidad to enter into reciprocity treaties with the United States and Canada, the colony's legislature rejected the measure as unnecessary and undesirable.[16] The prices for cane sugar, rum, and molasses continued to decline until 1901.[17]

Only slight relief was gained by shifting a large part of Trinidad's trade in cane sugar and its by-products from Great Britain to the United States, and the great hopes of an expanded trade with Canada and Venezuela in the 1890s proved illusory.[18]

But Trinidad managed better than the other sugar colonies in the West Indies to survive the economic depression of 1870–1901. Its economy was bolstered by increasing the production and export of cocoa and of high-quality asphalt drawn from the Pitch Lake at La-Brea.[19] American interests had secured rights to the lake in 1867, and by the end of the nineteenth century a vast network of roads and highways in the United States was paved with asphalt imported from Trinidad.[20]

The major breakthrough toward diversifying and stabilizing the economy of Trinidad came in 1897, when the Royal Commission headed by Sir Henry Norman addressed the matter. Attached to the commission was Dr. Daniel Morris, an agricultural expert who was serving at the time of his appointment as assistant director of the Royal Gardens at Kew. Drawing also upon his prior experience as director of the Botanical Department in Jamaica, Morris prepared for the commission an ancillary report on West Indies agriculture that was to have a great impact on the economic development of Trinidad.[21]

The Royal Commission made clear its antipathy toward the continental bounty system in Europe. But a majority refused to recommend the adoption of such retaliatory measures as countervailing duties or a bounty system for exports. The commission examined the collapse of cane sugar and pointed out that the failure to establish other industries, agricultural and nonagricultural, was due principally to the preference of most planters for a monoculture. Other crops had usually been introduced only when sugar fell on hard times. For example, in 1896, the economy of Trinidad was still dominated by cane sugar. Most of that crop was cultivated on only fifty-six estates, all but a few of which exceeded five hundred acres. Foreign interests continued to dominate the industry: Nonresident proprietors owned thirty-six (64 percent) of these large estates; among the fifty-six estates, thirteen (23 percent) were owned by firms based in Great Britain.[22]

The Royal Commission advised that a wide array of crops and manufacturing industries should be introduced as quickly as possible in the British West Indies to reduce the dependence on cane sugar and that the traditional resistance to instituting a system of peasant proprietorships should be ended.[23] (In 1898, there were only 18,000 such proprietorships in Trinidad, with holdings ranging from five to twenty acres. Lacking even a rudimentary knowledge of scientific agriculture, these cultivators usually achieved only marginal success.)[24] The commission advocated expanding the fruit trade between Trinidad and New York and recommended that further efforts be made to increase trade with neighboring Venezuela. (Nearly a decade earlier, Governor Sir William Robinson had tried to promote the export trade in fruit—especially citrus, coconut, and coconut oil—with mixed results.)[25] Strong encouragement was given to the Botanical Department in the Crown Colony to abandon decorative gardening in favor of experiments to develop more economic crops. Finding that Trinidad and Jamaica both had more resources than the other colonies in the British West Indies, the commission recommended against granting them any special relief. In the worst possible contingency, it advised, Trinidad should reduce public expenditures.[26]

Trinidad took to heart the findings and recommendations of the Royal Commission, and by 1900 its economic prospects had begun to brighten. New crops were introduced, among them coffee, plantain, rice, and rubber; eight new rubber plantations were in production that year. While the level of success varied among small cultivators, the planting of such crops helped to set Trinidad on a new course. The Colonial Office gave impetus to this development throughout the British West Indies, reflecting the influence of the Morris report. Dr. Morris had recommended the establishment of an Imperial Department of Agriculture for the West Indies, to help disseminate scientific knowledge to small cultivators and to spur the diversification of agriculture on the large estates. In 1898, Morris himself was appointed by Joseph Chamberlain to be the first imperial commissioner of the new department. To show its commitment, the British government allocated funds for the new undertaking from the imperial treasury in London.[27]

Manufacturing reached new heights in Trinidad by the turn of the century. Twelve sugar factories were operating, each fully modernized. There were also a brewery and a match factory, five rum distilleries, three coconut factories, and a cigarette factory whose production was based on Trinidad tobacco. A new Siegert's factory was exporting angostura bitters. Prospects were good also for petroleum and coal mining.[28] By 1900, the Crown Colony had achieved an economic buoyancy that set it apart from the other British West Indies colonies. The contrast was cited by Governor Sir Hubert Jerningham, who in 1900 told the Royal Colonial Institute in London, "Trinidad is in the position of a successful firm with premises too small for its growing business and it cannot with impunity be stopped growing in prosperity, only because, being part of the West Indies, it comes under the rule of rigid economy to be enforced by all West Indian colonies." [29]

Trinidad continued its economic advance during most of what remained of the period of urban nationalism, until 1914. In 1903, it enjoyed an unprecedented degree of prosperity, owing to such factors as the relaxation of restrictions on trade with Venezuela, the stimulus to local commerce of visits of many foreign warships, and the decision of the Royal Mail Steamship Company to move its headquarters from Barbados to Trinidad. (The last factor resulted from an epidemic of smallpox in Barbados.) [30] Sugar exports rose in 1902–3, as did trade in cocoa and asphalt. A temporary setback took place in 1903–4, when an epidemic of eruptive fever in Trinidad caused tourism to drop and other islands in the West Indies decided to curb their trade with the Crown Colony; exacerbating the economic situation was the decision of the Royal Mail Steamship Company to move its headquarters back to Barbados. The export trade in sugar, cocoa, and asphalt resumed its climb in 1904–5. [31] Production of rice, pineapples, coconuts, and bananas for export continued to expand through 1909, and the abolition of bounties on beet sugar in Europe augured well for West Indies cane sugar. [32]

But the most dramatic advance in Trinidad's economy involved petroleum. The industry began to boom in 1907, attracting foreign capital. The number of applications to prospect swelled in the period 1909–11. More on-shore wells were developed in southern Trinidad, and applications were received (and rejected) for prospecting under the sea. The Crown Colony government retained control over all oil refineries, in the interest of the empire and of the colony. [33]

From 1901 to 1914, the largest gains recorded were in the production for export of asphalt, cocoa, sugar, rum, coconut, citrus fruit, and petroleum, and their upward spiral continued through the First World War and beyond. Before the war, Trinidad's export trade was galvanized by the decision of Venezuela in 1909 to end its restrictions on trade and by the signing in 1912 of a preferential tariff agreement between Canada and the West Indies islands. [34]

III

Surveying the brightening economic landscape in Trinidad in the aftermath of the Port-of-Spain water riot, Joseph Chamberlain could find reason to doubt the report of the Riot Commission that the Crown Colony had suffered misrule and serious political division. By the turn of the century, the signals had become stronger that at last the colony was ready to emerge from its long economic stupor. Midyear in 1903, Chamberlain discerned in Trinidad an economy "conspicuously prosperous." Fixed now on a course of economic growth—generally steady, sometimes dramatic—Trinidad had the appearance down to the First World War and beyond of an oversized boom town. There was wealth to be acquired quickly, along with its trappings. For example, by 1912 the large number of imported motor-cars on the streets of Port-of-Spain posed a danger; in that year, the Legislative Council fixed the speed limit in the town at twelve miles per hour.[35]

But the appearance of prosperity was deceptive. After 1901, Trinidad bore more and more the hallmark of an extractive economy. Foreign capital would fuel economic growth in the Crown Colony for decades to come, so most of the profits were drained away by outside investors and speculators. Most motorcars that plied the streets of Port-of-Spain in 1912 were owned by the small affluent class in the colony and by foreigners who came to batten on the new sources of wealth. Labor gained little from the economic upturn; high levels of unemployment and underemployment, especially among blacks in Port-of-Spain and the other main towns, would remain a fixture of economic life for years. Weak and unorganized, labor had but one weapon, the wildcat strike.

By the end of the period of urban nationalism, which coincided with the onset of the First World War, concern over the food supply in Trinidad pushed prices up sharply. In an effort to prevent profiteering and consequent social unrest, the Trinidad government fixed the price of food, allowing increases of up to 33 percent on some commodities. While it was able by its intervention to discourage all but a few merchants and tradesmen from selling above the fixed prices,[36] the official ceilings were still high enough to inflict great hardship upon the lower classes who comprised the bulk of the population.

Wartime prosperity and inflation both rose sharply in Trinidad.

By 1919, prices had reached unprecedented high levels, triggering wildcat strikes among the restive laboring class. The wave of strikes that hit Trinidad began with the stevedores in Port-of-Spain. As it spread rapidly through the main towns and the country districts, thousands of blacks and Indians were caught up in the swell. Riots ensued, reportedly without loss of life. Alarmed by these developments, the government appointed a committee to consider wage rates for labor in the colony and the conditions of various categories of workers.[37] This concession had a quieting effect, at any rate for the short term. Labor unrest continued throughout the 1920s; its energies would be mobilized politically in the Great Depression to establish trade unions and found the Trinidad Labor Party.[38]

Popular discontent over the public's welfare waxed also in the period of urban nationalism, particularly over health, sanitation, and education. The West Indies had long been notorious for the squalor in which most of its people lived and worked and for the backwardness of its medical services. That Trinidad fared better than most of its neighbors in the region bore testimony to its greater, if still insufficient, labors to alleviate distress.

Soon after the turn of the century, the Crown Colony began to require that personal hygiene be taught in the schools. A campaign was also undertaken to fix in the public mind the relationship between disease-bearing mosquitoes and rats and recurrent outbreaks of yellow fever, malaria, and bubonic plague. But progress was slow, as indicated, for example, by data for the period 1907–9: thirty-eight cases of yellow fever were reported in 1907, resulting in twenty deaths, forty-seven cases in 1908, with twenty-eight deaths. Deaths from yellow fever declined in 1909, but fatalities from bubonic plague increased sharply that year, from seven to fifteen.[39]

Strict regulations were passed in 1910 to control mosquitoes, and hundreds of people were fined that year for failing to cleanse their premises of insect larva.[40] The following year, physicians examined more than 22,000 rats caught in Port-of-Spain as part of a campaign to reduce the risk of bubonic plague. But Trinidad was woefully lacking in medical services to meet the urgent needs of public health. For example, with a population of 333,552 in 1911, the Crown Colony had only twelve general and three special hospitals, one of the latter exclusively for victims of yaws. While the population of the colony increased by 21.8 percent in the decade 1901–11, government expenditure for medical services rose by only 12.3 percent, to £78,393. Greater strides were made in the next decade: population increased

9.7 percent—to 365,913—and government expenditure for medical services reached £156,797 in 1921, up 100.1 percent from 1911. Except for a decline in infant mortality in the decade 1911–21—from 149 per thousand population to 139.76[41]—overall results were disappointing.

The persistent high incidence of dysentery, hookworm, malaria, tuberculosis, typhoid fever, venereal diseases, and yaws led one observer to remark upon the period 1914–16, "There has been a good deal of enquiry, discussion, searching of minds and outlay of money in Trinidad in the effort to solve health and sanitation problems but hitherto with less practical result than in British Guiana."[42] The situation would not begin to show significant improvement until the Second World War.[43]

Problems in education in the period of urban nationalism derived from the need to adapt an English curriculum to a society with different categories of identity and affiliation, racial, religious, ethnic, and linguistic. Social heterogeneity was reflected in different types of educational institutions: in addition to the officially recognized, government-assisted primary and secondary schools, Trinidad had a wide array of private schools and language-training programs based on cultural groupings—Moslem, Hindu, Chinese, and Spanish. The educational system in the colony underwent many changes in the first half of the twentieth century to accommodate evolving needs and interests, and these changes were often sources of social tension.

Religious animosities and rivalries carrying over from the nineteenth century were exacerbated partly by the number of schools of different types.[44] For example, in 1902 there were 241 primary schools in Trinidad, of which only 51 were administered by the government and 72 by the Roman Catholic Church with government assistance. Of the remaining 118 schools—Protestant denominational, also run with government assistance—only the Presbyterian Church and the Church of England, with 50 and 48 schools, respectively, had large educational establishments. Fears that the Roman Catholic community might gain the ascendancy in educational affairs in Trinidad were exacerbated by the appointment of high officials who were Catholic.[45]

Social tension was a concomitant also of the changing occupational aspirations of educated youth in Trinidad. By the first decade of the twentieth century, students in the colony had become far less interested in the medical and legal professions than in securing employment as clerks, particularly in the public sector. But, based on the recommendations of the Royal Commission in 1897, the Trinidad government had sought to encourage students to enter agriculture, industry, and the crafts. Educational curricula were revised in the first decade of the century to promote that goal.[46] But there was resistance because agriculture and the manual arts lacked prestige and held little attraction for youth.

Yet other sources of social tension could be found in the patterns of school enrollment and attendance and of illiteracy. Because the first halting steps to make education compulsory in the Crown Colony were not taken until 1921—compulsory primary schooling was not fully implemented until the 1950s—school attendance rates remained low for many years after the turn of the century. For example, in 1911 there were 49,497 students enrolled in the schools, with an average daily attendance of 29,022 (58.4 percent). Among the general population of 333,552 that year, only 139,053 (41.6 percent) were literate. Of the remainder, 179,294 (53.7 percent) were illiterate and 15,205 (4.5 percent) semiliterate, capable only of reading.

Because most of the illiterates and semiliterates were unschooled members of the rural Indian community, patterns of school enrollment and attendance and of illiteracy worked to exacerbate tensions between rural Indian and urban non-Indian communities.[47]

The raw facts of general growth of the island economy to which Joseph Chamberlain alluded in July 1903 were misleading. On close inspection, his "conspicuously prosperous" Trinidad is revealed to have been throughout the period of urban nationalism, and for many years thereafter, a colonial society deeply divided along lines of wealth, class, and their social correlates.

IV

For more than a century down to the First World War, opposition politics in Trinidad turned on reformism. At different times after the middle of the nineteenth century, the reform movement was represented by the Legislative Reform Committee, the Reform Committee, the "no surrender party" in the Port-of-Spain Borough Council, the Ratepayers' Association, and the United Trinidad Committee— all small groupings founded by whites and mulattoes who were identified with a narrow economic and professional base in the tiny middle class. Eventually, some black professionals, mostly lawyers, joined the ranks of the reformers, prominent among them C. Prud-homme David of the Reform Committee and Emmanuel Lazare and Edgar Maresse-Smith of the Ratepayers' Association and the United Trinidad Committee.

Ironically, reformism advanced the cause of constitutional and po-litical change in Trinidad principally by its defects, the worst of which were the loose organization of the reform movement, a per-sistent, deep division within its ranks over concrete goals, and a longtime preference for an ineffectual pressure-group strategy over mass politics and political agitation. Not until March 1902, when the radical Emmanuel Lazare joined the Ratepayers' Association in Port-of-Spain, did any leading personality or grouping in the reform movement evince a willingness to use political agitation as a means of building broad-based political support. Their efforts were crowned by the water riot in Port-of-Spain on March 23, 1903.

But down to the end of the period of urban nationalism, in 1914, radicalism itself continued to mirror all the principal defects of the reform movement of which it was a part. Thus, even where individ-ual radicals and their followers were disposed to use political agita-tion to obtain mass support, they were never able—or willing—to move forward with an agenda that anticipated power sharing widely across the lines of economic and social divisions. For example, Em-manuel Lazare managed to radicalize the Ratepayers' Association in Port-of-Spain, albeit without clarifying the organization's goal of an enlarged role in public life for the politically powerless. Simi-larly, Richard Mole used the *Mirror* to hurl invectives at the system of Crown Colony government in Trinidad and to whip up radical sentiment grounded in a strategy of mass political agitation. But he persisted in giving expression to the deep distrust with which re-form circles had long regarded the "rabble" in Trinidad. Consistent with that elitist view, when it was time at last to reinstitute an elec-tive municipality in Port-of-Spain, the *Mirror* joined with its conser-vative rival, the *Gazette,* to endorse a much higher qualification for candidates in municipal elections than was desired even by the Co-lonial Office.

By 1914, reformism in all its shadings was a spent force in the Crown Colony, morally and politically. Its exhaustion was symbol-ized two years later by the demise of the *Mirror.* Trinidad would be ripe after the First World War for a new style of politics, one whose augury could be found in the period of urban nationalism that had recently drawn to a close.

V

For nearly two decades after its founding in 1897, the Trinidad Workingmen's Association continued to evince many of the failings that had long marked the reform movement in the colony: ineffectual leadership; a loose organizational structure to which neither black laborers nor colored professionals were attracted in large numbers; a dismal record of unsuccessful undertakings, including an abortive waterfront strike in 1902 against the backdrop of the water crisis in Port-of-Spain and a futile campaign in 1906 to persuade the Colonial Office and the Trinidad government to institute the elective principle simultaneously in the municipal authority in Port-of-Spain and in the Legislative Council. Despite this history, the association stood out in the period of urban nationalism as the only organization in public life whose goals and activities signaled the future course of radically oriented nationalist politics in the colony.

Nine years after its founding, the association established itself formally in the public life of the Crown Colony by registering as an incorporated body. Ostensibly a labor organization based on a narrow class interest, in fact it gave expression early of its intention to pursue certain larger political objectives. Thus, in addition to aiming to "promot[e] . . . measures calculated to benefit and protect the interest of its [mostly black] members, and the interest of working men in general,"[48] the organization promulgated an agenda for political action: abolition of the indenture system for Indian labor; repatriation of the only electricity company in Trinidad; and constitutional advance based on the principle of representative government in Port-of-Spain and the colony at large.

Despite frequent setbacks early in the period of urban nationalism, the Trinidad Workingmen's Association still managed to spring back with renewed zeal for the anticolonial fray. Defeated in 1906 in its campaign to promote the elective principle, a year later it petitioned the secretary of state, Lord Elgin, to improve the conditions of railway workers in Trinidad, and in 1908 it registered a sharp protest against the importation of indentured Indian labor.[49] Two years later it denounced the colony's government for failing to appoint a sufficient labor representation to the committee established to examine trade relations between the West Indies and Canada. In 1913, it protested the ban on matches between white and colored prizefighters.[50]

Oddly enough, the association seemed to be more politically effective outside the Crown Colony than at home. In 1913, it claimed an affiliation with the British Labor Party dating back to 1906.[51] While no evidence has ever been adduced of a formal tie between the two groups before the First World War, it is clear that by 1906, or not long after, it had found for itself a voice in British political circles. For example, in October 1907 Thomas Summerbell, the Labor member for Sunderland in the House of Commons, met with Governor Sir Henry Moore Jackson in London to discuss the grievances that the association had recently articulated on behalf of Trinidad railway workers.[52] Until his death in 1910, Summerbell frequently raised questions in Commons pertaining to economic and political issues in which the association had a strong interest.[53]

Succeeding Summerbell on Trinidad affairs in Commons was Joseph Pointer, the Labor member for Attercliffe in Sheffield, who was serving also as a junior party whip.[54] The close tie that developed between Pointer and the Trinidad Workingmen's Association could be discerned in his tour of the colony in October 1912 as a guest of the organization. He traveled widely in Trinidad, hailing the leadership of the association, presiding over the opening of new branches in the country districts, and speaking out against the system of Crown Colony government. He was received with great fanfare by large crowds who regarded him as an official of the imperial government sent from London to help meliorate their conditions.[55] Pointer's visit appeared to many ordinary Trinidadians to symbolize a growing sympathy in Great Britain for the plight of that colonial underclass.

The visit was significant also for two other reasons. First, it bore witness to an emergent dialectic in modern Trinidad: the largely rural Indian community was pitting itself against an urban black population straining for political power, a clash that would preoccupy the Crown Colony for a half century after the First World War.[56] Only two years before Joseph Pointer arrived in Trinidad, the Sanderson Commission reported that the Indian community had no wish to become politically engaged.[57] From his own experience, however, Pointer drew a different conclusion. Everywhere he went in the colony he was met by enthusiastic crowds of Indians; in Princes Town, he conferred with the leaders of the East Indian National Association, who pressed on him their political concerns. Speaking before a largely Indian audience in San Fernando, Pointer urged his listeners in their own interest to heed the lesson of their compatriots' drive in India for representative government.[58]

Second, Pointer's visit was significant as an occasion for radical elements in the reform movement to promote further organizational activity on public issues.

Shortly before its guest departed for London, the Trinidad Workingmen's Association held a mass meeting in Port-of-Spain. Attended by about 3,000 people, including "a fair number of [Indian] Coolies and 50 or 60 women respectably dressed,"[59] the meeting passed two resolutions calling for the adoption of the elective principle for municipal government in Port-of-Spain and for the Crown Colony. The *Mirror* hailed Pointer's visit, with its dramatic culmination, as "the first part of one of the most brilliant, rigorous and orderly political campaigns ever conducted in this colony." Taking a leaf from its issue of August 14, 1901, wherein it proposed the establishment of the Ratepayers' Association, the *Mirror* urged in October 1912 that other similar protest groups be founded throughout the colony; the time was propitious, it observed, for the formation of "'The Trinidad Reform League' or any other body called by another name."[60]

Spurred by this call to action, radicals in Port-of-Spain announced in early November 1912 that the Trinidad Democratic League had been established to foster the political education of the masses along democratic lines. A few days later, the Proprietors' Association was founded in the capital to promote the restoration of an elective municipality. Soon after, the Trinidad Reform League came into existence, its purpose to educate the masses politically and to press for local government reform in the colony on the elective principle; its leaders included such radical stalwarts as Emmanuel Lazare, Randolph Rust, and Richard Mole of the *Mirror*.[61]

Jubilant over these developments, the *Mirror* resolved to lend strong encouragement. In August 1901, the newspaper had drawn an analogy between the political struggles of the burgesses in Port-of-Spain and the Uitlanders in South Africa;[62] more than a decade later, in November 1912, it highlighted for the Trinidad radicals what it took to be the principal lesson of the Balkan agitation—that radicals must brace themselves for a long political struggle.[63]

But among the many protest groups that emerged in the aftermath of Pointer's visit, only the Trinidad Workingmen's Association seemed to heed that caveat; it alone retained any vitality until the end of the period of urban nationalism. By September 1913, its president, Alfred Richards, had founded a monthly journal, *The People,* to promote "Work in the Cause of Justice and Progress."[64] In order to strengthen ties between his organization and a small group

of black and mulatto university graduates who had recently returned to Trinidad to help radicalize its political life, Richards appointed one of their number, T. P. Achong, as editor of the journal.
The black Achong, who had already established himself in the pages
of the *Mirror* as a radical foe of the system of Crown Colony government,[65] helped briefly to energize the association with his political
and literary skills. Politically ambitious, he would be elected mayor
of Port-of-Spain during the Second World War.

VI

By the outbreak of the First World War, the Trinidad Workingmen's
Association could look back upon the period of urban nationalism as
its trial phase. Having survived the lean years since its inception in
1897, the organization had hope for a bright future in the colony.
Buoyed by the visit of Joseph Pointer in 1912, by its effort a year
later to strengthen itself organizationally with the new blood of returning graduates, and by the restiveness especially of urban black
labor in what was purportedly an era of economic prosperity, the association had cause to be optimistic about its prospects for rallying
the dispossessed and disaffected. By the end of the period of urban
nationalism, it was preparing to intensify the anticolonial struggle
on two fronts: it sought to replace the system of Crown Colony government with one of home rule organized on the principle of representative (elective) government and to displace the tiny group of
affluent whites, among them reformers, who had long stood *within*
the system of Crown Colony government as a barrier to the political
aspirations of the black laboring class. But the association was dealt
a lethal blow by the war.

The First World War evoked a rising tide of patriotism in the
colony, eclipsing for the duration its anticolonial struggle. Trinidad
came to the aid of Great Britain as a supplier of agricultural and
petroleum products, and it made a considerable financial grant—
£331,029—from government and private contributions to support
the war effort.[66] All told, 1,481 Trinidadians entered the British
armed forces during the war; the enlistees in the British West India
Regiment included some leaders, members, and supporters of the
Trinidad Workingmen's Association. By the war's end, the association was an anachronism, too enfeebled to attract support even from
urban black labor.

But the war and other major developments associated with it—at home the growing impoverishment of the lower classes, abroad the Bolshevik Revolution and the peace conference at Versailles, with their evocations of class conflict and strident anticolonial nationalism—had a galvanizing effect in Trinidad. In 1919, as we have seen, many thousands of ordinary Trinidadians—mostly black, with a large representation of Indian laborers—produced spontaneously a near general strike, bringing economic activity in Trinidad and Tobago almost to a standstill for a fortnight. Shortly before the strike began in December on the Port-of-Spain waterfront, another Trinidad Workingmen's Association was founded. Led by the irrepressible Captain Arthur A. Cipriani, an iconoclastic white creole whose popularity among blacks had soared during his wartime service as commander of the West India Regiment, the association rushed to organize the strike and articulate its goals. In barely a few weeks, its membership had grown to an astounding six thousand, spreading racial fears among the small white population akin to those aroused decades earlier by slave rebellions and by the excesses of the annual festivals of Carnival and Hosein.[67] With its base principally among urban black laborers, the new association signaled the racial struggle that would be the focus of nationalism in Trinidad in the half century after the First World War. Its promise, held out briefly in 1919, of a "grand alliance" of blacks and Indians in Trinidad's underclass in time gave way to a bitter political struggle among the nonwhite majority, which would be won by the blacks in the name of nationalism.[68]

VII

The study of history is the study of continuity and discontinuity in human affairs. Because the history of any society—country, tribe, or some other human aggregation—is not arranged "objectively" along a line clearly marked by temporal phases, the historian has to add his own delineations. The need to "arrange" history this way in order to be able to address it endows the enterprise of historical analysis with a certain arbitrariness, risking distortion. It can only be hoped that for all its perils the need to make analytic choices will enhance our understanding of the historical material at hand.

In *Urban Nationalism*, I have taken the analysis of Trinidad's history to the outbreak of the First World War, with a postscript, as it were, covering a half decade more. Because the period of urban nationalism, from 1895 to 1914, is distinctive and significant enough in the history of Trinidad to have merited a close rendering, and because what ensued politically in that society over the next half century—during the period of "decolonizing nationalism"—has already been chronicled admirably by others,[69] there is no need here to advance the historical narrative in detail. What is needed, rather, is a weighing of the period of urban nationalism in Trinidad, by itself and with regard to its implications for what came after and for various perspectives on Caribbean society held by social scientists.

The period was marked by an archaic constitutionalism—the system of Crown Colony government—against which there gathered in Trinidad considerable political momentum. It was the last phase in a long era of reformism which had been dominated by shifting alliances of middle-class whites and mulattoes, whose custom it was to seek modest constitutional gains principally by methods that had themselves come to symbolize constitutional legitimacy—the gentleman's petition, the discreet conversation. But the reformers had made little headway by 1895, the year Joseph Chamberlain came to the Colonial Office to set imperial conservatism in Trinidad and elsewhere on a retrogressive course. In turn, many in the reform camp rallied around festering municipal issues in Port-of-Spain— those of local governance and of water supply—whose roots could be traced back partly to the Spanish imperium in the island colony, when the cabildo often asserted its powers against gubernatorial authority. The reform agenda in the period of urban nationalism was one of anticolonialism based on issues of public policy that affected both the colony and its principal municipality. But reformism would be as ineffectual from 1895 to 1914 as it had been for nearly a century before. Constitutionally, in 1914 the system of Crown Colony government in Trinidad was essentially what it had been for almost six-score years—an artifact of British imperialism administered mostly by foreign-born officials in the name of trusteeship. Politically, the municipal question and the water issue in Port-of-Spain had both been resolved too nearly in the official interest to enhance the reformers' prestige or their influence. On its long record, then, reformism had acquitted itself poorly, becoming, in effect, a self-repudiating force in the public life of the colony.

Underlining the failure of the old reformism, urban nationalism sealed the fate of the white factor in Trinidad's politics. By 1919, the French community had lost its traditional influence, and many in the English community had come to identify their interests with the constitutional status quo. Arthur Cipriani would prove himself a "white renegade" over the next two decades, anathematizing the system of Crown Colony government. His appeal would be made principally to urban black labor, to a lesser extent—and less effectively—to the rural Indian community. The white community would split over this development, some wanting to suppress the new Trinidad Workingmen's Association, others to co-opt it.[70] By 1934, Cipriani would transform it into the "Fabian" Trinidad Labor Party, precipitating deep fissures in the movement that bore his name. Among the more radical defectors from his party were T. U. Butler, a black immigrant from Grenada, and the Trinidad Indian Adrian Cola Rienzi. "Butlerism" grew after 1937 through political demagogy directed toward black labor, beginning with the oilfield workers. Rienzi organized more widely, seeking an alliance of Indian and black labor based on two powerful trade unions, one for oilfield workers and the other for workers on sugar estates and in factories. After the Second World War, the nationalist struggle, down to independence in 1962, was fueled by the politics of race among the non-white majority; the leading protagonists were the black-dominated People's National Movement, headed by Dr. Eric Williams, and its principal foe, Dr. Radrunath Capildeo's Democratic Labor Party, based in the Indian community.

Urban nationalism also had ambivalent implications for the development of a national politics in Trinidad. The reform movement in the Crown Colony had long been divided by geography, among other things—as seen, by a north-south axis from Port-of-Spain to San Fernando.[71] Each town and its reform bloc usually showed a detachment toward the municipal problems of the other—even where some parochial interest in either town affected the reformers' common interest in the issue of Crown Colony government itself.

By 1919, the regional factor had been muted politically; urban nationalism having culminated with the resolution of the municipal question and the water issue in Port-of-Spain, parochial town and regional interests henceforth were subordinated to larger, colony-wide issues of race, class, and constitutional advance.[72] By the 1930s, Arthur Cipriani had come to symbolize an emergent "national tendency" in Trinidad's politics, playing the role of the first national political leader in the history of the colony. The process of nationalizing politics would not be uncontested, however. A strong countervailing force could be discerned especially where class or communal interests were organized on a distinctive regionalism; for example, the labor leader Adrian Cola Rienzi had his power base among the Indian community in southern Trinidad. After the Second World War, the national tendency was strengthened culturally in Trinidad when most of the population came to adopt the black-originated annual festival of Carnival as the symbol of Trinidad's modern identity.[73]

But the growing *political* consciousness and activism of black town dwellers, particularly after the founding of the old Trinidad Workingmen's Association in 1897, had by the end of urban nationalism begun to trigger a dialectical reaction among the rural Indian population; its long-term effect would be to weaken the national tendency in Trinidad's politics. The political roots of what would become antagonistic communal nationalisms in Trinidad were symbolized in the decade after the Port-of-Spain water riot by the appointment of C. Prudhomme David, Dr. Stephen Laurence, and George Fitzpatrick as unofficial members of the Legislative Council—David and Laurence to represent colored interests, Fitzpatrick as spokesman for his Indian community. Other roots can be discerned in the period of urban nationalism: the emergent political role of black women; a goal of the Trinidad Workingmen's Association, to forge a political alliance of urban black labor and colored professionals; and the alignment with the association of T. P. Achong and several other university graduates just before the outbreak of the First World War. The alliance envisaged by the association would be forged after the Second World War in the drive to power of the People's National Movement.

Urban nationalism ushered in a new style of politics. The methods of the old reformers having failed to achieve constitutional advance or significant social and economic development, there emerged in Trinidad near the end of the nineteenth century the confrontational politics of mass agitation, of the strike, of violence. The "no surrender party" earned its brief celebrity for agitating over the municipal question in Port-of-Spain in 1898 and 1899. In 1902, the Trinidad Workingmen's Association tried to foment a waterfront strike in the capital. Political agitation intensified in the ensuing months, finding its outlet in the water riot of 1903. Confrontational politics then became a fixture of public life in the colony, abating only occasionally over the next decade. Its fury was keenly felt during the half century after the First World War: in the near general strike of 1919; in the Butlerite labor strikes beginning in 1937; and, after the Second World War, in the rise of the People's National

Movement and the desperate attempt by elements in the Indian community to forestall a black hegemony either in Trinidad or in a proposed West Indies federation.[74]

In sum, the political ferment that surrounded municipal issues of public policy that affected both the colony and the capital can be seen as having made the period of urban nationalism both a testing time for an alternative strategy of anticolonialism and a watershed delineating two eras in the history of Trinidad's nationalism. The strategy of mass mobilization and political agitation that had been tried in the Borough Council and water issues in Port-of-Spain proved more effective in later years under a different anticolonial leadership. In its own time, urban nationalism helped pave the way for a largely discredited reformist nationalism based on constitutional proprieties which yielded after the First World War to a more strident revolutionary nationalism. Spearheaded increasingly in the next half century by charismatic black political leadership, revolutionary nationalism sought more programmatic goals throughout the Crown Colony (and, after 1962, in independent Trinidad and Tobago) by the mobilization of mass support, especially among the urban and peri-urban black population linked to Port-of-Spain and the other main towns. Urban nationalism heralded that development.

VIII

Social scientists are often charged—by other social scientists—with scanting history in the enterprise of social analysis. For example, the anthropologist M. G. Smith scores the influence of Parsonian sociology[75] in Caribbean studies, pointing out that his own conception of pluralism "explicitly enjoins a holistic view of societies and their cultures as units having historical continuity. Too often these historical and cultural dimensions are overlooked by [Parsonian] writers who simply assume that all social systems must be integrated by normative consensus, and hereafter only discuss those sociological aspects of the present system which support their initial assumption. Since the basic postulate is probably unverifiable, it may be possible to maintain it only by some such procedures."[76] Analogously, Bernard Johnpoll, a political scientist, criticizes the ahistorical orientation of contemporary scholarship on the American Left.[77]

Because history is indeed a great storehouse of signs and auguries and of lessons waiting to be discovered, it is appropriate to conclude this study by (1) examining from the perspective of nineteenth-century Trinidad relationships between different social factors— race, class, religion, ethnicity—and urban nationalism in the period 1895–1914, (2) drawing the implications of those relationships for various social science perspectives on Caribbean society, including social stratification, pluralism, social class in the Marxist tradition, democratic revolution, and Black Power, and (3) highlighting the principal lesson to be drawn from a study of urban nationalism in Trinidad regarding the process of social and political change.

1. Near the end of the Napoleonic Wars, Parliament established a Crown Colony government in Trinidad which would be directly responsible to London. By that action, imperial Britain signaled the political importance it attached to social heterogeneity in the colony it had seized from Spain. In 1797, the last year of Spanish rule, Trinidad had 17,718 inhabitants, only 12 percent of whom were whites (mostly French and Spanish Catholics). Eight years later, the population of black slaves in the island had doubled to about 20,000. The decision to ground colonial administration in Trinidad on the authoritarian principle of paternalistic trusteeship (and ad interim on Spanish law rather than on English civil law within a constitutional framework modeled on older British colonies) had several goals: to placate a large, potentially rebellious French and Spanish element; to check any attempt by an alliance of planter and mercantile interests in Trinidad and Great Britain to wrest control of the colony from Parliament; to prevent the rise of a white oligarchy based upon a slave economy; and to prepare the groundwork for the eventual abolition of slavery.

In the first generation after black manumission in 1834, the colony acquired an even more heterogeneous social cast. By midcentury, the population had grown to nearly seventy thousand, the overwhelming majority of whom were former black slaves and their descendants. There was a small minority of whites—mostly Roman Catholics of French, Spanish, and British descent—and of Indians— Hindu, Moslem, and Christian. And there were people of mixed race, runaway slaves and free blacks from the United States, immigrants and refugees from Portugal, China, West Africa, Venezuela, and other islands in the West Indies, and a remnant of native Amerindians. Over the next two decades, the immigrant Indian community swelled to nearly a third of the population. Trinidad was a collection of peoples and cultures, mostly nonwhite. The distinctiveness of the two largest nonwhite groups was partly racial and cultural, partly spatial: Most blacks clustered in Port-of-Spain and the other main towns, most Indians in the country districts and in small rural towns. The nonwhite majority was part also of a social pyramid whose upper echelon was dominated by two groups of whites, foreign-born officials appointed in London and an affluent class of planters (in cane sugar and cocoa), merchants, and professionals. By the last decade of the nineteenth century, a small knot of colored (mulatto) professionals—mostly lawyers—was poised to claim a share of offices in the government; its luminary at the time was Vincent Brown, who would become solicitor-general in the Crown Colony and later attorney-general.

Operating with a social pyramid in nineteenth-century Trinidad that bound most nonwhites at its base, the imperial government resolved to resist pressures, building principally among different groups of white reformers and their colored allies, for constitutional and political advance. Four-score years after the inception of Crown Colony government in Trinidad, a new secretary of state for the colonies affirmed that imperial Britain would continue to attach great political importance to social heterogeneity in the colony: Joseph Chamberlain contrasted imperial rule grounded on the principle of paternalistic trusteeship with rule either by "a local oligarchy of whites and half-breeds—always incapable and frequently corrupt . . .[or by] Negroes—totally unfit for representative institutions and the dupes of unscrupulous adventurers."[78]

These words were penned by Chamberlain in April 1896, at the dawn of the period of urban nationalism in Trinidad. At the time, he would not contemplate even the possibility that the large Indian community, isolated from the urban mainstream of public life and restive in its low social status as indentures, might someday press for its own political voice. Less than a year into his long stewardship at the Colonial Office, Chamberlain's sights had already turned backward. His political agenda for Trinidad, formulated as part of his grand design for imperial renewal, anticipated the disciplining of reform opinion: Instead of constitutional and political advance, the reformers would be made to suffer the indignity of losing even the meager gains in legislative affairs they had carved out over the last half century.

On taking up his office in 1895, Joseph Chamberlain had little cause to fear for the future of Crown Colony government in Trinidad. Looking back over the history of that British colony, he could take comfort from the fact that on the surface at least it had enjoyed remarkable political stability. Indeed, what social tension there was in nineteenth-century Trinidad appeared generally to strengthen its system of government along with its social pyramid. Cultural differences within the polyethnic white minority, for example, did not prevent the British and French communities from working together in the interest of reform, often loosely defined. By absorbing themselves in reform politics, the two communities gained time to work out a modus vivendi on other important issues that divided them. Thus, their conflict over sectarian education and Anglicization was largely resolved by the onset of the period of urban nationalism.[79] The high point of the "education wars" in the colony occurred in the third quarter of the nineteenth century. Just as Indian immigration was beginning to build, in 1851 the governor, Lord Harris, moved boldly to effect education reform in Trinidad. Under the new scheme, an extensive system of public primary education would be funded by local rates and would be accessible to all children; provision was made also for a government-appointed Board of Education to oversee the professional staff and a wholly secular curriculum. Not surprisingly, this initiative by government aroused bitter opposition from the Roman Catholic Church—especially from its members in the French community—and from other Christian denominations. The churches' long struggle against Harris's reform was capped by success: In 1870, a new Education Ordinance was enacted that allowed the various denominations to reassert their dominance over education in the Crown Colony—aided by a rising level of public subsidy. In that way, new life was injected into the old practice of integrating education with Christian missionary activity in an extensive system of denominational primary schools. (Passage of the ordinance that year did not end the struggle in Trinidad between church and state over ultimate authority in education. That struggle endured until the twilight of the colonial era nearly ninety years later.) Various government and denominational secondary schools (or colleges) were also established in the 1870s, but they were not intended to encourage mass education. All but a few of their students were drawn from the more affluent white population, another reinforcement of the social pyramid in the colony. Creole secondary school graduates were eligible for junior-level posts in the public service, affirming that high positions in the Trinidad government would still be filled mostly by foreign-born officials. Or they could continue their education in universities abroad. Talented sons of nonwhite families could attend secondary schools as scholarship students. In due course, the Island Scholarships program was instituted, based on rigorous, competitive examinations. It allowed a relatively small number of nonwhite graduates to matriculate in British universities.

By the time Joseph Chamberlain became secretary of state for the colonies, the spread of English as a lingua franca in Trinidad had combined with the reassertion by the churches of their dominant role in educational affairs to reduce the weight of the religious factor in day-to-day public life. The denominational issue did occasionally surface in the period of urban nationalism, albeit without its old force. For example, no public controversy was aroused by a letter in the Port-of-Spain *Gazette* (March 1, 1904) that expressed the fear that the Roman Catholic community might gain the ascendancy in education because high officials in the colony's government belonged to that religion. Doubtless this concern was offset in the public mind by the widespread approval of the Catholic Hugh Clifford, who had been acting in the year since the Port-of-Spain water riot as a stand-in for the discredited governor, Sir Alfred Moloney. The general decline in political influence of the Catholic French community down to the First World War also worked to limit the importance of the religious factor. What religious tension there was in the period of urban nationalism derived mostly from the missionary activities of rival Christian denominations.

On the record of reformism in nineteenth-century Trinidad, Joseph Chamberlain could also be confident that the movement lacked the political resources to force a basic change in the constitution of the Crown Colony or to check his retrogressive policy. The movement had been galvanized by the founding of the Legislative Reform Committee in 1854; by the press campaign of the *Gazette* and *Public Opinion* in Port-of-Spain in the late 1870s against the profligacy and the heavyhandedness of the administration of Governor Sir Henry Irving; and by the hue and cry raised by leading citizens in Trinidad against the high expenditures on public works and public service by Irving's successor, Sir Sanford Freeling. But all this political oppositionism had not stimulated any interest among the mass of impoverished nonwhites. The immediate reason is not difficult to fathom: With Trinidad locked since 1870 in a major economic depression that gave no sign of abating, that section of the population had much to gain from these initiatives taken by government. Irving had led the way for Freeling by opening vast tracts in the unoccupied Crown lands for free labor—black and Indian—and he had created more employment opportunities for free laborers with an ambitious program of public works. On these and kindred matters of public policy, conservative reformers were apt to align themselves with the sugar plantocracy in a continuing struggle in the colony between labor and capital. Long divided over public policy and regional interests, over personalities, and over political methods, the reform movement was compromised by the clear identification of many of its key members with the privileged class.

Individual reformers like the liberal Philip Rostant in Port-of-Spain and the radical Robert Guppy in San Fernando did establish their bona fides by pressing for, among other things, a wider franchise in the Crown Colony, abolition of the indenture system based on Indian immigration, and establishment of a large class of peasant landowners—all to check the political power of the planter interests. But neither those two luminaries nor any other prominent white reformer in nineteenth-century Trinidad ever espoused a strategy of anticolonial nationalism with a broad political coalition that spread across the major lines of social divisions. At times, liberal reformers even found themselves aligned with conservatives in the reform movement. The so-called Gorrie affair is instructive: It will be recalled that unlike their more radical colleagues in San Fernando, many reformers in Port-of-Spain bitterly resented the chief justice in Trinidad, Sir John Gorrie, for his highhanded, intemperate behavior in the interests of creole and Indian peasants. His opponents feared that his abuse of authority might be a portent of radical change in the colony, perhaps even of socialism. Conservative reformers in the capital who had rallied around the *Gazette* joined forces in 1891 with Henry Alcazar and other liberal reformers to press for Gorrie's removal from office. The entire incident can be seen in retrospect as having involved yet another, more significant augury: Nearly eight years later, Alcazar would again align himself with the *Gazette,* this time to denounce the majority radical "no surrender party" in the Port-of-Spain Borough Council for having, according to Alcazar, "strain[ed] every nerve to destroy" the main elective institution in Trinidad in its contest with Joseph Chamberlain. [80]

The Gorrie affair is significant also for what it symbolized about reformism in heterogeneous Trinidad over a century down to the First World War. An invention of the small white middle class in the colony chafing under rule from London, the reform movement remained tiny and fragmented over that period—and isolated from the large nonwhite majority with whose support it might have been able to force the pace of constitutional and political advance. Because public life in Trinidad was nearly monopolized by its white minority, collectively these attributes of the reform movement worked to strengthen authoritarian rule under the system of Crown Colony government. Constrained to stand outside the political arena, the low-status nonwhite population was left to register its own dissatisfaction with the status quo as best it could: in protest behavior—slave insurrections, prison unrest, and the rituals and violence of Carnival and Hosein—whose political message was sometimes difficult to grasp. Such behavior was likely to evoke in the white population feelings of revulsion and fear—perhaps intentionally. For most whites, the nonwhite cultures harbored a barbarous paganism whose menace was inverse to the small space of the island colony. Influenced by his Negrophobic companion James Froude, and convinced of the inherent superiority of the white race and of Anglo-Saxon culture, Joseph Chamberlain had taken great pains as secretary of state for the colonies to point out that tyranny would ensue if the Negro colonies in the West Indies were ever run by inept men of color. Deprecating also oligarchic rule based on local alliances of white men and colored, he had stressed the superiority of Crown Colony government grounded on the principle of paternalistic trusteeship. While Chamberlain's racialism fit well with white perceptions of the majority of color among whom they dwelt, the overall effect on the whites was deeply conflictive, politically and psychologically. Because the social imagery of color in Trinidad was bound up with its authoritarian political principle, there was fostered within the white community ambivalent feelings of dependence on and antipathy toward the system of Crown Colony government. Openly arrayed against that system was a tiny cohort of reformers, mostly white, who were themselves caught in the ambivalence that marked their community. Thus the workings of race and rule precluded a political assault on the status quo in the colony by a broad coalition bridging the great social divide. And it left the fragmented reform movement weak and isolated and ineffectual for an indefinite time. Encountering this situation in Trinidad, Chamberlain was encouraged to exploit it for his own political purposes. He would, for example, play on the whites' fear of a restive nonwhite majority in Port-of-Spain as he maneuvered in the Borough Council crisis of 1898–99 to secure for the colony's government tight control over municipal affairs in the capital.[81]

At the base of the pyramid in nineteenth-century Trinidad, the large majority of color might hope that some powerful whites would plead its interests in the political arena. But as the Gorrie affair pointed up, the effectiveness of even the most compassionate white surrogate could not be presumed. Accordingly, nonwhites sometimes had recourse to direct action, to collective violence or social disruption in some other form. By these means, they could express their antipathy toward a sociopolitical arrangement that threatened to render them permanently ineffective. But this, too, would avail them little. When violence or social disruption in the nonwhite community was on a scale that disturbed the white sensibility or posed a threat to its material interest, it would be swiftly countered with harsh repression—by self-styled vigilantes, by the Trinidad constabulary recruited mostly from among the immigrant Barbadian community of color, or by white military forces.

Because these outbreaks and their repression were sporadic, there was an appearance in Victorian Trinidad of social calm. (What outbreaks there were did, of course, confirm for the white minority the explosive potential in that heterogeneous society.) Everyday life in the colony gave little evidence of the pervasive repression that is often the hallmark of authoritarian rule. The British tradition of trial by jury was enshrined in the constitution of Trinidad, along with the rights of a free press. The government's patience might be sorely tried by the legal restraints imposed upon it—but patient it usually remained, as, for example, after the bloody water riot in Port-of-Spain. Despite the recommendation of the Riot Commission that a curb be instituted against various radical, inflammatory newspapers in the capital, and despite the revulsion that officials felt over a jury's quick acquittal of several leading figures in the riot, the colony's government took no action to restrict civil liberties.

But the appearance of calm was as deceptive as the claim by Joseph Chamberlain that Trinidad had entered the twentieth century as a "conspicuously prosperous" colony.[82] A troubling array of deep rifts in the Crown Colony along the lines of wealth, class, and their social correlates could be found at the human level among all sections of the population. The sociopolitical arrangement over a century in Trinidad had had a violent, brutalizing impact on the human spirit. Everyday life bore witness to a tragic distortion in relationships between white and nonwhite. The facts of inequality and social injustice based on race, class, and culture pervaded all private and public transactions. Despite the close proximity in which various groups in Trinidad often lived and worked and played, they were still strangers to each other. Except for the possibility of upward social mobility, which an expanding educational system had opened up to a few talented sons of the unprivileged class, there was no opportunity for the large majority of color to surmount the barriers raised by wealth and privilege. And always there was the powerful attraction of the metropolitan British culture in Trinidad and in Europe, pulling against the emotional tie that many nonwhites still had with West Africa and India. Among people of African descent and in the general population of the Crown Colony, the indignity of ascription was compounded by the assignment of a higher social prestige to the mulatto than to the black: The overall situation had a dispiriting implication: Because the offer of upward mobility for the talented few in the nonwhite community was an offer also of a new cultural identity, many of the "young colonials" who grasped it would display great arrogance in their newly acquired status.[83] How else to explain patterns in the politics of urban nationalism: the persistent refusal of colored professionals to align themselves with the black laboring class in the first Trinidad Workingmen's Association; the frequency with which radical reformers of color joined with white colleagues to express publicly their disdain for the "rabble" whose political radicalization they had promoted in the water issue in Port-of-Spain; and the failure of the black and colored literati to rally against the white publisher of the radical Port-of-Spain *Mirror* when in 1914 he campaigned for a higher qualification in the restored elective Borough Council than the one proposed by the Colonial Office? Could it have been otherwise in heterogeneous British Trinidad after more than a century of rule grounded on the authoritarian principle of paternalistic trusteeship?

2. Individually and as a group, the Caribbean societies—mostly island—manifest a rich diversity whose evocation can be found in the literature of social science. As the number of Caribbeanists in different disciplines has grown over the past generation, their diverse intellectual perspectives—conveyed in many case studies of individual societies and in works of regional and even global scope—have contributed to strengthening the link between area studies and the nomothetic social sciences. Because various social science perspectives on Caribbean society emphasize explicitly or by omission the importance of understanding the historical factor in social and political change, our attention is directed to two questions in the

context of this study. What are the implications of urban nationalism in British Trinidad in the two decades preceding the First World War for some of the more influential of those perspectives—social stratification, pluralism, social class in the Marxist tradition, democratic revolution, and Black Power? And what is the principal lesson to be drawn from *Urban Nationalism* for understanding the process of social and political change—in the Crown Colony of Trinidad and perhaps in other Caribbean societies and elsewhere?

Until independence in 1962, Trinidad and Tobago attracted little interest from social scientists. When an occasional scholarly monograph did appear, it was apt to be subjected to sharp criticism. For example, *Trinidad Village,* a study of rural life published by the anthropologists Melville Herskovits and Frances Herskovits in 1947, was scored some years later by the sociologist Lloyd Braithwaite for the low quality of its fieldwork and interpretation.[84] In 1953, there appeared Braithwaite's *Social Stratification in Trinidad,* a work he had originally conceived as part of a larger study that would integrate historical and documentary materials with a series of case studies of local communities. The objective of that "pioneering effort," according to the author, was "to depict in sociological terms the colonial society in Trinidad and Tobago as it passed to greater and greater autonomy." It was a preliminary analysis based on the larger study, which was never published. Following a brief sketch of colonial history in that society, the work presented a picture of culture and social structure frozen in time, along with some descriptive material on politics and the economy. Uncritically, Braithwaite drew upon Maslowian psychology and Parsonian sociology for a cursory treatment of human motivation and social organization in the colony. The promise held out by the author that his would be a careful study of the process of social change in Trinidad and Tobago did not materialize. Writing nearly a quarter century later, on the occasion of the reissue of his monograph, Braithwaite acknowledged that his study, too, "contains . . . many serious and gross imperfections."[85]

Braithwaite's leading critic among social scientists was M. G. Smith, who pointed out the limitations of Parsonian sociology in Caribbean studies, especially its preoccupation with normative consensus as a stabilizing factor in social systems and its shallowness in historico-cultural analysis. Smith registered his deep skepticism regarding a wide array of Marxist and non-Marxist theories of stratification based on the concept of social class. For him, the effort of the Parsonians to rescue those perspectives in social analysis with a structural-functional approach grounded on the notions of system stability and normative consensualism was hardly more useful. Instead he turned to the concept of pluralism,[86] as formulated earlier by J. S. Furnivall in his studies of various Far Eastern societies. Furnivall—and Smith, among other "pluralists"—challenged the more orthodox view in sociology and anthropology that a society cannot exist without a minimal sharing of common values or social will. Thus, writing in 1948 of prewar Burma and Java as plural societies, Furnivall observed that a wide array of ethnic groups "mix but do not combine. Each group holds its own religion, its own culture and language, its own ideas and ways. As individuals they meet, but only in the market place, in buying and selling. There is a plural society, with different sections of the community living side by side, but separately, within the same political unit." Writing in the period 1952–61 of plural societies in the British West Indies, Smith embraced Furnivall's notion that "in each section the sectional common will is feeble, and in the society as a whole there is no common will. There may be apathy, even on such a vital point as defence against aggression. Few recognize that, in fact, all the members of all sections have material interests in common, but most see that on many points their material interests are opposed."[87]

Along with other social scientists who have adopted a Furnivallian perspective in social analysis, Smith has been chastised for the vagueness of pluralism as a central, organizing concept, especially for his failure to specify the criteria for distinguishing between plural and heterogeneous but nonplural societies. This criticism is not without pointed irony. Just as Smith assailed the Parsonians—including Lloyd Braithwaite—for not being able to explain social change in Caribbean society from the perspective of structural-functionalism, the pluralist approach has been criticized for providing only limited explanations of culture (and, presumably, political) change.[88]

It should be noted, parenthetically, that, notwithstanding their different analytic perspectives, Smith shares with Braithwaite a keen sensitivity to the factor of inequality. For Braithwaite, inequality is a hallmark of social stratification in Trinidad; in Smith's writings on pluralism, there is a strong implication that pervasive inequality at every level of Caribbean society and culture lends credence to the Furnivallian conception of distinctive and nonsharing societies and cultures.

Worldwide the many interpretations of Marxism have drained it of meaning as a clearly delineated model of social development. Generally speaking, it can be defined as a theoretical perspective that holds that because property is the foundation of all power in society, social classes embodying antithetical interests will inevitably struggle for control over the means of production and therefore for power. Leninism, adapted partly from Marxism and partly from historical conditions in Tsarist Russia, is essentially a method for organizing political power on a single ruling party—Communist—which is presumed to embody the will of a dominant revolutionary class and on state control of the economy. Arguably the most important Marxist in Trinidad was the late C. L. R. James, a brilliant black "young colonial" whose life followed a shifting ideological and political course.[89] As a student in Great Britain in the 1920s he was swept up in the passions of the revolutionary left. Perceiving capitalism as the embodiment of social evil and Nazism as its most virulent expression, he fixed his gaze upon the Soviet Union as an alternative revolutionary society. But Stalin's excesses soon led him to Trotskyism. Still holding fast to Leninist principles, however, James continued to regard revolution in the Soviet Union and elsewhere as a "top-down" process, with the party vanguard at the center. By the 1950s he had lost confidence in both Trotsky and Lenin, rejecting their key notion that social revolution had perforce to be inspired and led by a party elite. On returning to Trinidad in the fifties, he was swept up in the politics of decolonizing nationalism that culminated in independence in 1962. Through all the twists and turns of his career on the left, there could be seen the great strengths and weaknesses of the Marxist perspective, especially as it bears upon the matter of developmental change in the so-called Third World. On the one hand, there is the incisiveness with which Marxism perceives property as the enemy of democracy, on the other, its failure to recognize that class struggle and a revolutionary outcome need not ensue wherever social classes exist and that the putative revolutionary party may in fact act as a barrier to revolutionary change. Weighing these considerations, among others, and notwithstanding the apparent success of Marxism in nearby Cuba, some social scientists have been led to conclude that Marxism is a doubtful model on which to base social development in the Caribbean region, especially in Trinidad and Tobago.[90] Other observers, however, have adopted a Marxist perspective in analyzing nationalism in the region as an expression of hostility to a persistent "colonial economic status" especially vis-à-vis the United States.[91]

238 / URBAN NATIONALISM

Yet another perspective on change in the Caribbean region centers on the idea of the democratic revolution. The concept came into vogue in Caribbean studies in the 1960s, when many European colonies in that region and in Africa and Asia gained political independence. It appealed especially to Caribbeanists who regarded the British West Indies as fertile soil for political democracy based on the Westminster model. For example, drawing on the landmark study by R. R. Palmer of *The Age of the Democratic Revolution* (in eighteenth-century Europe and America), the Jamaican scholar Wendell Bell wrote of his belief that such a revolution had indeed "spread and develop[ed] . . . through time and space from the eighteenth-century Atlantic community to the twentieth-century global society." In this conception, the Third World in particular had come to embrace the old revolutionary idea of political democracy, with its emphasis upon equality and social justice and representative systems rooted in an expansive political participation, in guarantees of public liberties, and in an institutionalization of the right of dissent.[92] For more than a decade, there would be an outpouring of scholarly monographs and articles on attitudinal, institutional, and behavioral developments in the Caribbean region as they pertained to the idea of the democratic revolution.[93] But political idealism was soon to be assailed by political events. Within that decade, most of the newly independent states in Africa and Asia succumbed to political authoritarianism—civilian or military, or both. And in the Anglophone Caribbean, the image of competitive partyism based on the Westminster model was blurred somewhat by "bashing" of the opposition by parties in power. Charles C. Moskos, Jr., observed of that period that "some nationalists were beginning to advocate the primacy of the state over the interests of its constituent members. In several West Indian territories the post-independence period was blemished by political surveillance of certain opponents of the government; and withdrawal of passport privileges from alleged political deviants. These developments, at least through 1966, did not seem to represent a consistent pattern, but their occurrence nevertheless did not bode well for the future."[94] In Trinidad particularly, civil liberties were curtailed in the early 1970s in response to a growing Black Power movement.[95]

These retrogressive developments nothwithstanding, the idea of the democratic revolution—defined as a gradually unfolding process, not as a fixed political position—appears to have taken hold in the Anglophone Caribbean in the postcolonial era. Over the past quarter century, the political arena has been enlarged in various territories to include a national citizenry based on the general population. From the onset of the period of independence in the early 1960s, regime legitimation could no longer be certified with authoritarian norms that had characterized the old colonial system. Even in the region's independent authoritarian systems—for example, Grenada under the administrations of Eric Gairy and the Marxist Maurice Bishop—rule by "popular regimes, in the name of the people" has been the principal basis for political legitimation. On balance, the Anglophone Caribbean is still noteworthy in the Third World for its tradition of public liberties and for its generally fair and honest elections within competitive party systems.[96]

Various British colonies in the West Indies had hardly gained their independence when the Black Power movement began to assert itself strongly. The context within which this development occurred was shaped by confluent forces: by a growing dissatisfaction in such countries as Jamaica and Trinidad and Tobago with the economic fruits of political independence and with abuses in a derivative system of parliamentary democracy;[97] by the influence of Frantz Fanon, the Francophone Negritude writers, and the civil rights and black consciousness movements in the United States;[98] and by the widespread unrest among university students in the late 1960s in North America and Western Europe. In the West Indies, the ideology of Black Power showed a growing alienation among black workers and black intellectuals and a feeling among some of the latter that henceforth their "class" must be more closely aligned with the former. Essentially diffuse and unfocused, the ideology had little programmatic content. Its essence was conveyed forcefully by the late Walter Rodney, a black Guyanese political historian:

> Black Power is a doctrine about black people, for black people, preached by black people. I'm putting it to my black brothers and sisters that the colour of our skins is the most fundamental thing about us. I could have chosen to talk about people of the same island, or the same religion, or the same class—but instead I have chosen skin colour as essentially the most binding factor in our world. In so doing, I am not saying that is the way things ought to be. I am simply recognising the real world—that is the way things are. Under different circumstances, it would have been nice to be colour blind, to choose my friends solely because their social interests coincided with mine—but no conscious black man can allow himself such luxuries in the world. . . .

Black Power in the West Indies means three closely related

things: (i) the break with imperialism which is historically white racist; (ii) the assumption of power by the black masses in the islands; (iii) the cultural reconstruction of the society in the image of the blacks. . . .

The black intellectual, the black academic must attach himself to the activity of the black masses.[99]

Notwithstanding its suppression in Trinidad and its political inefficacy elsewhere in the West Indies, the roots of the Black Power movement are likely to continue to sharpen the consciousness of blacks as blacks in that region and in the United States. Shared outlooks based on common origins, experiences, and dissatisfactions will probably continue to be mutually reinforcing for blacks across the boundaries of political sovereignty.

This discussion directs our attention to the first of the two questions posed: What are the implications of urban nationalism in Trinidad's history for the perspectives on Caribbean society held by social scientists? On the evidence here, there is warrant for the conclusion that the implications are ambivalent for each of the five perspectives—social stratification, pluralism, social class in the Marxist tradition, democratic revolution, and the ideology of Black Power.

The class system that Lloyd Braithwaite encountered in the Crown Colony in 1952, and that is a predicate of Marxist social analysis, could be discerned in the two decades of urban nationalism preceding the First World War. Consistent with Braithwaite's report in *Social Stratification in Trinidad* and with the Marxist perspective, the class factor did have a significant influence upon political life in that period. It is evidenced, for example, in the continuing struggle between labor and capital and in the dominant role of middle-class elements in the reform movement down to 1914, in the political controversy surrounding the Port-of-Spain Borough Council in 1898–99, and in the leadership of the Port-of-Spain Ratepayers' Association in the water issue in 1903. The influence of this factor could also be observed in the deprecating attitude of those middle-class elements toward the laboring class whose political radicalization they had helped galvanize. But the evidence from the period of urban nationalism does not establish the primacy of the class factor in political life; rather, it points up its dovetailing with the factors of race and culture as can be seen in these facts: White reformers in the middle class were ever conscious of their privileged status as members of the minority white community; the first Trinidad Workingmen's Association emphasized race over social class in its appeals for an alliance between black workers and colored professionals; and the East Indian National Association, founded shortly before the First World War as an expression of growing concern in the Indian community over the political assertiveness of urban blacks, sought to gather political strength in that community across the lines of class and denominational rifts. The complex interaction of race, class, and ethnicity in urban nationalism is a warning signal to those who would exaggerate the importance of any one social factor in the political life of the colony. Apropos of this cautionary note, it may be remarked that only weak evidence is available from the period of urban nationalism to substantiate Braithwaite's sweeping generalization that there is a tradition in Trinidad of the middle class supporting charismatic politicians.[100] In fact, few members of that class in Port-of-Spain were moved to support various charismatic radical politicians in the Borough Council and the Ratepayers' Association.

At first sight, the Furnivallian conception of the plural society, adapted for Caribbean studies by M. G. Smith and others, appears to be confirmed by the evidence from Trinidad in the century preceding the First World War. Black manumission in 1834 caused no significant change in the social pyramid. A small minority of whites— mostly foreign-born officials in the government and an affluent class of planters, merchants, and professionals—still stood atop an impoverished black majority. The durability of that arrangement was strengthened by the introduction of an indenture system based on Indian immigration. After mid-century, as seen, social tensions were exacerbated at the base of the social pyramid by the economics of free and indentured labor, by the high level of Indian immigration coupled with the soaring birth rate in that community, by the economic advances of rural Indian landlords and shopkeepers, and by a pattern of day-to-day relations between the black and Indian communities which, while never as explosive as in neighboring British Guiana, was still marked by mutual antagonism rooted in cultural and religious differences. The image conveyed by these data is of two communities rigidly compartmentalized in all but their most public, extracommunal transactions.

But was this really the case? What delineation of the private/communal and public/extracommunal would warrant that conclusion? A distinction is easiest to draw between the two spheres, of course, in the matter of cultural norms and practices having to do with religion, marriage, child-rearing, dress, diet, and so forth. But what of communal rituals of a highly public kind, as the festivals of Carnival and Hosein? With the passage of time, blacks and Indians came to participate more actively—as spectators and as principals—in each other's major festival. This tendency could be seen also in new rituals of political life in the period of urban nationalism as, for example, in 1903, when many hundreds of Indians joined a mostly black crowd rioting at Red House, and in 1912, when members of the Indian community appeared among the large crowds gathered to listen to a British parliamentarian touring the colony under the sponsorship of the black- and colored-dominated Trinidad Workingmen's Association. One can only speculate on what might have been the implications, short-term and long, had that distinguished speaker labored to get the black and Indian communities to forge a working alliance against the status quo in the Crown Colony or had the Trinidad Workingmen's Association and the East Indian National Association moved on the occasion of his visit at least to discuss the possibility. The gap between black and Indian political consciousness at the time was far narrower than the political chasm that divided the two communities in the half century after the First World War. By definition, Furnivallian pluralism sets itself as rigidly against the possibility of evolving toward political accommodation in intercommunal relations as it conceives communities based on racial and cultural differences to be set against each other. The record of urban nationalism in Trinidad in the period 1895–1914 suggests that it may have been political miscalculation in many quarters combined with the fact of communal differences that exacerbated the problem of intercommunal relations.

Those Caribbeanists who in the 1960s had warmed to the prospect of a democratic revolution spreading gradually in the British West Indies could look back upon the period of urban nationalism with a good feeling. Despite Joseph Chamberlain's retrogressive plans for the Crown Colony of Trinidad, a modest political advance had been forced by the water issue in Port-of-Spain. Violence had carried the day at Red House, obliging Chamberlain's successors at the Colonial Office to make piecemeal political concessions to reformist opinion in the colony. A black was quickly appointed to the Legislative Council and the first Indian some years later. After several false starts, an elective Borough Council was restored in Port-of-Spain near the end of the period of urban nationalism. But more basic constitutional change had to wait upon the recommendation of the Wood Report in the early 1920s that it was time at last to institute partially the elective principle in the colony's legislature—a development that anticipated a gradual enlargement of the electorate and of the number of elected legislators until representative government was introduced fully.

But the period of urban nationalism could also be seen to portend a growing political distemper, with an attendant risk of violence. This distemper was linked to frustration over the slow pace of constitutional advance and to persistent material deprivation in the lower classes in what the Colonial Office continued to insist was the most prosperous colony in the region. Privilege continued for a long time to define the parameters of politics in Trinidad, rendering the colony's slow evolution a "top-down" process from the perspective of London and Port-of-Spain. Given that reality, the politics of urban nationalism could be an augury not of a democratic revolution, as defined by R. R. Palmer, Wendell Bell, and others, but of a new institutionalism having to do less with genuine political democracy than with the ever more sophisticated manipulation of popular consent from above.

The Black Power movement that took root in Trinidad and elsewhere in the West Indies in the 1960s had as an ancestor, in the period of urban nationalism, the first Trinidad Workingmen's Association. Founded in 1897 by a small group of colored and black artisans, the association soon promulgated an agenda for political action centering on the black laboring class, especially in Port-of-Spain and the other main towns. Rebuffed in its efforts to forge an alliance with colored professionals, it managed by 1914 to gain the participation of a small group of blacks who had recently returned from university studies abroad.

Throughout its short life down to the end of the First World War, the association proved less stridently ideological than the Black Power movement of the 1960s and more programmatic in its orientation. It eschewed calls for black power as such, preferring to couch its racial appeals in more concrete proposals for public policy in the colony. Thus, it campaigned, among other things, for better working conditions for black labor and for an end to Indian immigration and the indenture system. It pressed, too, for the adoption of the elective principle in the Legislative Council and in various municipal councils and for a wider franchise at both levels. The association sometimes gave expression also to a "national impulse," for example, when it demanded an end to Canadian ownership of the only electricity company in Trinidad.

Yet another striking contrast between the Black Power movement and the Trinidad Workingmen's Association can be seen in their attitudes toward the building of racial alliances. Whereas Walter Rodney and other Black Power advocates embraced the goal of having black intellectuals reach out to the black masses, Alfred Richards and others in the association preferred a "bottom-up" approach by which they would appeal for the support of colored professionals and returning black university graduates.

But the radical, violence-prone Black Power movement in Trinidad and the Trinidad Workingmen's Association would be as one in political fate and political legacy. Riding a wave of popularity, the movement would be repressed by Dr. Eric Williams's People's National Movement government in the early 1970s; the association, politically ineffective throughout most of its life and weakened further in the wartime environment of the Crown Colony, would expire two decades after its founding. Their legacy was to have used the language of protest to heighten the racial and political consciousness of their common constituency.

3. Early in *Urban Nationalism,* I proposed that colonial rule (within the larger framework of imperial administration) was a system of power in which colonial governments, buffeted by conflicting pressures on many sides, acted on a bureaucratizing impulse—that is, they sought at once to consolidate their power over those whose lives they regulated and to ensure their own survival along with the tasks they performed. In that circumstance, conformity with abstract principles of imperial administration was apt to be less important than the push and pull between governor and governed that was reflected daily in their accommodation and adjustment to each other[101] —a political condition that pointed up the mutual adaptation of conflicting interests as change gradually took place against the background of persistence.[102] I further proposed that by widening our perspective on the network of imperial administration to include both the metropole and the colony, it should be possible to detail imperial administration better and to enhance our understanding of its historical corollary, anticolonial nationalism among subject peoples. With these considerations in mind, our attention is directed now to this question: What is the principal lesson to be drawn from *Urban Nationalism* regarding social and political change in the Crown

Colony of Trinidad and perhaps elsewhere? Consistent with the fore-going remarks, the answer is that there are limits to authoritarian rule, that is, political authoritarianism stimulates countervailing pressures to enlarge the political arena to accommodate a broader so-cial base of participation, and that within those limits social and po-litical change—toward equality, social justice, and political democ-racy—is apt to result as much from the actions of those who resist it as of those who instigate it.

The history of British rule in Trinidad over the century before the First World War militates against a simplistic assessment of the merits of conflicting political interests in the colony. Grounded on the principle of paternalistic trusteeship, Crown Colony government in that society sometimes found itself in the vanguard of progressive social change, at other times in staunch opposition. In the former case, as seen, Lord Harris incurred the wrath of the Roman Catholic community and other Christian denominations in the early 1850s when as governor he sought to promote secularization and Anglici-zation with a new system of universal public primary education. Over the next two decades, his successors felt themselves constrained by a combination of religious and ethnic pressures to allow the vari-ous Christian denominations to reassert their dominance over edu-cation in the colony—a development that served to fuel the long struggle between church and state to have the ultimate authority in that sphere.

Analogously, from the mid-1870s to the mid-1880s, Sir Henry Irv-ing and Sir Sanford Freeling aroused the bitter hostility of the sugar plantocracy and its conservative allies in the reform movement when the colony's government tried to counteract the worst effects of a deepening economic depression with two bold policy initiatives: the opening up of vast tracts in the Crown lands to peasant cultivators and the launching of a costly program of public works to benefit the impoverished urban laboring class, mostly black. Other evidence of the occasional interest of the imperial power in promoting progres-sive change in the colony can be found also in the period of urban nationalism. For example, the Colonial Office tried, over five years bracketing the turn of the century, to place municipal government and the administration of the water supply in Port-of-Spain on a sound financial basis, and in 1914, despite resistance in the Trinidad reform movement, it pushed hard to restore the elective Borough Council in the capital through relatively low qualifications for voting and officeholding.

At other times, however, imperial rule in Trinidad was more notable for its deep conservatism—for example, when the Liberal Rosebery cabinet maneuvered down to 1895 to deny to the appointive unofficial members of the Legislative Council their growing influence as the majority caucus in that body, and when for nearly a decade thereafter in the period of urban nationalism Joseph Chamberlain, secretary of state for the colonies in Lord Salisbury's Conservative-Unionist government, employed a retrogressive imperial policy to strengthen the hand of Crown Colony government in Trinidad.

But whether it acted as a progressive force or as the opposite, imperial rule in Trinidad was often scored for its heavyhanded methods and for its iron determination to advance politically and constitutionally only by small, halting steps. The sharpest criticism was registered, of course, by the reformers. But it availed them little, because the pattern of mixing progressivism with deep conservatism in imperial policy had the effect of keeping the reform movement divided and off-balance. Finding themselves in this condition throughout the century down to the First World War, the mostly white, middle-class reformers found it useful to try to accommodate themselves politically to the system of Crown Colony government which they professed to abhor. This tendency was encouraged by periodically rewarding key interests in the reform movement with minor political concessions—though always within the framework of the constitutional status quo.

Blending custom and interest, authoritarian rule in British Trinidad favored political accommodation, as necessary, over despotism. Whatever social and political change occurred during the first century of British rule in the island colony derived substantially from the pattern of political accommodation between government and the most influential private interests—supportive *and* antagonistic—that collected around government.

Based on a fundamental mutuality of interest that transcended even sharp differences over concrete issues of public policy, the pattern of political accommodation helped define the limits of authoritarian rule in Trinidad and encouraged a slow evolution in its constitutional and political life. The mostly white reformers knew that their status as members of a privileged racial minority was secure in a social pyramid bound up with the system of Crown Colony government—a system whose primacy over all other interests the mostly foreign-born high officials in the colony's government were expected by London to uphold. Under this sociopolitical arrangement, reformers would press publicly—or more discreetly in private—for some modest advance in Trinidad's public life, causing the imperial power either to grant the concession or to promise its future consideration. After much maneuvering on the matter, a concession might be granted in some form—such as the designation in the last quarter of the nineteenth century of the appointive unofficials as the majority caucus in the colony's legislature. Or the Colonial Office might itself propose a concession, which certain key elements in the reform movement would then denounce as immoderate. In that event, the imperial power might acquiesce in a more moderate political advance—such as the qualification to be adopted in 1914 for the restored elective Borough Council in Port-of-Spain. In this way, governmental or private interests that opposed social and political change on some matter of public policy could be confident that their opposition to the policy had had the effect that they intended, that of endorsing change by an acceptably small increment. This arrangement worked well until the 1890s, when, for the first time, reformist whites and colored creoles took up high offices in the colony's government. Their appointments were coincident with a growing political ferment among colored professionals and the black laboring class in the capital. The appointment of Chamberlain to the Colonial Office in 1895 instituted a retrogressive imperial policy toward reformism in Trinidad and in other crown colonies in the British Empire. Assertive and stubborn, Chamberlain abjured the old political arrangement in Trinidad that allowed even those who opposed social and political change on some matter of public policy the safety valve of a role in helping to moderate an inevitable advance. For his own immoderation, Chamberlain was rewarded with the explosive crises in Port-of-Spain over the Borough Council and the water issue. Soon after his departure from office in 1903, there was restored in Trinidad the old political game of integrating the slow pace of political advance in the Crown Colony with the process of political accommodation that encouraged even the resisters of change to help map its course.

By the time of the water riot in March 1903, other sections of the population had already begun to emerge from their long political somnolescence—urban blacks, who had been radicalized by the water issue in the capital, and Indians, whose political awakening in the country districts and in small rural towns had been stirred by black assertiveness.

By that time, too, new methods of political expression had been tried in Trinidad and found useful—agitation, mass mobilization, and violence. With these developments, urban nationalism had helped prepare the ground for the coming era of decolonizing nationalism, in which, as seen, the old political game was adjusted to accommodate a new class of political claimants with their new political methods. In the ensuing long nationalist struggle, which would culminate a half century later in political independence for the Crown Colony, there would be yet another affirmation of the principal lesson of *Urban Nationalism:* that there are indeed limits to authoritarian rule and that within those limits the future is apt to unfold as much from the actions of those who try to hold it back as from the actions of those who labor for it.

Notes

CHAPTER 1. *Imperial Administration and the Urban Factor in Nationalism*

1. References in this study to "British imperial administration" apply generally to the imperial network organized around the Colonial Office in London together with the governments in the various colonies. References to "colonial administration" and to "colonial government" apply specifically to the governments in the colonies.
2. J. Kelly, *Organizational Behavior,* 448–60. Complete citations can be found in the Bibliography.
3. R. V. Kubicek, *The Administration of Imperialism: Joseph Chamberlain at the Colonial Office,* 68–91.
4. P. Selznick, *Leadership in Administration,* 17, 21.
5. See, for example, the essays in A. Richards (ed.), *East African Chiefs: A Study of Political Development in Some Uganda and Tanganyika Tribes;* L. Fallers, "The Predicament of the Modern African Chief: An Instance from Uganda," 295–305.
6. See A. Magid, *Men in the Middle: Leadership and Role Conflict in a Nigerian Society,* 9–10, and "'Role Theory,' Political Science, and African Studies," 317–19.
7. The Crown Colony of Trinidad and Tobago, which obtained its independence from Great Britain in 1962, consists of the two islands named plus sixteen very small islands (twelve off the coast of Trinidad, four off the coast of Tobago). Trinidad, the most southerly island in the Caribbean archipelago, is situated about 10.4 kilometers (6.25 miles) off the northeast coast of Venezuela near the mouth of the Orinoco River; Trinidad and Tobago are located about 10–11 degrees north of the equator. The two islands have a total area of about 5,130 square kilometers (1,980 square miles), 4,825 square kilometers on Trinidad island and 300 on Tobago island. The island of Trinidad is generally flat with a mountain range spanning its northern sector; the highest peak is nearly 950 meters (3,100 feet). Tobago is situated northeast of Trinidad, separated from it by a channel about 30 kilometers (18 miles) wide. Tobago has a central chain of peaks, its main ridge reaching a height of about 550 meters (1,800 feet).

8. See, for example, Kubicek, *Administration of Imperialism*, passim; J. Rutherford, *Sir George Grey, 1812–1898: A Study in Colonial Government;* P. Knaplund, *James Stephen and the British Colonial System, 1813–1847;* R. Hyam, "The Colonial Office Mind 1900–1914."
9. Kubicek, 13–42; C. Parkinson, *The Colonial Office from Within, 1909–1945;* D. Young, *The Colonial Office in the Early Nineteenth Century;* R. Furse, *Aucuparius: Reflections of a Recruiting Officer.*
10. Kubicek, passim; R. Hyam, *Elgin and Churchill at the Colonial Office 1905–1908: The Watershed of the Empire-Commonwealth.*
11. See, for example, P. Reinsch, *Colonial Government: An Introduction to the Study of Colonial Institutions;* D. Cameron, *The Principles of Native Administration and Their Application;* F. Lugard, *The Dual Mandate in British Tropical Africa;* F. Lugard, *Political Memoranda, 1913–1918.*
12. See, for example, M. Perham, *Lugard: The Years of Authority, 1898–1945;* D. Cameron, *My Tanganyika Service and Some Nigeria;* G. Carmichael, *The History of the West Indian Islands of Trinidad and Tobago, 1498–1900.*
13. See, for example, R. Heussler, *The British in Northern Nigeria* and *Yesterday's Rulers: The Making of the British Colonial Service;* P. Woodruff, *The Men Who Ruled India;* K. Bradley, *Once a District Officer.*
14. W. J. Hanna and J. L. Hanna, *Urban Dynamics in Black Africa: An Interdisciplinary Approach,* 11–12.
15. P. R. Gould, "Problems of Structuring and Measuring Spatial Changes in the Modernization Process: Tanzania 1920–1963"; E. W. Soja, *The Geography of Modernization in Kenya: A Spatial Analysis of Social, Economic, and Political Change.* Social analyses based on the spatial conception of the modernization process can be found in R. H. Bates, "Ethnic Competition and Modernization in Contemporary Africa," 464–67; R. Dishman, "Cultural Pluralism and Bureaucratic Neutrality in the British Caribbean," 295–97; M. Hechter and M. Levi, "The Comparative Analysis of Ethnoregional Movements," 264–66.
16. Hanna and Hanna, *Urban Dynamics,* 2–6. Also see A. Toynbee, *Cities on the Move,* 67–152.
17. J. S. Coleman, *Nigeria: Background to Nationalism,* 178.
18. See, for example, R. Emerson, *From Empire to Nation: The Rise to Self-Assertion of Asian and African Peoples;* J. Kautsky (ed.), *Political Change in Underdeveloped Countries: Nationalism and Communism,* 30–56; B. C. Shafer, *Nationalism: Myth and Reality,* 3–11; L. L. Snyder, *The New Nationalism.*
19. Kautsky, 39.
20. See, for example, J. S. Coleman, "Nationalism in Tropical Africa."
21. See, for example, T. Hodgkin, *Nationalism in Colonial Africa,* 23.
22. A. Kalleberg, "The Logic of Comparison: A Methodological Note on the Comparative Study of Political Systems," 72.
23. A. Stinchcombe, *Constructing Social Theories,* 6.
24. It should be noted that other lesser municipalities in a colony may also be the foci of modernization and of "urban nationalism." From late in the era of

Spanish rule in Trinidad through the long era of British rule, Port-of-Spain was the principal urban "node" or "central place" from which modernity spread. Similarly, it was the center of urban nationalism in British Trinidad in the two decades preceding the outbreak of the First World War.

25. J. W. Cell, *British Colonial Administration in the Mid-Nineteenth Century: The Policy-Making Process*, 43, 220ff.; Kubicek, 24, 28, 30–33, 97, 108–9.

26. W. L. Strauss, *Joseph Chamberlain and the Theory of Imperialism;* Cell, 3–44; Kubicek, passim.

27. See chap. 3, sec. VII and VIII; chap. 5; chap. 7, sec. I; chap. 8, sec. I.

28. See chap. 4, sec. V and VI.

29. A. Bertram, *The Colonial Service*, 1n.; G. K. Lewis, "British Colonialism in the West Indies: The Political Legacy"; Cell, 45–77.

30. The governor was appointed by the secretary of state for the colonies and was subject to transfer or dismissal at his pleasure. The role of the secretary of state in making gubernatorial appointments was sometimes circumscribed by patronage considerations and by the political influence of special interests.

31. In the official ranking for Crown Colony officials, the governor was followed by the chief justice, the latter by the colonial secretary.

32. See chap. 8, sec. X and XI. Also see Bertram, 22–25; H. A. Will, *Constitutional Change in the British West Indies, 1880–1903, with Special Reference to Jamaica, British Guiana, and Trinidad*, 227–87. By 1903, unofficial members had been appointed to most Executive Councils in the British West Indies colonies. The Crown Colony of Trinidad was a notable exception.

33. See chap. 8, sec. X and XI.

34. Bertram, 31; Cell, 60–61. References in *Urban Nationalism* to "colonial secretary" apply specifically to that office in various British colonies, including Trinidad. This point is emphasized to avoid confusing the colonial secretary in any particular British colony with the secretary of state for the colonies in London—especially since the latter official was often referred to in the shorthand form as the "colonial secretary."

35. See chap. 8, sec. III, IV, X, and XI.

36. Great Britain, House of Commons, *British Sessional Papers*, vol. 7, *Cmd. 2884* (1927), 70. This passage is from the memorandum on secretariat organization that Clifford prepared for the Colonial Office Conference of 1927.

37. Bertram, 31.

38. Cell, 61–62. There are also parallels between the colonial secretary and the permanent secretary in a modern British ministry, especially with regard to their role in departmental administration and legislative affairs. See W. J. M. Mackenzie and J. W. Grove, *Central Administration in Britain*, 185–88.

39. Not all colonial secretaries were preoccupied with administrative details. Some preferred to delegate this responsibility to experienced subordinates. See, for example, Cameron, *My Tanganyika Service*, 145–52.

40. Will, x; S. Ryan, *Race and Nationalism in Trinidad and Tobago: A Study of Decolonization in a Multiracial Society*, 6.

CHAPTER 2. *Spanish Trinidad: Colonization, Town Life, and Constitutional Development*

1. E. L. Joseph, *History of Trinidad,* 117ff.; L. A. Newson, *Aboriginal and Spanish Colonial Trinidad: A Study in Culture Contact,* 71ff.
2. Newson, 107ff.; C. Reis, *A History of the Constitution or Government of Trinidad from the Earliest Times to the Present Day,* 29.
3. Reis, 30.
4. C. R. Ottley, *The Story of Port-of-Spain: Capital of Trinidad West Indies from the Earliest Times to the Present Day,* 11–12; Newson, 17.
5. Newson, 17.
6. See chap. 4, sec. VII. Also see L. M. Fraser, *History of Trinidad from 1781 to 1813,* 4–8.
7. Newson, 122.
8. The illegal slave trade brought the first black slaves to Trinidad early in the seventeenth century.
9. See chap. 4, sec. II.
10. Reis, 34–35; Joseph, 161; Newson, 118.
11. Joseph, 161; Newson, 184.
12. Newson, 180.
13. Fraser, 9.
14. G. Carmichael, *The History of the West Indian Islands of Trinidad and Tobago, 1498–1900,* 363–69; Joseph, 161–65.
15. The more benevolent Spanish law in the matter of slavery was destined to be an important factor in the decision to establish a system of Crown Colony government in Trinidad after the conquest by Great Britain. See chap. 3, sec. I and II.
16. See note 8 and chap. 3, sec. I–III.
17. Joseph, 172.
18. Capt. F. Mallet, *Descriptive Account of the Island of Trinidad.*
19. Ibid.
20. See chap. 3, sec. I; Fraser, 133–53.
21. CO 295/6 (1802).
22. Newson, 188.
23. CO 295/6 (1802).
24. Newson, 193.
25. Joseph, 172.
26. Ibid., 178.
27. G. K. Lewis, *The Growth of the Modern West Indies,* 39.
28. Reis, 45–46; Joseph, 177–81; Fraser, 95–106.
29. Newson, 107–10.
30. A. F. Ponte, *Bolivar y Ensayos,* 30.
31. H. E. Bolton, "The Mission as a Frontier Institution in Spanish American Colonies," 46.
32. See chap. 4, note 6.
33. The three terms refer to the offspring of, respectively, a white and a black, a white and an Amerindian, and a black and an Amerindian.

34. See chap. 2, sec. V.
35. Newson, 113.
36. See chap. 3, sec. II; chap. 4, sec. VII.
37. Reis, 35–37.
38. Ibid., 37.
39. Carmichael, 34–35; Joseph, 155–56.
40. The new policy direction was to involve liberalizing immigration and reorganizing colonial administration.
41. J. Lynch, *Spanish Colonial Administration, 1782–1810: The Intendant System in the Viceroyalty of the Río de la Plata,* 11.
42. Carmichael, 375–76.
43. Lynch, 46.
44. Newson, 178.
45. P. G. L. Borde, *Histoire de l'île de la Trinidad sous le Gouvernement Espagnol,* 141.
46. Ibid., 198–203.
47. Ibid.
48. Fraser, 106.
49. Great Britain, *Hansard,* 1801, 36, 96.
50. Throughout this study, references are made generally to the "reform movement," to a group of people who, whatever their specific goals and actions, were linked in nineteenth-century Trinidad by a common interest in "reform," often loosely defined. The concept of "reform movement" is not intended to denote a high degree of political organization, integration, or goal-sharing among the "reformers."

CHAPTER 3. British Trinidad: The Rise and Fall of Reform Politics in the Nineteenth Century

1. Great Britain, Cobbett, *Parliamentary Debates,* 1811, 20, 620.
2. For a critique of Spanish law in British Trinidad, see Great Britain, *Hansard,* 1822, new series, 7, 1815–38.
3. H. Wrong, *Government of the West Indies,* 137; *Hansard,* 1822, 1843. Also see G. K. Lewis, *Main Currents in Caribbean Thought: The Historical Evolution of Caribbean Society in Its Ideological Aspects, 1492–1900,* 94–238; and B. W. Higman, *Slave Populations of the British Caribbean 1807–1834.*
4. The principle of Crown Colony government is examined in P. Reinsch, *Colonial Government,* 167–237; Bertram, *The Colonial Sevice,* 1n. The establishment of Crown Colony government in Trinidad is examined in L. M. Fraser, *History of Trinidad;* J. Millette, *The Genesis of Crown Colony Government: Trinidad, 1783–1810;* and D. J. Murray, *The West Indies and the Development of Colonial Government, 1801–1834,* 67–88.
5. Its advisory role in colony affairs having been delimited under the administration of Governor José María Chacón, the cabildo looked upon the new Council of Advice as its principal rival for the ear of the British governor.
6. *Parliamentary Debates,* 1807, 9, 146, 147; T. Clarkson, *The History of the Rise, Progress, and Accomplishment of the Abolition of the African Slave Trade by the British Parliament,* 578.

7. The Act of Parliament abolishing slavery in the British Empire was passed on August 28, 1833, and took effect on August 1, 1834.
8. D. Hart, *Trinidad and the Other West India Islands and Colonies,* 200.
9. The evolution of municipal government in nineteenth-century Port-of-Spain is examined in chap. 4, sec. VII.
10. See Great Britain, House of Commons, "Report by the Hon. E. F. L. Wood, MP, on His Visit to the West Indies and British Guiana, December 1921–February 1922"; Ryan, *Race and Nationalism in Trinidad and Tobago,* 30–34; E. Williams, *History of the People of Trinidad and Tobago,* 215–20.
11. The aboriginal Amerindian population having been decimated under harsh Spanish rule, the two major nonwhite groups were the blacks, descendants of African slaves, and the Indians, who were brought from the Asian subcontinent to Trinidad as indentured labor for the sugar estates. Among the blacks in Trinidad was a small minority from other islands in the British West Indies, including Barbados, Grenada, St. Vincent, and St. Lucia. See I. M. Cumpston, *Indians Overseas in British Territories, 1834–1854;* Lewis, *The Growth of the Modern West Indies;* "Report from the West India Royal Commission with Appendices A and B, Appendix C Volumes 1 and 2, and Other Papers Relating to the Sugar Industry, 1877–1898," *British Parliamentary Papers 1898;* H. A. Will, *Constitutional Change in the British West Indies, 5;* Williams, *History of the People of Trinidad and Tobago,* 65–121, 151–66; E. Williams, *Capitalism and Slavery.*
12. The impoverishment of the laboring class in Trinidad and throughout the British West Indies in the mid-nineteenth century is examined in W. G. Sewell, *The Ordeal of Free Labor in the British West Indies.*
13. C. B. Franklin, *After Many Days: A Memoir, Being a Sketch of the Life and Labors of Rev. Alexander Kennedy,* 51 (emphasis in original).
14. The public debt grew rapidly in Trinidad largely as a result of the subsidies for Indian immigration. In 1871, Parliament voted a loan of £125,000 to help the Crown Colony to pay off its staggering debts. See Great Britain, *Parliamentary Papers,* 1847–48 (62), no. 10, 539, 540; ibid., 1871, 20 (1393), 41.
15. D. Wood, *Trinidad in Transition: The Years after Slavery,* 101–67.
16. By 1970, the Indians—who included Hindus, Moslems, and Christians—constituted 40.1 percent of the total population of 931,000, the blacks 42.8 percent. Because the Indians' birth rate is substantially higher than that of the rest of the population, they seem destined to become the largest—perhaps even the majority—group in Trinidad. This development is apt to intensify social and political strains in that small, plural society. See J. Harewood, *The Population of Trinidad and Tobago,* 95, 97; Y. K. Malik, *East Indians in Trinidad: A Study in Minority Politics;* and Ryan, 363–83.
17. Wood, 138, 153–57, 302–4.
18. By the mid-nineteenth century, black idleness throughout the island and particularly in Port-of-Spain was a matter of great concern to officials in the Crown Colony. See Great Britain, *Parliamentary Papers,* 1847, 38 (160), 19, no. 58, Harris to Grey, September 4, 1846; ibid., 1847–48, 23, Pt. 3 (245), 276, Harris to Grey, February 21, 1848; ibid., 1852–53, 67, Pt. 3 (936), 163, no. 21, Harris to Pakington, May 18, 1851.

19. See note 16.
20. Wood, 171–237.
21. The word "creole," from the Spanish "criollo," was first applied to any person, regardless of racial, ethnic, or religious background, who was born and raised in Trinidad. In time, it came to be applied more frequently throughout the West Indies to Negroes born there. The word is employed here in its original, broader sense. Thus, for example, French Catholic creoles are persons of French Catholic background who were born and raised in Trinidad.
22. B. Samaroo, "Constitutional and Political Development of Trinidad, 1898–1925," 19–23.
23. M. Duverger, *Political Parties: Their Organization and Activity in the Modern State,* 62–71.
24. The first president of the Trinidad Workingmen's Association was Walter Mills, another colored pharmacist in Port-of-Spain. By 1906, the leadership included Richards, who was part Chinese, part black (president); Adrien Hilarion, a black tailor (vice-president); and a steering committee whose members included a carpenter, a mason, a planter, and a commission agent. The association reportedly had 233 members that year, mostly black workers. CO 295/436. Clifford to Elgin, April 24, 1906, 108. Also see chap. 9, sec. II, and chap. 10, sec. V–VII.
25. Great Britain, *Parliamentary Papers,* 1882, 40 (C.3388), 153; ibid., 1898, 50 (C.8655), 105; ibid., 1902, 65 (C.788–9), 12. Also see the London *Times,* October 30, 1894. The Pitch Lake at LaBrea was proving to be a valuable economic resource. See chap. 10, sec. II.
26. See chap. 6, sec. I.
27. See, for example, Port-of-Spain *Gazette,* December 1, 1883.
28. Verteuil was a staunch defender of French creole and Trinidadian interests in social and economic affairs. For example, he pressed for liberalization of the Crown lands policy. Verteuil expected that the sale of large parcels of cheap land for cocoa cultivation would benefit younger French and other creoles, especially those who, working as managers and clerks on sugar estates controlled by expatriate British interests, had little opportunity for advancement. CO 295/235. Verteuil to Manners-Sutton, March 18, 1865. Also see A. de Verteuil, *Sir Louis de Verteuil: His Life and Times, Trinidad 1800–1900.*
29. See chap. 4, sec. VII, and chap. 9, sec. II.
30. Port-of-Spain *Gazette,* May 1, 1891.
31. See, for example, the reports of the commission meetings of February 10 and March 22, 1888, in Port-of-Spain *Gazette,* February 15 and March 24, 1888.
32. See, for example, CO 295/356. Broome to Ripon, no. 419, August 31, 1894. 16634. Minute by Wingfield, October 1, 1894; and CO 295/363. Broome to Ripon, no. 186, May 15, 1895. 9411. Minute by Selborne, August 3, 1895.
33. CO 295/321. Robinson to Knutsford, no. 5, January 2, 1889. 1407. Minute by Wingfield, January 23, 1889; CO 380/147/22. Additional instructions to the governor, February 8, 1889; and CO 380/147/22. Knutsford to Robinson, February 13, 1889.
34. CO 295/325. Knutsford to Robinson, no. 16, February 3, 1890. 1208.
35. CO 295/340. Ripon to Broome, no. 2, January 3, 1893. 23903; and CO

380/147/26. Additional instructions to the governor, February 8, 1893.

36. J. A. R. Marriott, *Modern England, 1885–1932: A History of My Own Times,* 75; J. A. Spender, *Great Britain: Empire and Commonwealth, 1886–1935,* 80.

37. Will, *Constitutional Change.*

38. CO 295/350. Ripon to Broome, August 29, 1893, enclosed with Broome to Ripon, August 13, 1893. A strong objection to the Ripon proposal to appoint reformers to the Legislative Council was registered by the planters' representative, the West India Committee, which claimed that such an action would incite class feeling in the colony. Its protest failed to sway the Colonial Office. CO 298/52. Lubbock to Ripon, November 14, 1893, in Council Paper 3 of 1894. Also CO 298/52. Wingfield to Lubbock, December 5, 1893, enclosed with Lubbock to Ripon, November 14, 1893.

39. J. L. Garvin, *The Life of Joseph Chamberlain,* 3–214.

40. See, for example, the comments on Chamberlain in B. Webb, *Our Partnership,* 123, 131, 190–91, 293.

41. For an examination of imperialism as a major factor in the declining British national economy after the 1870s, see B. Porter, *The Lion's Share: A Short History of British Imperialism, 1850–1970.* Great Britain's difficult relations with other imperial powers during Chamberlain's years as secretary of state for the colonies are examined in Spender, *Great Britain,* 118–95. His role during the South African crisis is examined in Kubicek, *The Administration of Imperialism,* 92–116. Despite Chamberlain's "pro-Americanism," relations between Great Britain and the United States, a growing power in the Caribbean, were not without difficulties. See, for example, the conflict between these two powers in the "Venezuelan crisis" of 1895, in E. R. May, *Imperial Democracy: The Emergence of America as a Great Power,* 33–55. Also see Spender, 84–85.

42. See chap. 5.

43. C. Lucas, *Historical Geography of the British Colonies,* 70–71.

44. J. Froude, *The English in the West Indies, or the Bow of Ulysses,* 262; Chamberlain to Dilke, April 15, 1896, *Chamberlain Papers,* JC5/24/563 (quoted in Will, 232). Froude's deprecating view of blacks and the West Indies is assailed in J. J. Thomas, *Froudacity: West Indian Fables by James Anthony Froude.*

45. CO 295/363. Broome to Ripon, no. 186, May 15, 1895. 9411. Minute by Chamberlain, November 3, 1895.

46. Ibid.

47. CO 295/363. Chamberlain to Broome, no. 323, November 14, 1895. 9411.

48. Ibid.; and CO 295/363. Broome to Ripon, no. 186, May 15, 1895. 9411. Minute by Selborne, August 3, 1895.

49. CO 295/369. Broome to Chamberlain, no. 10, January 14, 1896. 2786.

50. CO 295/386. Knollys to Chamberlain, no. 226, June 14, 1898. 15180. Knollys's contention was subsequently assailed by the governor of Trinidad, Sir Hubert Jerningham. CO 295/387. Jerningham to Chamberlain, no. 380, October 4, 1898. 24120.

51. CO 295/386. Knollys to Chamberlain, no. 226, June 14, 1898. 15180. Minute by Wingfield, August 13, 1898.
52. CO 380/147/29. Royal Instructions, October 31, 1898; and CO 295/386, Chamberlain to Jerningham, no. 370, November 1, 1898. 15180.
53. "Report from the West India Royal Commission."
54. CO 318/291. Colonial Office to Treasury Department, January 24, 1898. 761. Also see chap. 10, sec. II.
55. C. Lucas, "Memorandum on the Report of the West India Royal Commission," October 1896, CO 884/5, Confidential Prints, West Indian, no. 79.
56. Ibid.
57. Vincent Brown was not the first colored person to hold high office in the Crown Colony. Maxwell Phillip, a colored barrister, was mayor of Port-of-Spain in the years 1867–70. The first colored person to be nominated as an unofficial member of the Legislative Council was Dr. Stephen Laurence, who served from 1911 to 1924. Before Laurence, the first black nominated as an unofficial in the Legislative Council was C. Prudhomme David, a barrister who entered the legislature in 1904. See chap. 10, sec. V.
58. Will, 292. In the Crown Colony, the Indian population did not follow suit until a generation later, after the First World War. Evidence of a growing political consciousness in that community could be found before the outbreak of the war. See chap. 10, sec. V.

CHAPTER 4. *Port-of-Spain: The Strains of Growth in a Nineteenth-Century Colonial Capital*

1. Fraser, *History of Trinidad,* 124–29; Froude, *The English in the West Indies,* 63; C. Kingsley, *At Last: A Christmas in the West Indies,* 76; Sir W. Robinson, "Trinidad: Its Capabilities and Prominent Products," 273–74.
2. The data for the table and for the explication in the text are drawn from CO 295/6 (1802); Trinidad and Tobago, *Census Album,* 12–15; Mallet, *Descriptive Account of the Island of Trinidad.*
3. See chap. 3, note 16.
4. CO 295/156. Harris to Grey, January 16, 1847.
5. The development of Port-of-Spain particularly in the nineteenth century is highlighted in Wood, *Trinidad in Transition;* J. H. Collens, *A Guide to Trinidad: A Handbook for the Use of Tourists and Visitors,* 52ff.; Ottley, *The Story of Port-of-Spain,* 21–213.
6. While population data are not entirely reliable for the early years of Spanish rule in Trinidad, it is estimated that there may have been as many as 200,000 Amerindians in 1534 but fewer than 600 by 1840. Newson, *Aboriginal and Spanish Colonial Trinidad,* 29–33; Great Britain, *Parliamentary Papers,* 1839, 34 (35), 86.
7. Lawyers and estate managers in Trinidad administered the interests of the propertied class residing in Great Britain.
8. Great Britain, *Parliamentary Papers,* 1852–53, 67 (1936), 163, Pt. 3, no. 21, Harris to Pakington, May 18, 1851.

9. Resentments were directed especially against foreign-born officials in the upper echelons of the Crown Colony government.

10. *Parliamentary Papers,* 1884–85, 52 (C.4366), 50.

11. The depth of that alienation would be revealed in the period of urban nationalism, 1895–1914, particularly in the Port-of-Spain water riot of March 23, 1903. See chap. 6.

12. Carmichael, *The History of the West Indian Islands of Trinidad and Tobago, 1498–1900,* 376.

13. Hart, *Trinidad and the Other West India Islands and Colonies,* 140–41; London *Times,* November 3, 1849.

14. London *Times,* ibid.

15. Hart, 142.

16. Ibid.

17. Ibid. Governor Harris's outward calm may have been intended to disguise his frustration over the fact that because of the large nonwhite majority in the colony and the capital, he would have to tolerate a certain amount of antisocial behavior "for the sake of some little peace and quiet." He expressed that view more than a year before the riot. Great Britain, *Parliamentary Papers,* 1847–48, 23, Pt. 3 (245), 276, Harris to Grey, February 21, 1848.

18. London *Times,* November 3, 1849.

19. *Parliamentary Papers,* 1884–85, 53 (C.4366), 41.

20. The epithet "coolie" was applied generally to indentured laborers, Indian and non-Indian, and, among the former, to Hindus and non-Hindus. It was applied with particular scorn to the Indian laborers and often also to their descendants.

21. Fires had broken out frequently in Port-of-Spain from the earliest days of Spanish rule. The town was destroyed by a great conflagration in 1808, at a time when the British were trying to consolidate their control over the island colony.

22. Port-of-Spain *Gazette,* November 25, 1845.

23. Trinidad *Spectator,* February 25, 1846.

24. E. W. Daniel, *West Indian Histories,* 339.

25. Trinidad *Sentinel,* March 4, 1858.

26. Port-of-Spain *Gazette,* March 19, 1859; Trinidad *Sentinel,* March 10, 1859.

27. Trinidad *Free Press,* February 22, 1860.

28. Trinidad *Star of the West,* February 15, 1866, February 11, 1869, February 23, 1871.

29. Port-of-Spain *Gazette,* February 17, 1866; Trinidad *Star of the West,* February 23, 1871.

30. A. Cohen, "Drama and Politics in the Development of a London Carnival," 334 (emphasis in original). Also see A. Pearse, "Carnival in Nineteenth Century Trinidad."

31. Trinidad *Star of the West,* February 7, 1868.

32. *Parliamentary Papers,* 1870, 44 (C.85), 47.

33. Port-of-Spain *Gazette,* July 13, 1859.

34. Ibid., June 14, 1865.
35. *Parliamentary Papers,* 1882, 44 (C.3388), 105.
36. Daniel, 340.
37. *Parliamentary Papers,* 1882, 44 (C.3388), 105.
38. Ibid., 1884–85, 53 (C.4366), 73. Also see London *Times,* March 10, 1884.
39. *Parliamentary Papers,* 1884–85, 53 (C.4366), 41, 42, 45.
40. Ibid., 42–46. Also see London *Times,* December 2, 1884.
41. London *Times,* November 29, December 2, 1884.
42. *Parliamentary Papers,* 1884–85, 53 (C.4366), 68.
43. H. Craig, *The Legislative Council of Trinidad and Tobago,* 77–79.
44. Reis, *A History of the Constitution or Government of Trinidad,* 205.
45. Ibid., 201.
46. See chap. 4, sec. II.
47. Reis, 215ff. With the population of Trinidad concentrated in and around Port-of-Spain and the other main towns, priority was given in the first half of the nineteenth century to developing local government at the municipal level. In the 1870s, vast tracts were opened in the Crown lands to promote agricultural production and to end squatting in the countryside (mostly by poor blacks and by Indians who had concluded their indenture service on the estates). With the establishment by the colony government of new villages based on squatter communities, there arose the need to develop the machinery of rural local government. The first efforts to improve rural administration were made just before mid-century. In 1847, Trinidad was divided into new administrative units: divisions, counties, districts, and wards (CO 297/4. Ordinance 11 of 1847). This arrangement proved unsatisfactory, so in 1849 the colony was reorganized with only two divisions, northern and southern, each with four counties. Each county was comprised of two districts, and the latter were subdivided into wards. Provision was made for the appointment of wardens by the governor. Initially, the office of warden was honorary; the officeholder was usually a prominent landowner residing in the ward. He was responsible for maintaining peace and order in his jurisdiction, for collecting local rates and taxes, for registering lands, houses, births, deaths, and marriages, for preparing the list of jurors, for overseeing the maintenance of Crown lands and public roads, and for the care of indigents. Ward expenditure was based on ward revenues (CO 297/4. Ordinances 8 and 9 of 1849). Because these numerous responsibilities were soon found to be too complex and burdensome for a part-time honorary official, beginning in 1854 the office of warden was filled by salaried appointees. In order to enhance the efficiency of rural administration, two or more contiguous wards were combined to form ward unions, each administered by a warden (CO 297/5. Ordinance 14 of 1854). (With the merger of Trinidad and financially straitened Tobago in 1888, the island of Tobago was constituted a ward under the administration of a resident warden [CO 380/147/20. Order-in-Council of November 17, 1888].) Along with establishing the office of warden as the pillar of rural local administration, the colony's government sought to improve the administration of public roads in the countryside. To that end,

in 1854 there was established a system of rural road boards, road unions, and a central road board; the central board was empowered to exercise an overall supervisory function, which included allocating funds to the rural road boards for construction and maintenance (CO 297/5. Ordinance 15 of 1854). In 1894, the elective principle was established for the rural road boards, and those bodies were given a wider latitude for administrative initiative.

48. Reis, 215.

CHAPTER 5. *Urban Nationalism I: The Colony, the Capital, and the Politics of Municipal Governance in Port-of-Spain*

1. J. Chamberlain, "Municipal Government—Past, Present, and Future."
2. Reis, *A History of the Constitution or Government of Trinidad,* 196–202.
3. Ibid., 90, 203.
4. CO 297/8. Section 28. Port-of-Spain Borough Council Ordinance 28 of 1868.
5. CO 297/9. Section 15. Port-of-Spain Borough Council Ordinance 23 of 1872.
6. CO 297/9. Sections 3 and 4. Port-of-Spain Borough Council Ordinance 27 of 1875.
7. CO 297/13. Port-of-Spain Borough Council Ordinance 29 of 1893.
8. CO 297/14. Port-of-Spain Borough Council Ordinance 14 of 1894.
9. CO 295/380. no. 305. Chamberlain to Jerningham, February 8, 1898, in Jerningham to Chamberlain, August 20, 1897.
10. CO 298/58. Port-of-Spain town clerk to colonial secretary, January 24, 1896, in Council Paper 193 of 1896.
11. CO 298/58. Commission Report. Council Paper 193 of 1896.
12. Ibid.
13. Ibid., par. 3.
14. Ibid.
15. Ibid. Alcazar minority report, p. 41.
16. Ibid. Lange minority report, p. 32.
17. CO 295/377. Knollys to mayor of Port-of-Spain, December 14, 1896, in Knollys to Chamberlain, January 11, 1897.
18. CO 295/377. Port-of-Spain town clerk to Knollys, December 21, 1896, enclosed with Knollys to Chamberlain, January 11, 1897.
19. CO 295/380. Jerningham to Chamberlain, August 20, 1897. This dispatch finally arrived at the Colonial Office on September 16, 1897.
20. CO 295/377. Knollys to Chamberlain, January 11, 1897. Minutes by Harris, August 9, 1897, and Ellis, August 10, 1897.
21. CO 295/380. no. 305. Jerningham to Chamberlain, August 20, 1897.
22. Ibid.
23. Ibid., encl. 4.
24. CO 295/380. no. 305. Jerningham to Chamberlain, August 20, 1897.
25. CO 295/380. no. 306. Jerningham to Chamberlain, August 20, 1897.
26. CO 295/380. no. 307. Jerningham to Chamberlain, August 21, 1897.
27. CO 295/380. no. 305. Jerningham to Chamberlain, August 20, 1897. Minute by C. P. L., September 20, 1897.

28. Ibid. Minute by E. W., October 3, 1897.
29. CO 295/380. no. 305. Chamberlain to Jerningham, February 8, 1898.
30. See chap. 3, sec. VIII and IX. See also Chamberlain, "Municipal Government," esp. pp. 656ff.
31. See chap. 3, sec. IX.
32. See chap. 4, sec. VII, and chap. 9, sec. II.
33. Chamberlain, "Municipal Government," 649.
34. See chap. 4, sec. VII, and chap. 9, sec. II.
35. Port-of-Spain *Gazette*, March 3, 1898.
36. Ibid.
37. CO 295/385. Jerningham to Chamberlain, March 26, 1898. Commission Report. Encl. 3.
38. CO 295/385. Jerningham to Lucas, March 31, 1898. Enclosed with Jerningham to Chamberlain, March 27, 1898.
39. CO 295/385. Jerningham to Chamberlain, March 26, 1898. Minute by W. D. E., April 19, 1898.
40. Ibid. Minute by J. C., April 29, 1898.
41. Port-of-Spain *Gazette*, editorial, April 7, 1898.
42. Ibid.
43. CO 295/385. Jerningham to Chamberlain, April 25, 1898. Minute by J. C., June 9, 1898.
44. CO 295/385. Chamberlain to Jerningham, August 31, 1898.
45. CO 295/385. Chamberlain to Jerningham (confidential), August 31, 1898.
46. CO 295/388. Jerningham to Chamberlain (confidential), October 27, 1898. Also see Port-of-Spain *Gazette*, October 20, 27, 1898.
47. CO 295/388. Jerningham to Chamberlain, November 24, 1898. Encl. 1.
48. Port-of-Spain *Gazette*, editorial, October 23, 1898.
49. Ibid., editorial, October 21, 1898.
50. Ibid.
51. Ibid., editorial, October 26, 1898.
52. Ibid., November 2, 1898.
53. CO 295/391. Jerningham to Chamberlain, January 5, 1899.
54. CO 295/388. no. 447. Jerningham to Chamberlain, December 8, 1898.
55. Ibid. Also see Port-of-Spain *Gazette*, December 6, 1898.
56. Sir H. Jerningham, "Crown Colony Government," 91ff.
57. CO 295/388. Jerningham to Chamberlain, December 22, 1898.
58. CO 297/16 (1899).
59. Port-of-Spain *Gazette*, editorials, January 17, 21, 25, 1899.
60. Trinidad and Tobago, *Royal Gazette*. Council Paper no. 203 of 1895, Broome to Ripon, May 15, 1895.
61. See chap. 3, sec. VIII.
62. Port-of-Spain *Gazette*, editorial, March 8, 1898. It should be noted that this statement appeared in the *Gazette* when the newspaper was a leading critic of Chamberlain's hardline policy toward the municipality. Its attitude toward the secretary of state became more affirmative six months later when radical sentiment began to take hold within the Borough Council and among the population of the capital. See chap. 5, sec. III.

63. Despite his apparent conciliatoriness toward the Port-of-Spain Borough Council on the municipal question, in fact Chamberlain had moved decisively against the reform movement in Trinidad at the colony and municipal levels. He had pursued a similarly retrogressive policy against Jamaica and British Guiana, albeit in a somewhat more cautious, hesitant manner. See Will, *Constitutional Change in the British West Indies,* 229–73.

64. It was expected by the imperial power that the appointed unofficials in colony legislatures would routinely support the Crown on important matters of policy. (See CO 854/9. Circular Despatch, August 17, 1868.) Desiring for reasons of prestige and politics to be reappointed, most unofficial members would usually fulfill that expectation.

65. Great Britain, *Parliamentary Papers,* 1884–85, 52, 67.

66. San Fernando and Arima were also in chronic financial distress, the result of insufficient revenues and jurisdictional conflicts with the Crown Colony government. See, for example, CO 298/521. Council Paper 60 of 1894 and Minutes of the Legislative Council, 1894, p. 35; CO 298/521. Minute no. 115, Council Paper 220 of 1894; and CO 297/15. Ordinance 24 of 1896. The ordinance empowered the governor to amend or revoke any municipal charter in the colony upon the signed petition of one-third of the burgesses. It was inspired by a public protest in Arima against the worsening financial condition of the municipality.

67. See chap. 3, sec. V.

68. See chap. 3, sec. IV.

69. Many reformers in the Crown Colony did finally admit that they had not been organized to deal effectively with a hostile, obdurate secretary of state at the Colonial Office. They urged that the reform movement work to establish itself as a political organization with a broad popular constituency. See, for example, the letter by W. G. Hales in the December 7, 1898, issue of the Port-of-Spain *Mirror,* the leading radical newspaper in Trinidad in the period of urban nationalism.

CHAPTER 6. *Urban Nationalism II: The Colony, the Capital, and the Politics of Water in Port-of-Spain*

1. See chap. 4, sec. II and III.

2. *The Commission of Enquiry into the Water Riots* (Port of Spain: Diocesan 1903), 534. (The official record of the Proceedings and Report is contained in Great Britain, House of Commons, "Report of the Commission of Enquiry into the Recent Disturbances at Port-of-Spain, Trinidad.")

3. See chap. 4, sec. II and III.

4. *The Commission of Enquiry,* 535.

5. Ibid., 536–37.

6. Ibid., 539–40.

7. See chap. 3, sec. V.

8. Port-of-Spain *Gazette,* editorial, April 29, 1899.

9. See chap. 5, sec. II–IV.

10. Port-of-Spain *Gazette,* April 22, 1897.

11. In fact, the record on civil liberties in Trinidad and the British West Indies was more positive than that encountered in most other colonial and post-colonial societies in the Third World. The extent of the difference may be marked by noting that in one pertinent study no reference is even made to Trinidad or to the British West Indies; see D. H. Bayley, *Public Liberties in the New States.*
12. Port-of-Spain *Gazette,* editorial, February 10, 1897.
13. Ibid., editorial, July 21, 1897.
14. See chap. 3, sec. VIII.
15. See chap. 5, sec. IV.
16. See chap. 3, sec. IV.
17. See chap. 5, sec. III.
18. Great Britain, *Parliamentary Papers,* 1898 (C.8657), Appendix C, Vol. 2, Pt. 4, 1795–1884 and 1883.
19. See chap. 10, sec. V. The Trinidad Workingmen's Association was destined to become a more effective organization after the First World War under the radical leadership of Arthur A. Cipriani, a Corsican creole. See Ryan, *Race and Nationalism in Trinidad and Tobago,* 28ff.; Williams, *History of the People of Trinidad and Tobago,* 212ff.
20. Port-of-Spain *Mirror,* September 10, 1901.
21. Ibid., October 30, 1901.
22. Report of the secretary of the Ratepayers' Association, cited ibid., October 7, 1902.
23. *The Commission of Enquiry,* 548.
24. Ibid., 548–49.
25. London *Times,* July 7, 1900; editorial in *Pan-African,* vol. 1, no. 1 (1901), 1.
26. Port-of-Spain *Mirror,* June 8, 1901.
27. Ibid., July 4, 1901.
28. Ibid., editorial, August 12, 1901.
29. See chap. 3, sec. VII.
30. See chap. 3, sec. IV.
31. The *Mirror* had a short but sparkling life as a radical newspaper. In December 1916, Richard Mole went bankrupt, forcing the newspaper to close after eighteen years of publication.
32. Port-of-Spain *Mirror,* March 10, 1902.
33. *The Commission of Enquiry,* 550–51.
34. See chap. 6, sec. III–V; chap. 7, sec. V and VII; chap. 8, sec. IV.
35. CO 295/388. Jerningham to Chamberlain, December 8, 1898.
36. CO 295/391. Jerningham to Chamberlain, January 19, 1899.
37. CO 295/391. Enclosed with Jerningham to Chamberlain, January 5, 1899.
38. Ibid.
39. Port-of-Spain *Gazette,* January 18, 1899. Also see chap. 5, sec. III.
40. CO 295/301. Enclosed with Jerningham to Chamberlain, February 2, 1899.
41. See chap. 5, sec. III.
42. Great Britain, *Hansard,* 4th series, 68, 1899, 1374–75.
43. See chap. 3, sec. V.

44. Port-of-Spain *Mirror,* editorial, August 10, 1901.

45. Ibid., editorial, August 14, 1901.

46. Ibid., September 4, 1901.

47. Ibid.

48. See chap. 3, sec. IV.

49. See chap. 6, sec. I.

50. Wrightson to the secretary of the Ratepayers' Association, March 21, 1902, cited in the Port-of-Spain *Mirror,* March 29, 1902.

51. C. P. David, "Loyalty in British Colonies."

52. London *Daily Telegraph,* March 29, 1902, cited in the Port-of-Spain *Mirror,* April 24, 1902.

53. Honorary secretary of the Trinidad Chamber of Commerce to the secretary of the Ratepayers' Association, cited in the Port-of-Spain *Mirror,* April 17, 1902.

54. Ibid., June 9, 1901.

55. Ibid., September 20, 1902.

56. Ibid., October 18, 1902.

57. See chap. 3, sec. VIII.

58. Port-of-Spain *Mirror,* October 18, 1902.

59. See chap. 6, sec. I.

60. Report of the secretary of the Ratepayers' Association, cited in the Port-of-Spain *Mirror,* October 18, 1902.

61. See chap. 2, sec. II and V.

62. P. Selznick, *TVA and the Grassroots,* 13–15.

63. See, for example, the notices in the Port-of-Spain *Mirror,* February 14, 28, 1903.

64. Great Britain, House of Commons, "Papers Relating to the Recent Disturbances at Port-of-Spain, Trinidad" (July 1903), encl. 1 in no. 12, 20–31.

65. CO 295/416. Moloney to Chamberlain, March 24, 1903.

66. *The Commission of Enquiry,* 545.

67. "Papers Relating to the Recent Disturbances," encl. 2 in no. 1, 2–6.

68. Port-of-Spain *Mirror,* editorial, February 28, March 6, 7, 1903; Port-of-Spain *Pioneer,* editorial, March 7, 1903.

69. Port-of-Spain *Mirror,* March 16, 1903.

70. CO 295/416. par. 5. Moloney to Chamberlain, March 24, 1903.

71. Port-of-Spain *Mirror,* March 17, 1903; Port-of-Spain *Gazette,* editorial, March 21, 1903.

72. CO 295/416. Enclosed with Moloney to Chamberlain, March 24, 1903.

73. The government notice appearing in the press characterized the ticket regulation as "in accordance with the practice of the Imperial Parliament." See Port-of-Spain *Mirror,* March 21, 1903.

74. Ibid., March 23, 1903.

75. CO 295/416. par. 13. Moloney to Chamberlain, March 24, 1903.

76. *The Commission of Enquiry,* 519.

77. Port-of-Spain *Mirror,* March 23, 25, 1903.

78. The remainder of this chapter is a summary of the events surrounding the

water riot, based upon the official record. Many more details are contained in that voluminous record, especially in the "Report of the Commission of Enquiry," 515–59.

79. Ibid., 521–22.
80. Ibid., 523.
81. Ibid., 524.
82. Ibid., 525.
83. The role of the warden in rural local government is highlighted in chap. 4, note 47.

CHAPTER 7. *Urban Nationalism III: A Painful Stocktaking*

1. See chap. 2, sec. I, and chap. 4, sec. IV.
2. See chap. 4, sec. IV–VI.
3. Froude, *The English in the West Indies*, 75.
4. See chap. 4, sec. III.
5. Great Britain, House of Commons, "Papers Relating to the Recent Disturbances at Port-of-Spain, Trinidad" (July 1903), no. 10, 8.
6. Ibid., no. 2, 6.
7. In his interesting study of imperial administration under Joseph Chamberlain, Robert Kubicek points out how colonial governors did sometimes use telegraph communication to heighten political tension in their own interest. The study of urban nationalism in Trinidad illustrates that that mode of communication could be used for their own purposes by diverse political interests, official and nonofficial. See Kubicek, *The Administration of Imperialism*, 32.
8. "Papers Relating to the Recent Disturbances," no. 3, 6–7.
9. See, for example, the Port-of-Spain *Mirror*, editorial, April 4, 1903.
10. "Papers Relating to the Recent Disturbances," no. 4, 7.
11. Ibid., no. 5, 7.
12. Ibid., no. 12, 15–20.
13. Ibid., no. 6, 8.
14. Ibid., no. 7, 8.
15. Ibid., no. 10, 9.
16. See chap. 3, sec. VII.
17. London *Times*, May 7, 1903.
18. "Papers Relating to the Recent Disturbances," no. 8, 8.
19. Ibid., no. 9, 8.
20. Ibid., no. 10, 9.
21. Ibid., no. 1, enclosure 1, 1–6; no. 11, 9; no. 12, enclosure 1, 20–31.
22. Ibid., no. 11, enclosure, 10–15.
23. Ibid., no. 12, 19–20 (emphasis in original).
24. See chap. 3, sec. I and VIII.
25. See chap. 3, sec. VIII.
26. CO 295/416. Moloney to Chamberlain, March 24, 1903. Minute by C. P. L., April 11, 1903.
27. "Papers Relating to the Recent Disturbances," no. 13, 45–46.

28. Ibid., no. 14, 47–62.
29. Ibid., no. 15, 62–63.
30. Ibid., no. 16, 63.
31. Ibid., no. 18, 63.
32. Ibid., no. 19, 64, no. 21, 65–66.
33. Ibid., no. 20, enclosure, 65. A full report from Captain Robertson is contained ibid., no. 22, enclosure, 66–68.
34. CO 295/417. Report by Major Johnstone. Enclosed with Moloney to Chamberlain (confidential), April 20, 1903.
35. CO 295/419. no. 380. Moloney to Chamberlain, August 14, 1903, 40.
36. Port-of-Spain *Mirror,* March 30, April 17, 1903.
37. Ibid., April 22, 28, 1903.
38. Ibid., April 24, 27, 1903.
39. See chap. 3, sec. V.
40. Port-of-Spain *Mirror,* April 4, 8, 1903.
41. Ibid., April 16, 1903.
42. CO 295/417. Enclosure 1 with Moloney to Chamberlain (confidential), April 20, 1903.
43. Port-of-Spain *Mirror,* April 17, 1903.
44. CO 295/417. Moloney to Chamberlain, April 24, 25, 1903.
45. CO 295/417. Moloney to Chamberlain, April 25, 1903.
46. CO 295/417. Moloney to Chamberlain (confidential), May 8, 1903. The Commission of Enquiry would also underline the need to regulate private firearms in the colony. See chap. 7, sec. VII.
47. "Papers Relating to the Recent Disturbances," no. 15, 62.
48. "Report from the West India Royal Commission ... Relating to the Sugar Industry."
49. *The Commission of Enquiry,* 505–6.
50. The major points in the Chadwick Report are highlighted ibid., 534ff.
51. See chap. 4, sec. II.
52. See chap. 6, sec. I and II.
53. "Papers Relating to the Recent Disturbances," no. 11, enclosure, 10–15.
54. *The Commission of Enquiry,* 536–38.
55. W. H. Mercer and A. E. Collins, *The Colonial List for 1905,* 534. The colonial secretary served as officer administering the government when the governor was absent from the colony or incapacitated or when a new appointee had not yet arrived to take up his post as governor. Also see chap. 1, sec. V.
56. See chap. 3, sec. VIII.
57. *The Commission of Enquiry,* 170.
58. Ibid., 358.
59. Ibid., 360.
60. Ibid., 488–505.
61. See chap. 3, sec. V. The cost of public works projects had long inspired political controversy in the colony.
62. *The Commission of Enquiry,* 475, 476, 481.
63. Ibid., 479.

64. Ibid., 480.
65. Ibid., 481.
66. See chap. 3, sec. VI.
67. *The Commission of Enquiry,* 482.
68. See chap. 5, sec. III.
69. Ibid.
70. The findings and recommendations of the commission are contained in *The Commission of Enquiry,* 518–59.
71. Ibid., 548; "Papers Relating to the Recent Disturbances," no. 5, 7.
72. *The Commission of Enquiry,* 545.
73. Ibid., 556.
74. Ibid., 558.
75. Ibid.
76. Ibid., 533.
77. Ibid., 38.
78. See chap. 7, sec. I.
79. *The Commission of Enquiry,* 548.
80. CO 295/419. Crown Law Officers Report in Moloney to Chamberlain, April 13, 1903.
81. CO 295/424. Wrightson to Bourne, July 13, 1903. Enclosed with the Report of the Commission of Enquiry sent to Chamberlain, July 2, 1903.
82. "Papers Relating to the Recent Disturbances," no. 23, 68–70; no. 24, enclosure, 70–71.
83. CO 295/424. James to Lucas (private letter), July 7, 1903. Enclosed with the Report of the Commission of Enquiry sent to Chamberlain, July 2, 1903.
84. *The Commission of Enquiry,* 548–49.
85. See note 83.
86. See chap. 3, sec. VIII and IX.

CHAPTER 8. Urban Nationalism IV: A New Normalcy

1. Port-of-Spain *Mirror,* May 25, 1903.
2. Lewis, *The Growth of the Modern West Indies,* 95–117.
3. Great Britain, House of Commons, "Papers Relating to the Recent Disturbances at Port-of-Spain, Trinidad" (July 1903), no. 26, 72.
4. CO 884/7. Chamberlain to Moloney, July 21, 1903. no. 124 in West Indian 122.
5. House of Commons, "Further Papers Relating to the Recent Disturbances at Port-of-Spain, Trinidad, in March 1903" (April 1904), no. 1, 3 (emphasis added). This passage is contained in a letter written by Chamberlain to Moloney on July 21, 1903.
6. See note 4.
7. Mercer and Collins, *The Colonial List for 1905,* 534.
8. Mercer and Collins, *The Colonial List for 1903,* 526.
9. CO 295/420. Moloney to Lyttelton, November 3, 1903. Lyttelton took charge of the Colonial Office on October 9, 1903.
10. See, for example, Clifford's *In Court and Kampong* (1897); *Since the Begin-*

ning (1898); *In a Corner of Asia* (1899); *Bushwhacking* (1901); *A Free-Lance of Today* (1903); *Further India* (1904); *Sally, A Study* (1904); *Heroes of Exile* (1906); *Saleh: A Sequel* (1908); *The Downfall of the Gods* (1911); *Malayan Monochromes* (1913); *The Further Side of Silence* (1916); *In Days That Are Dead* (1926); *A Prince of Malaya* (1926). Clifford was a friend of the novelist Joseph Conrad; they each periodically reviewed the other's manuscripts and published work. See F. R. Karl and L. Davies, eds., *The Collected Letters of Joseph Conrad,* 57–58, 129–30, 179–81, 189, 193–94, 199–202, 226–27, 404–5, 459–63.

11. *The Dictionary of National Biography, 1941–1950,* 158; also see Mercer and Collins, *The Colonial List for 1907,* 509.
12. Mercer and Collins, *The Colonial List for 1906,* 540.
13. J. de V. Allen, "Two Imperialists: A Study of Sir Frank Swettenham and Sir Hugh Clifford," 43–44.
14. H. Clifford, "Life in the Malay Peninsula: As It Was and Is" and "British and Siamese Malaya."
15. See the Foreword (especially ix–xi) in Clifford's book *Sally, A Study.*
16. H. Clifford, *The German Colonies: A Plea for the Native Races.*
17. Clifford's role as governor of Nigeria is examined in H. A. Galley, "Sir Hugh Clifford (1856–1941)"; I. F. Nicolson, *The Administration of Nigeria, 1900–1960: Men, Methods, and Myths,* 216ff.; I. M. Okonjo, *British Administration in Nigeria, 1900–1950: A Nigerian View,* 83–124.
18. For his distinguished service in the British Empire, Clifford was awarded the C.M.G. in 1900, the K.C.M.G. in 1909, the G.C.M.G. in 1921, and the G.B.E. in 1925.
19. *The Dictionary of National Biography,* 158.
20. A warm appreciation of Clifford as a ladies' man can be found in the memoirs of Leonard Woolff, who as a cadet would later serve under him in Ceylon. See L. Woolff, *Growing: An Autobiography of the Years 1904–1911,* 170. The first Mrs. Clifford died several months after having been thrown from a horse. Her many social activities in Trinidad were extolled in an obituary in the Port-of-Spain *Catholic News,* January 19, 1907.
21. In its issue of July 25, 1903, the Port-of-Spain *Pioneer* predicted that, as the new special colonial secretary, Clifford would "to all intents and purposes . . . be the real Governor of the Colony."
22. House of Commons, *British Sessional Papers,* vol. 7 (1927), 69–72. This citation is of a memorandum by Clifford on the modernization of administration in British Crown Colonies. At the time, he was governor of Ceylon. Also see chap. 1, sec. V.
23. Port-of-Spain *Mirror,* editorial, September 29, 1903.
24. Trinidad and Tobago, *Hansard,* 1903, 158.
25. On the eve of his departure from the Crown Colony, Governor Moloney expressed high praise for Clifford to the secretary of state. See Trinidad and Tobago. *Despatches to Secretary of State, 1904,* Moloney to Lyttelton, March 25, 1904; also see the tribute to Clifford from the Trinidad Chamber of Commerce in Port-of-Spain *Mirror* (Supplement), March 16, 1904. Clifford also

had detractors, among them Dr. Stephen M. Laurence, a colored physician who served as an unofficial member in the Legislative Council from 1911 to 1921. See K. O. Laurence, "The Trinidad Water Riot of 1903: Reflections of an Eyewitness," 15, 17.

26. Port-of-Spain *Mirror,* August 31, 1904.

27. Trinidad and Tobago. National Archives. 7304/1903. Mole to Clifford (private letter), November 17, 1903; Clifford to Mole (private letter), November 18, 1903 (emphasis in original); Mole to Clifford (private letter), November 25, 1903.

28. See chap. 7, sec. VIII.

29. CO 295/424. Wrightson to Bourne, July 13, 1903. Enclosed with the Report of the Commission of Enquiry sent to Chamberlain, July 2, 1903.

30. "Further Papers Relating to the Recent Disturbances," no. 1, 4.

31. CO 295/419. Moloney to Lyttelton, October 7, 1903.

32. Ibid; CO 295/421. Moloney to Lyttelton, December 2, 1903.

33. CO 295/424. James to Lucas (private letter), July 7, 1903. Enclosed with the Report of the Commission of Enquiry sent to Chamberlain, July 2, 1903.

34. CO 295/419. Moloney to Lyttelton, October 7, 1903. Minute by R. V. V., October 24, 1903 (emphasis in original); minute by H. C. B., October 26, 1903.

35. See chap. 5, sec. II.

36. CO 295/419. Moloney to Lyttelton, October 7, 1903. Minute by A. L., October 28, 1903.

37. See chap. 3, sec. III. Fires of unexplained origin, regarded by many as incendiarism (in Port-of-Spain in 1883, 1884, and 1895, and in San Fernando in 1884), were of great concern. See Great Britain, *Parliamentary Papers,* 1884–85, 52, 65; ibid., 1897, 59, 12. Also see C. A. Stoddard, *Cruising among the Caribees,* 180.

38. See chap. 4, sec. IV.

39. See chap. 4, sec. IV–VI.

40. CO 295/426. Moloney to Lyttelton (confidential), February 10, 1904.

41. See chap. 4, sec. VI.

42. See note 40.

43. David's background and career are highlighted in an interesting article by Samaroo, "Cyrus Prudhomme David."

44. See chap. 3, sec. IX, and chap. 6, note 51.

45. CO 295/421. Moloney to Lyttelton, December 2, 1903.

46. Ibid. Minute by C. A. H., January 1, 1904. The "black A. G." in the passage was the colored attorney-general, Vincent Brown.

47. See, for example, Port-of-Spain *Mirror,* editorial, October 2, 1903.

48. CO 295/427. Clifford, officer administering the government, to Lyttelton (confidential), May 19, 1904. High praise for the appointment was given, for example, by the Port-of-Spain *Mirror* in its editorial of April 15, 1904.

49. CO 295/426. Lyttelton to Moloney (secret and confidential), March 15, 1904. Enclosed with Moloney to Lyttelton (confidential), February 10, 1904.

50. See chap. 7, sec. I.

51. See chap. 7, sec. VIII.

52. CO 295/417. Moloney to Chamberlain (confidential), May 8, 1903. Minute by C. P. L., May 22, 1903.
53. Ibid., May 22, 1903.
54. "Papers Relating to the Recent Disturbances," no. 26, 72.
55. CO 295/419. Deputy Inspector-General of Police to Moloney. Enclosed with Moloney to Chamberlain, August 28, 1903.
56. CO 295/417. Inspector-General of Police to Moloney. Enclosed with Moloney to Chamberlain (confidential), May 8, 1903.
57. CO 295/419. Moloney to Chamberlain, August 28, 1903. Minute by H. C. B., August 29, 1903.
58. CO 295/419. Lucas to Crown Law Officers, September 10, 1903.
59. CO 884/7. Moloney to Lyttelton, November 16, 1903, no. 203 in West Indian 122.
60. Port-of-Spain Mirror, editorial, November 27, 1903.
61. "Papers Relating to the Recent Disturbances," no. 25, 71.
62. CO 298/75. Council Paper 19 of 1904.
63. CO 884/7. Moloney to Chamberlain, July 17, 1903, no. 135 in West Indian 122.
64. CO 884/7. Chamberlain to Moloney, August 17, 1903, no. 150 in West Indian 122; also see CO 297/18. (Additional House Tax) Ordinance 4 of 1904. The unpopular tax was abolished in February 1907. See Port-of-Spain Mirror, February 19, 1907.
65. CO 295/426. Enclosed with Marryat to Bourne (private letter), January 26, 1904. The protests from several organizations and from Marryat were, in turn, enclosed with Moloney to Lyttelton, January 28, 1904.
66. Their denunciations were published on, respectively, January 22, 29, and 30, 1904.
67. See note 65.
68. CO 295/426. Moloney to Lyttelton, January 28, 1904. Minute by C. P. L., February 17, 1904.
69. CO 295/426. Lyttelton to Moloney, March 1, 1904. Enclosed with Moloney to Lyttelton, January 28, 1904.
70. CO 884/7. Moloney to Lyttelton, December 19, 1903, no. 209 in West Indian 122.
71. CO 295/430. War Office to Colonial Office, February 24, 1905. Minute by R. V. V., March 8, 1905.
72. See chap. 4, sec. V.
73. CO 295/428. Clifford, officer administering the government, to Lyttelton, August 10, 1904.
74. See, for example, Port-of-Spain Mirror, editorial, July 4, 1904.
75. CO 295/428. Enclosed with Clifford, officer administering the government, to Lyttelton, August 12, 1904.
76. Port-of-Spain Mirror, editorial, August 30, 1904.
77. See chap. 8, sec. IV.
78. This development grew out of the abolition of the Borough Council in Port-of-Spain. See chap. 5, sec. III.

79. CO 297/18. Ordinances 13 and 18 of 1904.
80. CO 295/436. Jackson to Elgin, May 29, 1906. Par. 2. Enclosed with Clifford, officer administering the government, to Elgin (confidential), April 24, 1906. This document can also be found in Trinidad and Tobago, Minute Paper 850/1906 on "The Municipal Government of Port-of-Spain" (hereafter referred to as "Jackson on Municipal Government").
81. CO 297/18. Ordinance 13 of 1904.
82. CO 295/436. 108. Clifford, officer administering the government, to Elgin, April 24, 1906. This document can also be found in Trinidad and Tobago. Council Paper no. 86 of 1906 on the "Municipal Authority in Port-of-Spain," 3–8 (hereafter referred to as "Clifford on Municipal Government, open despatch").
83. Governor Jackson underlined the urgency of the matter in a minute to Elgin. See note 80.
84. Cited in Trinidad and Tobago, National Archives, *Secret and Confidential Despatches to Secretary of State, 1903–1909,* Clifford, officer administering the government, to Elgin (confidential), April 24, 1906, sec. 2 (hereafter referred to as "Clifford on Municipal Government, confidential despatch").
85. "Jackson on Municipal Government," par. 3.
86. "Clifford on Municipal Government, confidential despatch," sec. 8; "Jackson on Municipal Government," par. 18 and 19.
87. In "Clifford on Municipal Government, confidential despatch," sec. 3.
88. Ibid.
89. Ibid., sec. 4.
90. *The Commission of Enquiry into the Water Riots,* 548.
91. See note 30.
92. "Clifford on Municipal Government, confidential despatch," sec. 2. Also see Port-of-Spain *Mirror,* editorial, July 4, 1905. The report of the Special Committee and other pertinent documents can be found in Trinidad and Tobago, Council Paper no. 86 of 1906 on the "Municipal Authority in Port-of-Spain," 1–3, iii–v, Appendix.
93. "Clifford on Municipal Government, confidential despatch," sec. 2.
94. Trinidad and Tobago, *Hansard,* 1906, 97ff.
95. "Clifford on Municipal Government, confidential despatch," sec. 2.
96. *Hansard,* 1906, 101, 103.
97. Similar remarks were made by other officials in the Legislative Council, including, for example, R. H. McCarthy, collector of customs in Trinidad. See ibid., 135–36. When it was time for the division, McCarthy was the only official who voted against a proposal to restore the Borough Council as a wholly appointive institution. See chap. 8, sec. X.
98. Ibid., 123, 133.
99. See notes 82 and 84.
100. "Clifford on Municipal Government, confidential despatch," sec. 5.
101. See chap. 3, note 24.
102. Council Paper no. 86 of 1906, 8, 9.
103. "Jackson on Municipal Government," par. 24.

104. Council Paper no. 86 of 1906, 9–10.
105. "Clifford on Municipal Government, confidential despatch," sec. 6.
106. Ibid., sec. 6, 7.
107. Ibid., sec. 7.
108. "Jackson on Municipal Government," par. 5, 6.
109. Ibid., par. 9.
110. Ibid.
111. Ibid., par. 18, 19.
112. Ibid., par. 21.
113. Ibid., par. 22.
114. Ibid., par. 20.
115. Ibid., par. 25.
116. CO 298/80. Elgin to Clifford, officer administering the government, June 21, 1906. This document can also be found in Council Paper no. 86 of 1906.
117. CO 297/18. Ordinance 19 of 1907.

CHAPTER 9. *Urban Nationalism V: The Municipal Question Resolved*

1. Port-of-Spain *Mirror,* editorial, November 29, 1906.
2. Mercer and Collins, *The Colonial List for 1904,* 525.
3. Trinidad and Tobago, *Hansard,* 1909, minute 8 (1909), 294.
4. See chap. 8, sec. XI.
5. *Hansard,* 1909, 294.
6. CO 298/88. Council Paper 31 of 1910.
7. Ibid., 6.
8. Trinidad and Tobago, *Hansard,* 1910, 122.
9. Ibid., 123.
10. Ibid., 142.
11. CO 295/463. LeHunte to Crewe, October 14, 1910.
12. Ibid. Minute by R. V. V., November 11, 1910.
13. See chap. 8, sec. X and XI.
14. CO 295/445. Fenwick to Knaggs, officer administering the government, July 22, 1908, in Knaggs to Crewe, July 25, 1908; Crewe to Knaggs, October 5, 1908, in Knaggs to Crewe, August 25, 1908.
15. Great Britain, House of Commons, *Hansard,* 1909, fourth series (8), 1134.
16. CO 295/463. Harcourt to LeHunte, November 5, 1910. Enclosed with LeHunte to Crewe, October 14, 1910.
17. See chap. 4, sec. VI.
18. See chap. 3, note 57.
19. See chap. 8, sec. V.
20. Port-of-Spain *Mirror,* December 7, 1912.
21. CO 298/96. Council Paper 107 of 1912.
22. CO 295/483. LeHunte to Harcourt, June 30, 1913.
23. CO 295/483. Knaggs, officer administering the government, to Harcourt, July 7, 1913.
24. CO 298/98. Harcourt to LeHunte, July 29, 1913. Council Paper 115 of 1913.
25. See chap. 10, sec. V.

26. See chap. 4, sec. VII.
27. CO 295/489. Pointer to Harcourt, September 11, 1913.
28. CO 295/485. LeHunte to Harcourt, October 20, 1913.
29. CO 298/98. Council Paper 182 of 1913.
30. See note 27.
31. House of Commons, "Papers Relating to the Recent Disturbances at Port-of-Spain, Trinidad" (July 1903), no. 12, enclosure 15, 36–39.
32. See, for example, CO 295/476. Knaggs, officer administering the government, to Harcourt, October 16, 1912.
33. Spender, *Great Britain: Empire and Commonwealth,* 436–39.
34. Port-of-Spain *Mirror,* letter, September 20, 1913.
35. Trinidad and Tobago, *Hansard,* 1914, 254.
36. CO 295/485. LeHunte to Harcourt, December 22, 1913. Minute by L. H., January 20, 1914.
37. CO 298/99. Harcourt to LeHunte, January 27, 1914. Council Paper 24 of 1914.
38. CO 295/491. LeHunte to Harcourt, May 4, 1914.
39. Port-of-Spain *Mirror,* editorial, April 24, 1914; Port-of-Spain *Gazette,* editorial, August 22, 1913.
40. CO 295/492. LeHunte to Harcourt, June 6, 1914.
41. CO 295/491. LeHunte to Harcourt, May 4, 1914. Minute by R. A. W., June 1, 1914, and E. R. D., June 2, 1914.
42. CO 297/20. Ordinance 24 of 1914.
43. *Hansard,* 1914, 270.
44. See chap. 4, sec. VII.
45. *Hansard,* 1914, 270.
46. See, for example, ibid., 259–60.
47. CO 295/485. LeHunte to Harcourt, December 22, 1913. Minute by G. G., January 15, 1914.

CHAPTER 10. *Urban Nationalism in Trinidad: Concluding Observations, Pointing Ahead*

1. E. Williams, *History of the People of Trinidad and Tobago;* see also two other works by Williams, *British Historians and the West Indies* and *Capitalism and Slavery.* The rise of the People's National Movement to power is examined in Ryan, *Race and Nationalism in Trinidad and Tobago,* 120ff.
2. G. K. Lewis, *The Growth of the Modern West Indies,* 116; Williams, *History of the People of Trinidad and Tobago,* 167ff.
3. Williams, ibid., 189–95.
4. Great Britain, House of Commons, "Further Papers Relating to the Recent Disturbances at Port-of-Spain, Trinidad, in March 1903" (April 1904), no. 1, 3–4.
5. See chap. 3, sec. V.
6. London *Times,* November 2, 1899.
7. Great Britain, *Parliamentary Papers,* 1898, 50 (C.8655), 18.
8. Ibid., 101.

9. See chap. 10, sec. II.

10. Robinson, "Trinidad: Its Capabilities and Prominent Products," 276.

11. C. S. Salmon, "Depression in the West Indies."

12. J. E. Tyler, *The Struggle for Imperial Unity, 1868–1895,* 86.

13. *Parliamentary Papers,* 1893–94, 60 (C.6857–24), 4; ibid., 1895, 69 (C.7629), 4.

14. "Report from the West India Royal Commission ... Relating to the Sugar Industry, 1877–1898"; CO 318/291. Colonial Office to Treasury Department, January 24, 1898. Also see chap. 3, sec. IX.

15. Great Britain, *Hansard,* 1899, 75, 4, 494.

16. *Parliamentary Papers,* 1902, 65 (C.788-8), 12.

17. Ibid., 16.

18. Ibid., 1896, 50 (C.8655), 329; 1900, 54, 10.

19. Ibid., 1902, 12. Also see chap. 3, sec. V.

20. London *Times,* October 30, 1894.

21. The major implications of the Morris report for Trinidad are examined in chap. 10, sec. II and III.

22. "Report from the West India Royal Commission," 105, 106.

23. See chap. 3, sec. III.

24. *Parliamentary Papers,* 1898, 105.

25. Ibid., 1892, 55 (C.6563), 16.

26. Ibid., 1898, 36–41.

27. Sir H. Jerningham, "Trinidad and Its Future Possibilities," 222.

28. *Parliamentary Papers,* 1899, 54, 12; ibid., 1902, 15–17.

29. Jerningham, 230.

30. It will be recalled that public fear of such epidemics helped fuel the water crisis in Port-of-Spain. See chap. 6, sec. I, and chap. 7, sec. IV.

31. *Parliamentary Papers,* 1905, 52 (C.2238-19), 3.

32. Ibid., 1906, 75 (C.2684-15), 19.

33. Ibid., 1908, 69 (C.3729-51), 8; ibid., 1909, 58 (C.4448-30), 7, 8; ibid., 1911, 52 (C.5467-35), 12; ibid., 1912–13, 58 (C.6007-45), 13.

34. Ibid., 1914–16, 44 (C.7622-10), ll; ibid., 1911, 4; ibid., 1913, 45 (C.6674), 3.

35. Ibid., 1912–13, 13.

36. Ibid., 1916, 19 (C.8173-2), 23.

37. Ibid., 1921, 24 (C.1103-12), 5.

38. Ryan, *Race and Nationalism,* 28–69. Also see chap. 10, sec. VI and VII.

39. *Parliamentary Papers,* 1909, 16, 17; ibid., 1911, 16.

40. Ibid., 1911, 21.

41. Ibid., 1917–18, 22 (C.8434-17), 19; Trinidad and Tobago, *Census Album,* 12–14.

42. *Parliamentary Papers,* 1914–16, 47 (C.7744), 34.

43. Colonial Office, *Development and Welfare in the West Indies,* 1950.

44. The historical roots of the problem of education in Trinidad are examined in Wood, *Trinidad in Transition,* 212–37.

45. See, for example, Port-of-Spain *Mirror,* letter from "Common Sense," March 1, 1904.

46. *Parliamentary Papers,* 1905, 14; ibid., 1911, 17.
47. Ibid., 1914, 58 (C.7050-31), 13–14.
48. CO 295/436. "Articles of Association," enclosed with Clifford, officer administering the government, to Elgin, April 24, 1906.
49. CO 295/441. Carter, officer administering the government, to Elgin, June 18, 1907; CO 295/444. Knaggs, officer administering the government, to Elgin, March 21, 1908.
50. CO 295/456. LeHunte to Crewe, January 10, 1910; CO 295/490. LeHunte to Harcourt, January 26, 1913.
51. Report of the secretary of the association, Port-of-Spain *Mirror,* January 13, 1913.
52. CO 295/441. Carter, officer administering the government, to Elgin, June 18, 1907. Minute by T. C. M., October 31, 1907.
53. See, for example, Great Britain, *Hansard,* 1906, fourth series, 10063, 1324, and 1908, fourth series, 10083, 1527.
54. See, for example, ibid., 1910, fifth series, 16, 861–63. See also CO 295/463. Pointer to Harcourt, July 21, 1910, and CO 295/472. Pointer to Harcourt, June 2, 1911.
55. Port-of-Spain *Mirror,* October 2, 4, 5, 1912.
56. Ryan, *Race and Nationalism,* 28ff.
57. *Parliamentary Papers,* 1910, 27 (C.5192), 294. The commission report dealt with emigration from India to the various Crown Colonies and Protectorates in the British Empire.
58. Port-of-Spain *Mirror,* October 5, 7, 14, 1912.
59. CO 295/476. Knaggs, officer administering the government, to Harcourt, October 16, 1912.
60. Port-of-Spain *Mirror,* October 12, 1912, and editorial, October 16, 1912.
61. Ibid., November 7, 18, 1912.
62. See chap. 6, sec. III.
63. Port-of-Spain *Mirror,* editorial, November 25, 1912.
64. Ibid., October 1, 1913.
65. Ibid., letter, December 10, 1912.
66. *Parliamentary Papers,* 1920, 32 (C.508-2), 6.
67. See chap. 4, sec. IV and V, and chap. 6, sec. V and VI.
68. Ryan, *Race and Nationalism,* 128ff.
69. Ibid., 28ff. Also see Craig, *The Legislative Council of Trinidad and Tobago,* 28ff.; Lewis, 197–225.
70. Trinidad *Guardian,* December 1, 4, 1919. This newspaper was closely tied to the business community in the colony.
71. See chap. 3, sec. V.
72. See chap. 10, sec. VII.
73. See chap. 1, sec. V.
74. While there was evidence of a growing political consciousness within the Indian community even before the First World War (see chap. 10, sec. V), the range of political opinion did not begin to be clarified until 1921, the year the Colonial Office sent Major E. F. L. Wood to the colony to investigate political

conditions. Four years before, the system of indentured immigration had been abolished, anticipating the end of indentured Indian labor in 1922. With these developments, and with the growing politicization of the black population, the Indian community had perforce to weigh its political future in Trinidad. The urgency of the matter was pointed up when, on the basis of the Wood Report, the constitution of Trinidad was modified in 1925 to allow for a partially elective Legislative Council (see chap. 3, sec. II). With that action, pressure built for further constitutional advance in the colony. The political attitudes and behavior of different elements in the Indian community are examined in Ryan, *Race and Nationalism,* 30–32 and passim. Also see House of Commons, "Report by the Hon. E. F. L. Wood, MP, on His Visit to the West Indies and British Guiana."

75. See, for example, T. Parsons, *The Social System;* T. Parsons, R. F. Bales, and E. A. Shils, *Working Papers in the Theory of Action;* T. Parsons and E. A. Shils, *Toward a General Theory of Action.*

76. M. G. Smith, *The Plural Society in the British West Indies,* xvi. The influence of the Parsonian perspective in political science has also been a matter of great intellectual controversy in that discipline. See R.H. Chilcote, ed., *Theories of Comparative Politics: The Search for a Paradigm,* 139–216.

77. B. Johnpoll, *The Impossible Dream: The Rise and Demise of the American Left,* 4.

78. See chap. 3, note 44.

79. See chap. 3, sec. III.

80. Port-of-Spain *Gazette,* editorial, January 25, 1899.

81. See chap. 5, sec. III.

82. See chap. 7, note 20.

83. Williams, *History of the People of Trinidad and Tobago,* 196–214; I. Oxaal, *Black Intellectuals Come to Power: The Rise of Creole Nationalism in Trinidad and Tobago,* 56–79. Some of the "young colonials" became important figures in the history of Trinidad nationalism. For example, the historian Eric Williams, as leader of the People's National Movement party, became the first prime minister of independent Trinidad and Tobago. C. L. R. James and Malcolm Nurse (whose political pseudonym was George Padmore) would build substantial reputations as professional revolutionary organizers and intellectuals. See Oxaal, 61.

84. M. Herskovits and F. Herskovits, *Trinidad Village;* L. Braithwaite, *Social Stratification in Trinidad: A Preliminary Analysis,* iv.

85. Braithwaite, iii.

86. See note 76. Also see J. S. Furnivall, *Colonial Policy and Practice: A Comparative Study of Burma and Netherlands India;* M. G. Smith, "Social and Cultural Pluralism"; L. Despres, *Cultural Pluralism and Nationalist Politics in British Guyana.* A broad survey of the social science literature on pluralism can be found in C. Young, *The Politics of Cultural Pluralism;* also see C. Young, "The Temple of Ethnicity."

87. Furnivall, 304, 308.

88. See the remarks by V. Rubin in Rubin, "Social and Cultural Pluralism in the

Caribbean," 780–85; also the comments on M.G. Smith's paper (see note 86) by R. T. Smith in his book review, 155–57.

89. C. L. R. James, *State Capitalism and World Revolution;* Ryan, *Race and Nationalism,* passim; Oxaal, 61ff.

90. See, for example, Ryan, 416.

91. See chap. 1, sec. IV. Also see J. Pearce, *Under the Eagle: U.S. Intervention in Central America and the Caribbean.*

92. R. R. Palmer, *The Age of the Democratic Revolution: A Political History of Europe and America,* 1760–1800; W. Bell, ed., *The Democratic Revolution in the West Indies: Studies in Nationalism, Leadership, and the Belief in Progress,* 1–4.

93. See essays by the different contributors in Bell, 20–223. Also see C. C. Moskos, Jr., and W. Bell, "Emergent Caribbean Nations Face the Outside World"; Moskos and Bell, "Attitudes Towards Democracy among Leaders in Four Emergent Nations"; Moskos and Bell, "West Indian Nationalism"; Moskos and Bell, "Some Implications of Equality for Political, Economic, and Social Development"; Moskos and Bell, "Cultural Unity and Diversity in New States"; J. A. Mau, *Social Change and Images of the Future: A Study of the Pursuit of Progress in Jamaica;* W. Bell, "Equality and Social Justice: Foundations of Nationalism in the Caribbean."

94. C. C. Moskos, Jr., *The Sociology of Political Development,* 72.

95. Ryan, 365ff.

96. See chap. 6, note 11.

97. I. Oxaal, *Race and Revolutionary Consciousness: A Documentary Interpretation of the 1970 Black Power Revolt in Trinidad.*

98. S. C. Gilman, "Black Rebellion in the 1960s: Between Nonviolence and Black Power."

99. W. Rodney, *The Groundings with My Brothers,* 16, 28, 63 (emphasis in original). Rodney's sweeping denunciation of European imperialism is further developed in his study of *How Europe Underdeveloped Africa.*

100. Braithwaite, 114.

101. See, for example, Heussler, *The British in Northern Nigeria;* M. Gluckman, *Analysis of a Social Situation in Modern Zululand;* H. Kuper, *The Uniform of Color: A Study of White-Black Relationships in Swaziland,* 92–96.

102. See, for example, L. I. Rudolph and S. H. Rudolph, *The Modernity of Tradition: Political Development in India;* C. S. Whitaker, Jr., "A Dysrhythmic Process of Political Change"; R. Nisbet, *Social Change and History: Aspects of the Western Theory of Development,* 270–71.

Bibliography

I. OFFICIAL DOCUMENTS — A: *Great Britain*

1. Public Record Office, London (Colonial Office Records, selected volumes)
   1802–1914: CO 295/6 to 492
   1847–1914: CO 297/4 to 20
   1893–1914: CO 298/52 to 99
   1898: CO 318/291
   1888–1898: CO 380/147/20 to 29
   1868: CO 854/9
   1897–1903: CO 884/5 to 7
2. Foreign and Commonwealth Office Library, London (*Parliamentary Papers,* selected volumes)
   1839–1927: XXXIV, 35 to VII, *Cmd. 2884*
3. *Miscellaneous*
   Cobbett, *Parliamentary Debates* (selected volumes: 1803–1812).
   Hansard (selected volumes: new series, 1820–1830; third series, 1830–1891; fourth series, 1892–1908; fifth series, 1892–1950).
   (1903) House of Commons, "Papers Relating to the Recent Disturbances at Port-of-Spain, Trinidad," *Cmd. 1661.*
   (1903) House of Commons, "Report of the Commission of Enquiry into the Recent Disturbances at Port-of-Spain, Trinidad," *Cmd. 1662.*
   (1904) House of Commons, "Further Papers Relating to the Recent Disturbances at Port-of-Spain, Trinidad, in March 1903," *Cmd. 1988.*
   (1922) House of Commons, "Report by the Hon. E. F. L. Wood, MP, on His Visit to the West Indies and British Guiana, December 1921–February 1922," *Cmd. 1679.*
   (1927) House of Commons, *British Sessional Papers,* vol. 7, *Cmd. 2884.*
   (1951) Colonial Office, *Development and Welfare in the West Indies, 1950.* London: H.M.S.O.
   (1971) "Report from the West India Royal Commission with Appendices A and B, Appendix C Volumes 1 and 2, and Other Papers Relating to the Sugar Industry, 1877–1898," *British Parliamentary Papers 1898: Colonies, West Indies, 7.* Shannon, Ireland: Irish University.

279

I. OFFICIAL DOCUMENTS — B: *Trinidad and Tobago*

1. National Archives, Port-of-Spain
   Royal Gazette, 1895.
   Hansard, 1903–1914 (selected volumes).
   (1903) *Private Letters, 7304/1903.*
   (1904) *Despatches to Secretary of State, 1904.*
   (1906) Council Paper No. 86 of 1906 on the "Municipal Authority in Port-of-Spain."
   (1906) *Minute Paper 850/1906* on "The Municipal Government of Port-of-Spain."
   (1909) *Secret and Confidential Despatches to Secretary of State, 1903–1909.*
2. Miscellaneous
   (1948) *Census Album.* Port-of-Spain: Government Printer.

II. NEWSPAPERS AND PERIODICALS — A: *Great Britain* (*British Museum Newspaper Library*)

London *Daily Telegraph*
London *Times*

II. NEWSPAPERS AND PERIODICALS — B: *Trinidad and Tobago* (*National Archives, Port-of-Spain; British Museum Newspaper Library*)

Port-of-Spain *Catholic News*
Port-of-Spain *Gazette*
Port-of-Spain *Mirror*
Port-of-Spain *Pioneer*
Port-of-Spain *Public Opinion*
Trinidad *Free Press*
Trinidad *Guardian*
Trinidad *Magazine*
Trinidad *Sentinel*
Trinidad *Spectator*
Trinidad *Star of the West*

III. OTHER SOURCES AND SECONDARY WORKS

Allen, J. de V. (1964), "Two Imperialists: A Study of Sir Frank Swettenham and Sir Hugh Clifford," *Journal of the Royal Asiatic Society of Great Britain and Ireland (Malayan Branch),* 38 (Part 1): 41–73.

Bates, R. H. (January 1974), "Ethnic Competition and Modernization in Contemporary Africa," *Comparative Political Studies* 6: 457–84.

Bayley, D. H. (1964), *Public Liberties in the New States.* Chicago: Rand McNally.

Bell, W. (June 1980), "Equality and Social Justice: Foundations of Nationalism in the Caribbean," *Caribbean Studies* 20: 5–36.

Bell, W., ed. (1967), *The Democratic Revolution in the West Indies: Studies in Nationalism, Leadership, and the Belief in Progress.* Cambridge, Mass.: Schenkman.

Bertram, A. (1930), *The Colonial Service.* Cambridge: Cambridge University.

Bolton, H. E. (1917), "The Mission as a Frontier Institution in Spanish American Colonies," *American Historical Review* 23: 42–61.

Borde, P. G. L. (1882), *Histoire de l'île de la Trinidad sous le Gouvernement Espagnol,* vol. 2. Paris: Maisoneuve et Cie.

Bradley, K. (1966), *Once a District Officer.* New York: St. Martin's.

Braithwaite, L. (1975), *Social Stratification in Trinidad: A Preliminary Analysis.* Kingston, Jamaica: University of the West Indies Institute of Social and Economic Research. (Reprinted from the Institute's journal [October 1953], *Social and Economic Studies* 2, 2 and 3.)

Cameron, D. (1934), *The Principles of Native Administration and Their Application.* Lagos, Nigeria: Government Printer.

―――― (1939), *My Tanganyika Service and Some Nigeria.* London: Allen and Unwin.

Carmichael, G. (1961), *The History of the West Indian Islands of Trinidad and Tobago, 1498–1900.* London: Redman.

Cell, J. W. (1970), *British Colonial Administration in the Mid-Nineteenth Century: The Policy-Making Process.* New Haven: Yale University.

Chamberlain, J. (June 1894), "Municipal Government—Past, Present, and Future," *The New Review* 10: 649–61.

Chilcote, R. H. (1981), *Theories of Comparative Politics: The Search for a Paradigm.* Boulder, Col.: Westview.

Clarkson, T. (1808), *The History of the Rise, Progress, and Accomplishment of the Abolition of the Slave Trade by the British Parliament,* vol. 2. London: Hurst.

Clifford, H. (1898-99), "Life in the Malay Peninsula: As It Was and Is," *Proceedings of the Royal Colonial Institute* 30: 369–401.

―――― . (1902–3), "British and Siamese Malaya," *Proceedings of the Royal Colonial Institute* 34: 45–75.

―――― . (1904), *Sally, A Study.* London: Blackwood.

―――― . (1918), *The German Colonies: A Plea for the Native Races.* London: Murray.

Cohen, A. (1982), "Drama and Politics in the Development of a London Carnival," in *Custom and Conflict in British Society,* ed. R. Frankenberg, 313–43. Manchester: Manchester University.

Coleman, J. S. (June 1954), "Nationalism in Tropical Africa," *American Political Science Review* 48: 404–26.

―――― . (1958), *Nigeria: Background to Nationalism.* Berkeley: University of California.

Collens, J. H. (1888), *A Guide to Trinidad: A Handbook for the Use of Tourists and Visitors.* London: Stock.

Commission of Enquiry into the Water Riots (1903), *Report.* Port-of-Spain: Diocesan.

Craig, H. (1952), *The Legislative Council of Trinidad and Tobago*. London: Faber and Faber.

Cumpston, I. M. (1953), *Indians Overseas in British Territories, 1834–1854*. London: Oxford University.

Daniel, E. W. (1936), *West Indian Histories,* Book 3. London: Nelson.

David, C. P. (April 1902), "Loyalty in British Colonies," *Trinidad Magazine* 1: 168–72.

de Verteuil, A. (1973), *Sir Louis de Verteuil: His Life and Times, Trinidad 1800–1900*. Port-of-Spain: Columbus.

Despres, L. (1967), *Cultural Pluralism and Nationalist Politics in British Guyana*. New York: Rand McNally.

Dictionary of National Biography, 1941–1950, The. London: Oxford University, 1959.

Dishman, R. (1978), "Cultural Pluralism and Bureaucratic Neutrality in the British Caribbean," *Ethnicity* 5: 274–99.

Duverger, M. (1955), *Political Parties: Their Organization and Activity in the Modern State*. New York: Wiley.

Emerson, R. (1960), *From Empire to Nation: The Rise to Self-Assertion of Asian and African Peoples*. Boston: Beacon.

Fallers, L. (1955), "The Predicament of the Modern African Chief: An Instance from Uganda," *American Anthropologist* 57: 290–305.

Franklin, C. B. (1910), *After Many Days: A Memoir, Being a Sketch of the Life and Labors of Rev. Alexander Kennedy*. Port-of-Spain: Greyfriar's Church.

Fraser, L. M. (1891), *History of Trinidad,* vol. 1 (*1781–1813*). London: Cass, 1971.

Froude, J. (1888), *The English in the West Indies, or the Bow of Ulysses*. New York: Scribner's, 1900.

Furnivall, J. S. (1948), *Colonial Policy and Practice: A Comparative Study of Burma and Netherlands India*. New York: New York University.

Furse, R. (1962), *Aucuparius: Reflections of a Recruiting Officer*. London: Oxford University.

Galley, H. A. (1978), "Sir Hugh Clifford (1856–1941)," in *African Proconsuls: European Governors in Africa,* ed. L. H. Gann and P. Duignan, 265–89. New York: Free Press.

Garvin, J. L. (1932), *The Life of Joseph Chamberlain*. Vol. 1, *1836–1885: Chamberlain and Democracy*. London: Macmillan.

Gilman, S. C. (1981), "Black Rebellion in the 1960s: Between Nonviolence and Black Power," *Ethnicity* 8: 452–75.

Gluckman, M. (1968), *Analysis of a Social Situation in Modern Zululand*. Manchester: Manchester University.

Gould, P. R. (1968), "Problems of Structuring and Measuring Spatial Changes in the Modernization Process: Tanzania 1920–1963," *Proceedings of the Annual Meeting of the American Political Science Association,* Washington, D.C., September 2–7, 1–23.

Hanna, W. J., and J. L. Hanna (1981), *Urban Dynamics in Africa: An Interdisciplinary Approach*. New York: Aldine.

Harewood, J. (1975), *The Population of Trinidad and Tobago*. Paris: CICRED Series.

Hart, D. (1866), *Trinidad and the Other West India Islands and Colonies*. Port-of-Spain: "Chronicle."

Hechter, M., and M. Levi (July 1979), "The Comparative Analysis of Ethnoregional Movements," *Ethnic and Racial Studies* 2: 260–74.

Herskovits, M., and F. Herskovits (1947), *Trinidad Village*. New York: Knopf.

Heussler, R. (1963), *Yesterday's Rulers: The Making of the British Colonial Service*. Syracuse: Syracuse University.

——. (1968), *The British in Northern Nigeria*. London: Oxford University.

Higman, B. W. (1984), *Slave Populations of the British Caribbean 1807–1834*. Baltimore: Johns Hopkins University.

Hodgkin, T. (1956), *Nationalism in Colonial Africa*. New York: New York University.

Hyam, R. (1968), *Elgin and Churchill at the Colonial Office 1905–1908: The Watershed of the Empire-Commonwealth*. London and New York: Macmillan and St. Martin's.

——. (October 1979), "The Colonial Office Mind 1900–1914," *Journal of Imperial and Commonwealth History* 8: 30–55.

James, C. L. R. (1950), *State Capitalism and World Revolution*. Detroit, Mich.: Facing Reality Publishing Committee.

Jerningham, Sir H. (1901), "Crown Colony Government," *The Empire Review* 1: 87–95.

——. (1901), "Trinidad and Its Future Possibilities," *Proceedings of the Royal Colonial Institute* 32: 215–31.

Johnpoll, B. (1981), *The Impossible Dream: The Rise and Demise of the American Left*. Westport, Conn.: Greenwood.

Joseph, E. L. (1838), *History of Trinidad*. London: Cass, 1970.

Kalleberg, A. (October 1966), "The Logic of Comparison: A Methodological Note on the Comparative Study of Political Systems," *World Politics* 19: 69–82.

Karl, F. R., and L. Davies, eds. (1986), *The Collected Letters of Joseph Conrad*, vol. 2, 1898–1902. Cambridge: Cambridge University.

Kautsky, J., ed. (1962), *Political Change in Underdeveloped Countries: Nationalism and Communism*. New York: Wiley.

Kelly, J. (1969), *Organizational Behavior*. Homewood, Ill.: Irwin/Dorsey.

Kingsley, C. (1871), *At Last: A Christmas in the West Indies*. New York: Harper.

Knaplund, P. (1953), *James Stephen and the British Colonial System, 1813–1847*. Madison: University of Wisconsin.

Kubicek, R. V. (1969), *The Administration of Imperialism: Joseph Chamberlain at the Colonial Office*. Durham, N.C.: Duke University.

Kuper, H. (1947), *The Uniform of Color: A Study of White-Black Relationships in Swaziland*. Johannesburg: Witwatersrand University.

Laurence, K. O. (March 1969), "The Trinidad Water Riot of 1903: Reflections of an Eyewitness," *Caribbean Quarterly* 15: 5–22.

Lewis, G. K. (April 1967), "British Colonialism in the West Indies: The Political Legacy," *Caribbean Studies* 7: 3–22.

_____. (1968), *The Growth of the Modern West Indies.* New York: Monthly Review.

_____. (1983), *Main Currents in Caribbean Thought: The Historical Evolution of Caribbean Society in Its Ideological Aspects, 1492–1900.* Baltimore: Johns Hopkins University.

Lucas, C. (1905), *Historical Geography of the British Colonies,* vol. 2. London: Oxford University.

Lugard, F. (1923), *The Dual Mandate in British Tropical Africa.* London: Blackwood.

_____. (1970), *Political Memoranda, 1913–1918.* London: Cass.

Lynch, J. (1958), *Spanish Colonial Administration, 1782–1810: The Intendant System in the Viceroyalty of the Río de la Plata.* London: Athlone, University of London Historical Studies No. 5.

Mackenzie, W. J. M., and J. W. Grove (1957), *Central Administration in Britain.* London: Longmans, Green.

Magid, A. (1976), *Men in the Middle: Leadership and Role Conflict in a Nigerian Society.* Manchester and New York: Manchester University and Africana.

_____. (January 1980), "'Role Theory,' Political Science, and African Studies," *World Politics* 32: 311–30.

Malik, Y. K. (1971), *East Indians in Trinidad: A Study in Minority Politics.* London: Oxford University.

Mallet, Capt. F. (1802), *Descriptive Account of the Island of Trinidad.* London: Faden.

Marriott, J. A. R. (1934), *Modern England, 1885–1932: A History of My Own Times.* London: Methuen.

Mau, J. A. (1968), *Social Change and Images of the Future: A Study of the Pursuit of Progress in Jamaica.* Cambridge, Mass.: Schenkman.

May, E. R. (1973), *Imperial Democracy: The Emergence of America as a Great Power.* New York: Harper and Row.

Mercer, W. H., and A. E. Collins (1903), *The Colonial List for 1903.* London: Waterlow.

_____. (1904), *The Colonial List for 1904.* London: Waterlow.

_____. (1905), *The Colonial List for 1905.* London: Waterlow.

_____. (1906), *The Colonial List for 1906.* London: Waterlow.

_____. (1907), *The Colonial List for 1907.* London: Waterlow.

Millette, J. (1970), *The Genesis of Crown Colony Government: Trinidad, 1783–1810.* Curepe, Trinidad: Moko.

Moskos, C. C., Jr. (1967), *The Sociology of Political Development: A Study of Nationalist Attitudes among West Indian Leaders.* Cambridge, Mass.: Schenkman.

Moskos, C. C., Jr., and W. Bell (January 1964), "West Indian Nationalism," *New Society* 23: 16–18.

_____. (Summer 1964), "Emergent Caribbean Nations Face the Outside World," *Social Problems* 12: 24–41.

_____. (December 1964), "Attitudes Towards Democracy among Leaders in Four Emergent Nations," *British Journal of Sociology* 15: 317–37.

_____. (1965), "Some Implications of Equality for Political, Economic, and Social Development," *Community Development* 13–14: 219–46.

_____. (May 1965), "Cultural Unity and Diversity in New States," *Teachers College Record* 66: 679–94.

Murray, D. J. (1965), *The West Indies and the Development of Colonial Government, 1801–1834.* Oxford: Clarendon.

Newson, L. A. (1976), *Aboriginal and Spanish Colonial Trinidad: A Study in Culture Contact.* New York: Academic.

Nicolson, I. F. (1969), *The Administration of Nigeria, 1900–1960: Men, Methods, and Myths.* London: Clarendon.

Nisbet, R. (1969), *Social Change and History: Aspects of the Western Theory of Development.* London: Oxford University.

Okonjo, I. M. (1974), *British Administration in Nigeria, 1900–1950: A Nigerian View.* New York: NOK.

Ottley, C. R. (1962), *The Story of Port-of-Spain: Capital of Trinidad West Indies from the Earliest Times to the Present Day.* Port-of-Spain: Ottley.

Oxaal, I. (1968), *Black Intellectuals Come to Power: The Rise of Creole Nationalism in Trinidad and Tobago.* Cambridge, Mass.: Schenkman.

_____. (1971), *Race and Revolutionary Consciousness: A Documentary Interpretation of the 1970 Black Power Rebellion in Trinidad.* Cambridge, Mass.: Schenkman.

Palmer, R. R. (1959, 1964), *The Age of the Democratic Revolution: A Political History of Europe and America, 1760–1800,* 2 vols. Princeton: Princeton University.

Pan-African (1901), editorial, 1: 1.

Parkinson, C. (1947), *The Colonial Office from Within, 1909–1945.* London: Faber and Faber.

Parsons, T. (1959), *The Social System.* Glencoe, Ill.: Free Press.

Parsons, T., and E. A. Shils (1951), *Toward a General Theory of Action.* Cambridge: Harvard University.

Parsons, T., R. F. Bales, and E. A. Shils (1952), *Working Papers in the Theory of Action.* Glencoe, Ill.: Free Press.

Pearce, J. (1982), *Under the Eagle: U.S. Intervention in Central America and the Caribbean.* Boston: South End.

Pearse, A. (1956), "Carnival in Nineteenth Century Trinidad," *Caribbean Quarterly* 4: 175–93.

Perham, M. (1950), *Lugard: The Years of Authority, 1898–1945.* London: Collins.

Ponte, A. F. (1919), *Bolivar y Ensayos.* Caracas: Cosmos.

Porter, B. (1975), *The Lion's Share: A Short History of British Imperialism, 1850–1970.* London: Longman.

Reinsch, P. (1926), *Colonial Government: An Introduction to the Study of Colonial Institutions.* New York: Macmillan.

Reis, C. (1929), *A History of the Constitution or Government of Trinidad from the Earliest Times to the Present Day.* Port-of-Spain: Reis.

Richards, A., ed. (1960), *East African Chiefs: A Study of Political Development in Some Uganda and Tanganyika Tribes.* New York: Praeger.

Robinson, Sir W. (1898-99), "Trinidad: Its Capabilities and Prominent Products," *Proceedings of the Royal Colonial Institute* 30: 272–97.

Rodney, W. (1969), *The Groundings with My Brothers*. London: Bogle-L'Ouverture.

_____. (1974), *How Europe Underdeveloped Africa*. Washington, D.C.: Howard University.

Rubin, V. (1960), Remarks on M. G. Smith's "Social and Cultural Pluralism," in "Social and Cultural Pluralism in the Caribbean," ed. V. Rubin, *Annals of the New York Academy of Sciences* 83: 780–85.

Rudolph, L. I., and S. H. Rudolph (1969), *The Modernity of Tradition: Political Development in India*. Chicago: University of Chicago.

Rutherford, J. (1961), *Sir George Grey, 1812–1898: A Study in Colonial Government*. London: Cassell.

Ryan, S. (1972), *Race and Nationalism in Trinidad and Tobago: A Study of Decolonization in a Multiracial Society*. Toronto: University of Toronto.

Salmon, C. S. (1884), "Depression in the West Indies," *Cobden Club Publication* 1: 10–22.

Samaroo, B. (1969), "Constitutional and Political Development of Trinidad, 1898–1925." Ph.D. diss., University of London.

_____. (November 1971), "Cyrus Prudhomme David—A Case Study on the Emergence of the Black Man in Trinidad Politics," *Journal of Caribbean History* 3: 73–89.

Selznick, P. (1957), *Leadership in Administration*. New York: Harper and Row.

_____. (1966), *TVA and the Grassroots*. New York: Harper.

Sewell, W. G. (1862), *The Ordeal of Free Labor in the British West Indies*. London: Sampson Low.

Shafer, B. C. (1955), *Nationalism: Myth and Reality*. New York: Harcourt, Brace, and World.

Smith, M. G. (1960), "Social and Cultural Pluralism," in "Social and Cultural Pluralism in the Caribbean," ed. V. Rubin, *Annals of the New York Academy of Sciences* 83: 763–77.

_____. (1965), *The Plural Society in the British West Indies*. Berkeley: University of California.

Smith, R. T. (1961), Book Review, *American Anthropologist* 63: 155–57.

Snyder, L. L. (1968), *The New Nationalism*. Ithaca: Cornell University.

Soja, E. W. (1968), *The Geography of Modernization in Kenya: A Spatial Analysis of Social, Economic, and Political Change*. Syracuse: Syracuse University.

Spender, J. A. (1973), *Great Britain: Empire and Commonwealth, 1886–1935*. Westport, Conn.: Greenwood.

Stinchcombe, A. (1968), *Constructing Social Theories*. New York: Harcourt, Brace, and World.

Stoddard, C. A. (1895), *Cruising among the Caribees*. New York: Scribner's.

Strauss, W. L. (1971), *Joseph Chamberlain and the Theory of Imperialism*. New York: Fertig.

Thomas, J. J. (1890), *Froudacity: West Indian Fables by James Anthony Froude*. Philadelphia: Gebbie.

Toynbee, A. (1970), *Cities on the Move*. New York: Oxford University.

Tyler, J. E. (1938), *The Struggle for Imperial Unity, 1868–1895*. London: Longmans, Green.

Webb, B. (1948), *Our Partnership*. London: Longmans, Green.

Whitaker, C. S., Jr. (January 1967), "A Dysrhythmic Process of Political Change," *World Politics* 19: 190–217.

Will, H. A. (1970), *Constitutional Change in the British West Indies, 1880–1903, with Special Reference to Jamaica, British Guiana, and Trinidad*. Oxford: Clarendon.

Williams, E. (1964), *British Historians and the West Indies*. Port-of-Spain: PNM.

_____. (1964), *History of the People of Trinidad and Tobago*. New York: Praeger.

_____. (1966), *Capitalism and Slavery*. New York: Putnam.

Wood, D. (1968), *Trinidad in Transition: The Years after Slavery*. London: Oxford University.

Woodruff, P. (1953, 1954), *The Men Who Ruled India*, 2 vols. New York: Schocken.

Woolff, L. (1961), *Growing: An Autobiography of the Years 1904–1911*. New York: Harcourt, Brace, and World.

Wrong, H. (1923), *Government of the West Indies*. London: Oxford University.

Young, C. (1976), *The Politics of Cultural Pluralism*. Madison: University of Wisconsin.

_____. (July 1983), "The Temple of Ethnicity," *World Politics* 35: 652–62.

Young, D. (1961), *The Colonial Office in the Early Nineteenth Century*. London: Longmans.

Index

Abercrombie, Gen. Sir Ralph, conqueror of Spanish Trinidad, 31, 40
Achong, T. P., black reformer, 221, 225
Agostini, Leon, white reformer, solicitor-general, 91, 99, 117
Alcazar, Henry, white reformer, unofficial in Legislative Council, 50, 54, 84, 87, 95–98, 101, 127, 138, 174, 180, 182, 199, 201, 203, 231; opposes system of Crown Colony government, 147–53; role in municipal crisis over Borough Council, 88–89, 91
Allen, J. deV., 166

Barbados, 68, 71, 132, 212
Bell, Wendell, 238, 243
Bertram, Anton, 16
Black Power, 227, 235, 238–40, 243–44
Bodu, Ignacio, white reformer, member of "no surrender party," 98, 110, 118, 126
Borough Council, Port-of-Spain: municipal crisis over, 80–84; resolution of crisis, 197–206
Bourne, H. C., colonial official, 91–92, 174, 177–78
Bowen, A. S., warden, 129
Braithwaite, Lloyd, 235–36, 240–41
Brake, Lt.-Col. H. E., head of Trinidad police and military, 125–26, 128–29, 146–47, 176
British Guiana, 174, 182–84, 191–92, 215, 241

Broome, Gov. Sir Napier: role in legislative reform, 53, 58–59; role in municipal crisis, 87–89, 92–93, 95, 102; role in water crisis, 107, 119, 141
Brown, Vincent, colored reformer, solicitor-general and attorney-general, 53, 61, 84–85, 96, 121, 123, 175–76, 228, 257 n.57, 269 n.46
Butler, T. U., black labor and nationalist leader, 224–25

Cabildo (municipal council): in British Trinidad, 41, 80–82, 223, 253 n.5; in Spanish Trinidad, 25–26, 30, 35, 37, 120
Carnival (festival), 72–80, 104, 131, 170–71, 174, 222, 225, 232, 242
Cell, John W., 16
Chacón, Gov. Don José María: capitulates to British, 31, 38, 40; reformer, 28, 36–38, 253 n.5
Chadwick, Osbert, engineer, 106, 118–19, 135, 141–44, 148–49
Chamberlain, Joseph, secretary of state for the colonies, 10, 18, 53–54, 59–60, 62, 83–84, 107, 169, 172–74, 184, 200, 211, 216, 223, 228, 230–32, 242, 246, 256 n.41, 261 n.62; advocates protectionism, 56, 209; background of, 54–56; friendship with Negrophobic writer James Froude, 57–58, 232; pursues retrogressive policy for Trinidad,

289

Phillip, Maxwell, colored Port-of-Spain mayor, 257 n.57
Picton, Lt.-Col. and Gov. Thomas, 40
Pluralism, concept of, 21, 235–36, 241–42
Pointer, Joseph, Labor MP, House of Commons, 202–3; tours Trinidad, 219–21
Political authoritarianism: civil liberties in Trinidad and British West Indies, 108, 233, 263 n.11; limits of, 21, 233–34, 245–46, 248
Population: in British Trinidad, 65–67; decimation of Amerindians, 22–23, 68, 227, 254 n.11, 257 n.6; mixed-race groups, 252 n.33; in Spanish Trinidad, 23, 25–31
Port-of-Spain: colonial capital, 24–26, 29, 35–38, 64–83; politics of municipal governance in, 84–104; politics of water in, 105–30; Ratepayers' Association in, 111–13, 116–19, 121–23, 125–26, 129, 132–34, 137–40, 144–45, 148, 153, 156, 158, 161, 172, 177–80
Prada, Dr. E., white reformer, unofficial in Legislative Council, 201–2
Prison riot, Port-of-Spain, 71–72

Race, 68, 80, 95–96, 104, 233–34, 239–40, 244
Rapsey, J. A., white reformer, Port-of-Spain mayor, member of "no surrender party," 99, 180, 182
Ratepayers' Association. *See* Port-of-Spain
Red House, destroyed in water riot, 129–30
Reform movement: definition of, 253 n.50; in Port-of-Spain politics, 64–206 passim; in Trinidad, 39–63
Religion, 27–28, 80, 227, 229–30, 245; and education, 229, 245, 274 n.44
Richards, Alfred, colored president of Trinidad Workingmen's

Association, 46, 188, 220, 244, 255 n.24
Rienzi, Adrian Cola, Indian labor leader, 224–25
Ripon, Lord, secretary of state for the colonies, 52–53, 59, 102, 256 n.38
Robertson, Capt. Hope, R.N., commander of H.M.S. *Pallas* during water riot, 128, 138
Robinson, E. A., member United Trinidad Committee, 147
Robinson, Gov. Sir William: and Port-of-Spain water issue, 141; promotes agricultural development, 211
Rodney, Walter, Guyanese Black Power advocate, 239, 244, 277 n.99
Rosebery, Lord, Liberal prime minister: and Crown Colony system in Trinidad, 53, 59, 84–85, 246; hostile to protectionism, 209
Rostant, Philip, white reformer, publisher of Port-of-Spain *Public Opinion*, 49–50, 113, 231
Royal Commission of Enquiry, investigates water riot, 133–35, 140–60
Royal Commission of Enquiry, investigates West Indies sugar industry, 94, 209–11
Rust, Randolph, white reformer, 182, 220

Salisbury, Lord, Conservative prime minister: appoints Chamberlain, 53, 56–57, 246; hostile to protectionism, 60
San Fernando, town of, 72, 78, 81, 83, 87, 103, 219, 224, 231, 262 n.66, 269 n.37
Selznick, Phillip, 120
Slavery, 68–70, 227, 252 n.8, 254 n.11; black manumission, 39–41, 65, 68, 241
Smith, Adam, unofficial in Legislative Council and chairman, Port-of-Spain Town Board, 204
Smith, M. G., 226, 235–36, 241, 276 n.88